Praise for *Michael Amaladoss and the Quest for Indian Theology*

Enrico Beltramini has accomplished a herculean task. He has written the definitive account of Michael Amaladoss: an esteemed Indian academic polymath, who faithfully served the Jesuit order and became globally renowned. Beltramini's familiarity with Amaladoss, his Indian context, and his massive corpus of writing makes this volume indispensable for those wanting to understand Indian Christian theology over the last century.
—Dyron B. Daughrity, William S. Banowsky Chair and Professor of Religion, Pepperdine University, and coauthor of *Understanding World Christianity: India*

Theologizing in the Indian context is a spiritual experience rooted in the Christian faith and grown in the soil of India, with its plurality of religions, cultures, languages, ethnicities, and socioeconomic conditions. Dr. Enrico Beltramini has succeeded in introducing readers not only to the contours of Indian Christian theology, but also to its breadth, length, depth, and height, by delving deep into the theological reflections and articulations of a great Indian theologian, Michael Amaladoss, SJ.
—Jacob Parappally, MSFS, chief editor, *Journal of Indian Theology*

I congratulate Prof. Enrico Beltramini for his scholarly monograph, *Michael Amaladoss and the Quest for Indian Theology*. Michael Amaladoss's theological writings are a mosaic of Indian life experiences, reflected as a pilgrim with an optic of God and God's people. They are pastorally positioned for the third-millennium church in Asia/India.
—Pudota Rayappa John, SJ, former principal of Vidyajyoti College of Theology, New Delhi

Michael Amaladoss and the Quest for Indian Theology

Michael Amaladoss and the Quest for Indian Theology

Enrico Beltramini

FORTRESS PRESS
MINNEAPOLIS

MICHAEL AMALADOSS AND THE QUEST FOR INDIAN THEOLOGY

Copyright © 2024 Fortress Press, an imprint of 1517 Media. All rights reserved. Except for brief quotations in critical articles and reviews, no part of this book may be reproduced in any manner without prior written permission from the publisher. Email copyright@1517.media or write to Permissions, Fortress Press, PO Box 1209, Minneapolis, MN 55440-1209.

29 28 27 26 25 24   1 2 3 4 5 6 7 8 9

Unless they are incorporated in quoted materials, Greek and Latin Scriptural passages from the New Testament cited in this book are from *Novum Testamentum Graece et Latine*, 28th ed. (Nestle-Aland Greek and New Vulgata Latin). Stuttgart: Deutsche Bibelgesellschaft, 2014.

Library of Congress Control Number: 2024938834

Cover image: Ornaments from "L'Ornement Polychrome" published in 1873 by Albert Charles Auguste Racinet (1825-1893) a french designer, lithographer and art historian. Photographed and edited by J. C. Rosemann, from Getty Images
Cover design: Emily Harris

Print ISBN: 978-1-5064-8713-7
eBook ISBN: 978-1-5064-8714-4

For Dyron,
in celebration of our friendship

CONTENTS

Foreword	ix
Sebastian Painadath, SJ	
Acknowledgments	xiii
Premise	xix
Abbreviations	xxi
Introduction	1
About This Book	1
Argument	8
Structure	21
Terminology	22
Method	27
1 The Man and the Theologian	31
Profile	31
Further Details	33
An Indian Theologian	39
Free Thinker	45
Self-Determination	51
2 Amaladoss and Indian Theology	55
Between Brahminical and Dalit Theologies	55
Between Moderates and Progressives	61
Inculturation and Religious Dialogue	70
Building Our Own Christianity	75
3 Inculturation and Dialogue	79
Theology in Context	79
Inculturation	86
Dialogue	94
One Last Thought	101
4 Christology	105
The Uniqueness of Jesus Christ	105
Jesus, the Word, and the Spirit	114

VIII   CONTENTS

The Religions	119
The Church and the Kingdom	122
De-Dogmatization	126

5 A True Indian Theology — 131
Indian Tradition	131
Dehellenization	134
Tradition and Modernity	139
Tradition and Magisterium	145
Vatican II	150

Conclusion — 155
Amaladoss and India	155
Amaladoss and the West	159
Amaladoss and the Church	164
What Has Been Left Out	170
Unanswered Questions	173
Legacy	177
In Place of a Conclusion	181

Post Scriptum — 183
Excusatio	183
Exegetical Problem	183
Western-Indian Theological Divide	187
Epistemic Frameworks	192
Politics of Identity	200
Intra-Catholic Theological Dialogue	205

Bibliography — 213
Books by Michael Amaladoss	213
Books Edited by Michael Amaladoss	214
Articles and Other Material by Michael Amaladoss (Quoted in This Book)	215
Books, Articles, and Other Material on Michael Amaladoss (Quoted in This Book)	217
Books (Quoted in This Book)	217
Articles, Book Chapters, and Book Reviews (Quoted in This Book)	221
Church Documents (Quoted in This Book)	225

Index of Names	227
Index of Scriptures	231

FOREWORD

Michael Amaladoss would like to be called an Asian-Indian theologian. During his long years of formation in the Jesuit Order, he grew up with the Second Vatican Council (or Vatican II), which took place from 1962 to 1965. He imbibed the "spirit of the Council," especially in the areas of inculturation and interreligious dialogue. Most of his writings revolve around these two themes, which he considers to be pivotal for developing an Asian-Indian theology. For him, Vatican II was more pastoral than dogmatic.

I remember that when Peter-Hans Kolvenbach, the superior general of the Society of Jesus, thanked Amaladoss for his tenure as general assistant, he described Amaladoss as "the man of wisdom from the East." In fact, it was Amaladoss's ongoing interest to fertilize Western theology with the wisdom of the East. In the years he remained in Rome, he was much more an *Indian*; this is evident in his writings of that period. Often, one discovers the depth of Asian-Indian spirituality when one stays abroad.

For Amaladoss, Asia/India has to liberate itself from the doctrinal formulations of the West. Doctrine is a culturally conditioned reflection of the primal faith-experience. Naturally, political, economic, and colonial interests of the local culture flow into this articulation process. One cannot develop a truly Asian-Indian theology as long as one hangs on to the apron strings of the West. We cannot move forward with the divine Spirit with the principle of "back to past." He considers the living experience of the people and the ongoing guidance of the divine Spirit as sources of an Asian-Indian theology. In fact, there is no separation between the two when we pay attention to the *sensus fidelium*.

Tradition is a Spirit-guided process. *Traditio* is a verbal noun in Latin; it is not merely looking back to the past and seeing in it only a static *depositum fidei*, but seeing the depth of the present moment in which the divine

X FOREWORD

Spirit vibrates. Tradition is an ongoing process. Hence, the living experience of the people of all religions belongs to the interior movements of the Spirit. That is why, for Amaladoss, it becomes the *locus theologicus* for Asian-Indian theology.

In 1954, Amaladoss met Ignatius Hirudayam, SJ, and this meeting gave him a deeper love for Indian cultural traditions. He devoted a year to learning Carnatic music. Father Irudayam was a scholar in *Saivasiddhānta*. To promote Indian cultural studies, he established the center called Aikialayam in Chennai, and Amaladoss was very much associated with this center.

Amaladoss never wanted to be an academic theologian in the sense of Western academics. While teaching at Vidyājyoti in Delhi, he was very close to the students. As rector of the college, he insisted on real contact with the poor: all students should have contact with the people of the slums in Delhi. Based on their experience with the poor, he reflected on the themes he had to teach. He did not believe in a top-down method, but rather in a bottom-up method in theology, which emphasizes experience with the poor. With this perspective, Amaladoss was the main brain behind establishing the regional theology centers in the Jesuit provinces in India. In the 1970s and 1980s, there was a great deal of interest in developing a genuinely Indian theology.

In the area of theological inculturation, Amaladoss made significant contributions in the spirit of Vatican II. For him, inculturation means Gospel encountering culture. The divine Spirit vibrates in the hearts of all humans, and the divine Logos pulsates in all things of the cosmos. We Christians experience this universal divine presence in Jesus Christ. Others experience it through other symbols, which we respect. When the Gospel comes in deep contact with a local culture, the divine Spirit inherent in it finds an ever-fresh articulation. This gives rise to local theologies. Inculturation unfolds itself with a Christological axis, but on a pneumatological horizon. To uphold the tension between the two has been Amaladoss's great achievement. The Kingdom of God, not Christianity, is the ultimate goal of inculturation.

Amaladoss is a theological stalwart in the area of interreligious harmony. For him, the encounter of Gospel and culture, especially in Asia, also becomes an interreligious process because the plurality of religions has been a part of the salvific plan of God. According to him, all religions communicate salvation experiences, not merely Christianity. In world religions, deep down, each believer has to discover *Spirit*uality: one has to discern the movements of the divine Spirit in cultures and religions. The divine Spirit makes all things new. All religions want to communicate this message in a symbolic language. Faith affirmations and doctrinal reflections have to be made in the context of religious pluralism. Dogmas can be very static; however, the Spirit is dynamic. For Amaladoss, dialogue is for mutual enrichment and discerning the work of the Divine in bringing about a new humanity.

The divine presence is invisible; yet the mind and the body need names, forms, and symbols to make the invisible into a visible reality. The divine presence is vibration, but the mind cannot perceive the vibrant reality. It is only through the *nous/buddhi,* which functions as a door to the heart, that we experience the Divine as Spirit, as vibration. The divine Spirit vibrates in every human heart. In all religions, the spiritual masters want to communicate the message that we are called to a higher consciousness, to a divine consciousness. The awareness that *we are divine* (*theosis*) is the deepest mystical meeting point of all religions.

I hope that Enrico Beltramini's critical study on Michael Amaladoss will have a large audience of readers, especially those who are interested in Asian-Indian theological developments. I consider it an honor to write a foreword to the study of a great Asian-Indian theologian in the post–Vatican II era.

Sebastian Painadath, SJ
Sameeksha Ashram
Kalady, India

ACKNOWLEDGMENTS

This book is the result of a patient and meticulous reading of the colossal intellectual production of Michael Amaladoss, SJ—which consists of thirty-six books in English and over 500 articles so far—merged with long, dense, in-person conversations with their author. I met with Amaladoss (henceforth also Father Amal, or simply Amal, as his friends call him) at his place in the Jesuit Residence at Loyola College in Chennai during a period of one week in April 2022. I felt immediately at home at Loyola. Father Amal made himself available to answer my questions about the events of his life and the nuances of his thought. The encounter between Father Amal, who proudly defines himself as an Indian who happens to be a theologian, and the author of these notes, who humbly proceeds into a theological journey across worlds, could not have been more improbable, yet it worked out beautifully. It is a testimony to Father Amal's love for intellectual discussion that we spent long hours in his room or mine discussing both high and less high theological themes. I must recognize Father Amal's simple and unassuming presentation of his immense intellectual work. He defends his ideas with no affectation whatsoever. He never readily conceded a point, but when he did, he did so with disarming simplicity. He found the time to escort me to St. Thomas Cathedral Basilica, and we visited the National Shrine of Saint Thomas, which was rebuilt by the Portuguese in 1523 over the tomb of Thomas the Apostle. I am grateful to Amaladoss and the Jesuit Chennai Province for their warm welcome and kind hospitality. Loyola College is an outstanding university with several schools and faculties and a beautiful cricket field, which brought back memories of some funny experiences from when I was a graduate student in England. I enjoyed visiting the Loyola campus and meeting the entertaining local students during my stay there.

XIV ACKNOWLEDGMENTS

The search for Father Amal's writings and their collection was a job in itself. By his own admission, he never tried to systematically publish in Western scholarly journals; however, this does not mean that some aspect of his work is not present in the content that Western scholars interested in Christianity in South Asia usually consult. I gained access to Father Amal's publications in Western outlets through the legendary staff of the Graduate Theological Union library in Berkeley, California, who not only offered assistance during the troubled times of Covid restrictions but remained available for questions and addressed my scholarly needs. It remains to be said, however, that a systematic study of Father Amal requires access to the Indian publications, which de facto host the majority of his contributions.

Most of Father Amal's work has been published in Indian outlets, particularly in *Vidyajyoti Journal of Theological Reflection* (henceforth *VJTR*), the prestigious journal of theology of Vidyajyoti College of Theology (or simply Vidyajyoti College), the Jesuit seminary of Delhi. Father Amal spent two long periods there, both as a teacher and an administrator. It is from Vidyajyoti College that I received my doctoral degree in theology. The college's library conserves a large portion of Father Amal's publications, particularly articles. I thank the Jesuits of Vidyajyoti College for their friendly hospitality and concrete help in supplying all the relevant material regarding Father Amal. I recognize the critical assistance of Pudota Rayappa (or P. R.) John, SJ, who is a professor of systematic theology and the principal of the college. Father John was a student of Amaladoss, although now he is a recognized theologian. Leonard Fernando, SJ, kindly provided material on Father Amal that was otherwise nowhere to be found. Father Fernando, who was my doctoral supervisor at Vidyajyoti College, was the editor of the 2002 Festschrift in honor of Father Amal and knows him well. When I was working on this book, Father Fernando was the rector of St. Joseph's College in Tiruchirappalli. He graciously hosted me in a spacious room at the center of a naturally beautiful yard between the Jesuit Residence and the gothic church. Father Sebastian Painadath, SJ, who lives in Sameeksha, which is an ashram, research center, and school on the banks of Poorna River, generously agreed to write the foreword. I thank the editor of *VJTR*, Father Edwin Rodrigues, SJ, for his indispensable assistance in recovering sources from the large library of Vidyajyoti College. Finally, I recognize the work of the anonymous librarians at Vidyajyoti College and St. Joseph's

ACKNOWLEDGMENTS   XV

College who physically provided the material and helped me take notes and make copies.

Apart from the direct interaction with Father Amal and the study of his work, I benefited from conversations with theologians, priests, and Father Amal's friends. Usually, these conversations happened casually at dinner or during teatime, a routine that brought me back, once again, to my days in the United Kingdom. I took down some of their names, but I lost track of others. M. A. Joe Antony, SJ, for example, introduced himself simply as a "friend of Amal." Jesuits are notoriously restrained when it comes to sharing personal anecdotes or opinions of people and other facts of life, but Father Antony was adamant in his praise of Father Amal and celebrated their friendship. When Father Amal turned sixty-five, Father Antony, who is a journalist, compiled a piece that was both a personal recollection and a psychological introspection on Father Amal—the type of article that only a friend dares to publish. I collected comments, insights, and suggestions both in Delhi and Tiruchirappalli, from Jesuits and non-Jesuits alike. I thank Dorathick Rajan, OSB Cam, the prior of Saccidananda Ashram in Kulithalai, for sharing his thought on the present state of Indian theology and the necessary bridge between spiritual search and social concern. I must mention that Father Dorathick cut short an appointment he had in Bangalore to welcome me at the ashram; I am grateful for the generous gesture and honored by his friendship.

Outside the perimeters of the Roman Catholic community in India, I was lucky enough to share ideas with Rev. Dr. V. S. Varughese, the principal of Mar Thoma Syrian Theological Seminary in Kottayam, and Metropolitan Geevarghese Mar Coorilose, former bishop of the Syrian Orthodox Church, through a trip to Kerala. During my visit, I had the great honor of briefly introducing Father Amal and his theology to the graduate students of the Mar Thoma Theological Seminary in Kottayam. Before the address, the students celebrated the vespers with a melancholic liturgy that touched my heart. Jesudas Athyal, who was the acquisitions editor at Fortress Press in world and South Asian religious topics, organized the meetings in Kerala. Throughout my scholarly life, I have met outstanding editors who went well beyond the established boundaries of their job to help me write good books, but I have never had an editor who pushed the limits of engagement to the point of supporting an author on the ground.

XVI ACKNOWLEDGMENTS

It probably helped that Doctor Athyal is a scholar on his own terms; as a son and a son-in-law of pastors, he has a profound love for religion and enjoys ecumenical interfaith dialogues. Born in California and at home in Kerala, he sees himself as a living bridge between the East and West; mastering the two cultures, he is a natural nexus of both.

I am indebted to Gavin Flood, who is now an internationally known emeritus professor of Hindu Studies and Comparative Religions at Oxford University. I met him in Scotland at the University of Stirling where he was the head of the religion department and my research project supervisor when I was pursuing a master of letters degree. It is through his now classic *An Introduction to Hinduism* that I encountered Hinduism for the first time. His love for Hinduism and his encyclopedic knowledge permanently shaped my view on the subject, and his influence on my work is unmistakable.

Like my previous titles, this book also profits from the extensive and, in the end, transformative work of my editor Sarah Tyrrell. After all these years, she knows what I am trying to say, and she closes the gap between that and what I actually wrote. She is the reason I can publish in a language that I am still learning.

This book took shape during the long nights of a California winter, and I credit my wife, Laura, for the atmosphere of serenity that empowered me while I was writing this book. On these nights, there was a cup of tea on the table and a fire going; while Laura struggled with her gigantic puzzle game, the cats gave themselves a bath, and the dogs pretended to sleep but never failed to lose sight of our every movement.

This book is possible because Dyron Daughrity helped me find a press. I have known Professor Daughrity for many years and met him well before he became a celebrated author and respected scholar in the field of world Christianity. During these years, we had innumerable meals together, in which we rapidly exchanged opinions about theological issues but dedicated most of the conversation to family matters and ordinary subjects. He has helped me several times, this project being the most recent. I should pay my debt to him, as scholars usually do, but Dyron and I are friends, and in friendship, there is no accounting, only love and respect. This book is dedicated to Dyron, the best of friends. But I would add that this book is also dedicated to friendship, because friendship is what links all the people

I mentioned above and all the others I did not, either because I forgot their names or because they desire anonymity. Friendship is the invisible, sacramental tapestry that made this book possible.

***

During my work on Michael Amaladoss, I have presented papers at conferences and published essays in academic journals. Portions of chapters 2 and 5 of this text were previously published as academic papers: "The 'Wisdom Writer': Michael Amaladoss and His Thought," *Religions* 12, no. 6, article 396 (2021) and "The Historical Revolution of Vatican II and Post-Western Christianity in India," *Rupkatha Journal* 15, no. 3 (2023). In both cases, I own the copyright of the articles.

PREMISE

The Church encourages the charism of the theologians . . .
As long as they are not content with a desk-bound theology.

—Pope Francis[1]

Father Amal is a gentle, reflective, reserved man. He maintains a daily routine and, like me, always eats the same food. He is highly disciplined and keeps a remarkable schedule for a man of his age. When I met him the first time, he was eighty-six, the same age as my mother. This coincidence suggested I might approach him as I approach her: I make myself available and leave her to control the agenda. I did the same with Father Amal, and it worked out well. We spent long sessions discussing primary and marginal topics related to his theological work. His intellectual integrity is disarming. To his credit, he never avoided a subject or failed to provide an answer. When we disagreed on something, he became tense, his face more concentrated, his eyes fixed on an invisible point behind me. I took advantage of these rare moments to try to guess what he was like as a younger man, when he was full of energy and ideas, and how much richer his reasoning probably was then. I found ample notes about him in the secondary literature, where it seems that Father Amal has left a mark on an entire generation of Indian authors, theologians, historians, and social theorists. Several told me that he impressed them not only with his thought but with his personality, too. He is clearly interested in his intellectual legacy, but

---

[1]   The epigraph is an extraction from a letter Pope Francis penned to Archbishop Víctor Manuel Fernández, Prefect of the Dicastery for the Doctrine of the Faith, Vatican City, Catholic News Agency, July 1, 2023, https://tinyurl.com/yck4e45e.

he has reached a point in life when there are things more important than a legacy. He prays often and intensely. His best moments are after dinner, when memories of his youth resurface from the past, and he tirelessly narrates about villages, Carnatic music, and the multitude of languages that constitute India.

Father Amal's theology is for anybody who cares to read his books and meditate on his message. But his message is primarily for the sons and daughters of India. His message is for the communities of the villages in Tamil Nadu, the state where he was born almost nine decades ago and where he still lives out his busy days. His message is for the nuns, the priests, and the missionaries in the villages who need theological tools they can understand and, more importantly, that their audience can understand. His message is for those who feel uncomfortable and ultimately troubled by the loss of Indian roots in Indian society. Finally, his message is for Indian theologians, or at least those who read his work and are not busy either teaching in seminaries or addressing dramatic social issues. Thus, Father Amal speaks to common people about topics of theological relevance while he speaks to his fellow theologians about topics of common people. In brief, Father Amal is an Indian theologian who is first and foremost concerned about his people.

ABBREVIATIONS

The following are abbreviations used in this book:

SJ	Society of Jesus
Vidyajyoti College	Vidyajyoti College of Theology
VJTR	*Vidyajyoti Journal of Theological Reflection*
Congregation	Congregation for the Doctrine of the Faith
FAPA	For All the Peoples of Asia
FABC	Federation of the Asian Bishops' Conferences
OTC	Office of Theological Concerns of FABC

BOOKS (BY MICHAEL AMALADOSS)

(For complete citations, see the bibliography at the end of this book.)

Beyond Inculturation	*Beyond Inculturation: Can the Many Be One?*
Beyond Dialogue	*Beyond Dialogue: Pilgrims to the Absolute*
Peoples' Theology in Asia	*Peoples' Theology*
The Asian Jesus	*The Asian Jesus*
Lead Me On	*Lead Me On*
Experiencing	*Experiencing God in India*
Interreligious Encounters	*Interreligious Encounters: Opportunities and Challenges*
Life in Freedom	*Life in Freedom: Liberation Theologies from Asia*
Quest for God	*Quest for God: Doing Theology in India*
Making All Things New	*Making All Things New: Dialogue, Pluralism and Evangelization in Asia*

ARTICLES (BY MICHAEL AMALADOSS)

(For complete citations, see the bibliography at the end of this book.)

"My Pilgrimage in Mission"	*"My Pilgrimage in Mission"*
"Toward an Indian Theology"	*"Toward an Indian Theology"*
"The Mystery of Christ"	*"The Mystery of Christ and Other Religions: An Indian Perspective"*
"Together Toward the Kingdom"	*"Together Toward the Kingdom: An Emerging Asian Theology"*

INTRODUCTION

ABOUT THIS BOOK

Michael Amaladoss is one of the few theologians—Raimon Panikkar (1918–2010) and Jacques Dupuis, SJ (1923–2004) also come to mind—who has reached international notoriety in Western circles through his work in India. Unlike Panikkar and Dupuis, however, Amaladoss was born in India and has spent most of his life there. Outside of India, he is known mostly for some books that Western presses have published and for his lectures at theological institutes in Asia, Europe, and the United States. His international status has been confirmed by important appointments such as being a consultant to the Pontifical Council of Interreligious Dialogue and the Pontifical Council of Culture as well as the World Council of Churches and being the president of the International Association of Mission Studies. In India, he has been active as an influential thinker for decades, well known inside and outside the context of Roman Catholicism (henceforth, simply Catholicism). Generations of theologians, both in Catholic and non-Catholic seminaries, have learned from his texts, often enthusiastically embracing them, sometimes struggling with them, but rarely rejecting them. His work is an inescapable step in the coming-of-age path of Indian theologians, regardless of their scholarly interests, political positions, and Christian denominations. His influence extends beyond India and reaches Asian countries like Indonesia, the Philippines, and Sri Lanka.

Despite being an internationally renowned thinker with critical influence on the development of a native theology in India, Amaladoss's life, and most importantly, his thought has never been studied comprehensively. Of course, Indian theologians have frequently engaged his work and entered in conversation with his ideas, and some have tried to summarize his thought on this or that subject. Outside of India, he is recognized as a master of inculturation and a champion of interreligious dialogue: he would agree with these labels, as inculturation and religious dialogue have occupied much of his theological reflection. But Amaladoss's thought cannot be reduced to his works on these two themes, relevant as they may be. He has a grand vision of Christianity's role in India and, more importantly, of India in Christianity; moreover, he has articulated a peculiar interpretation of theology, summarized in terms of "our search for a better understanding of our faith in relation to our lives."[1] Here the word *our* does not only identify professional theologians or religious men and women, but all people who want—as he puts it—to understand their faith in relation to their life.

His definition of theology as it is known in India may be less familiar in the West. According to Amaladoss, theology is more properly "encountering God in the way God challenges our lives and our relationships. This is affected by the historical, geographical, cultural, and religious circumstances in which we live."[2] Thus, theology is not necessarily faith seeking understanding but rather one's response to God's self-revelation in the context of one's life in the historical, geographical, cultural, and religious circumstances in which they live. At this point, Amaladoss concludes, "For those of us living in Asia, our situation will affect our experience of God and the way we speak about it."[3] For those who live in Asia, the particular situation to being Asian produces consequences related to their experience of God and the modes through which they understand that experience. This is theology according to Amaladoss: to consider the circumstances in which one lives and how they affect one's experience of God and the way one speaks about that experience. Thus, Asian theology, and its progenitor, Indian theology, are different from other theologies not only because they place faith in dialogue with the present and concrete circumstances of life, but also because these circumstances are specifically Asian.

---

[1]   Michael Amaladoss, *Peoples' Theology in Asia: Collection of the Lectures: East Asia Theological Encounter Program (2006–2018)* (Phnom Penh: Jesuit Conference of Asia Pacific, 2021), back cover.

[2]   Amaladoss, *Peoples' Theology,* back cover.

[3]   Amaladoss, *Peoples' Theology,* back cover.

INTRODUCTION 3

By his own admission, Amaladoss is an Indian Catholic theologian. Apart from that, he rejects classifications:

> I would consider myself an Indian Catholic theologian. Beyond that, I would reject categories like Brahminical, Dalit, etc. I am neither a Brahmin nor a Dalit. My theological reflection would be classified much more under the Asian triple dialogue of the Gospel with the poor, the cultures and the religions, though my own interests follow a reverse order: dialogue with religions, Indian culture and the poor. I tackle questions as they come to me. I have not developed a system, nor do I belong to a school or a group.[4]

Easy classifications of Amaladoss—liberation theologian, Dalit theologian, or pioneer of religious dialogue—often fail to fully capture the mystique of a creative and prolific thinker like Amaladoss. He calls himself a Hindu Christian not in the sense of double belonging (Hindu is the adjective, Christian the noun), but rather as a Christian who is generated by a civilization matrix called "Hinduism," which is at once metaphysical and existential.[5] Hinduism refers to the people of Hindustan.[6]

---

4   Here, Amaladoss referred to the Federation of the Asian Bishops' Conferences (or FABC), which at their first General Assembly in 1974 in Taipei, Taiwan, described "mission" as the building up of local churches in Asia through a dialogue with the many poor, the rich cultures, and the living religions of Asia.

5   For the reference to Hindu Christian, see Michael Amaladoss, "My Pilgrimage in Mission," *International Bulletin of Missionary Research* 31, no. 1 (2007): 24. He told me that the notion of double belonging is a theological invention. In one of his articles, he articulates the notion of "double religious identity"; see Michael Amaladoss, "Double Religious Identity and Pilgrim Centres," *Word and Worship* 43, no. 1 (2010): 5–22. Amaladoss repeatedly returns to this notion of a double identity. See "Can One Be a Hindu-Christian?" *Ishvani Documentation and Mission Digest* 15, no. 1 (1997): 88–93; "Double Religious Identity: Is It Possible? Is It Necessary?" *VJTR* 73, no. 7 (2009): 519–32; "Being a Hindu-Christian," in *Toward A Planetary Theology: Along the Many Paths of God*, ed. Jose Maria Vigil (Montreal: Dunamis, 2010), 3–37; "Attaining Harmony as a Hindu-Christian," in *In Search of the Whole*, ed. John Haughey (Washington, D.C.: Georgetown University Press, 2011), 99–110.

6   Manan Ahmed Asif, *The Loss of Hindustan: The Invention of India* (Cambridge, MA: Harvard University Press, 2020).

4   MICHAEL AMALADOSS AND THE QUEST FOR INDIAN THEOLOGY

This study is about Amaladoss's theology. Only a detailed and at the same time comprehensive engagement with Amaladoss's complex and ever-evolving thought can do justice to its nuances and distinctions. Only a study that encompasses the entire intellectual production of an author of thirty-six books and over 500 articles on theology—some that have been translated into other languages and some that have never crossed Indian borders—can clarify his overall theological vision. Here, his theology is placed in the context of his life and of the history of Indian theology: as they say, it takes a village. However, this is a study of historical theology, not the history of theology. A simple summary of Amaladoss's thought seems too limited in scope for a monograph that, at least for now, stands as the first monograph dedicated to the subject. Some degree of valuation of Amaladoss's place in the history of Indian theology, and eventually beyond, must be considered; moreover, the Western audience needs to be aware of the assumptions hidden in Amaladoss's frameworks. I am not content to offer only a synthetic picture of Amaladoss's theology; I dare to enter into dialogue with his theology and offer interpretations.[7] Because of who I am—that is, a Western theologian—this book is inevitably, although not exclusively, a West-East, intra-Catholic dialogue on the status of Indian theology. Some Indian theologians might deem this a kind of intrusion. However, for reasons explained at the end of this book (see Post Scriptum), I think this intra-Catholic dialogue is not only necessary but urgent. India is assuming its place among the hegemonic powers of the world, and Indian theology is no longer relevant only to India. With more power comes greater responsibilities. Indian theologians must accept this fact.

The aim of this book is to provide both Indian and Western readers a synthetic understanding of Amaladoss's theological thought. I disclose the intellectual roots of his main contributions as well as his overall vision

---

7   Even though I cannot match the theological precision and philosophical depth of von Balthasar, I have been captivated by his essential overviews of Henri de Lubac's and Romano Guardini's works. Well written and equipped with copious notes and excellent bibliographies, von Balthasar's overviews also contain critical comments. Those overviews are the model of this study. See Hans Urs von Balthasar, *Romano Guardini: Reform from the Source* (San Francisco: Ignatius, 2010) and *The Theology of Henri de Lubac: An Overview* (San Francisco: Ignatius, 1991).

INTRODUCTION 5

and how it took shape in the distinct fields in which it was applied. The quality of his theology, the range of topics he addresses, and the impact he maintains on Indian theology legitimates exhaustive coverage of his work. A synthesis of his theological vision is crucial and at the same time difficult. It is crucial because the level of his reflection justifies that his work becomes known beyond India; it is difficult because Amaladoss is a creative thinker in the sense that he is both evolving and fluid, which is expected from a thinker who rejects the option of theologizing from above. He lives his life and recognizes the thick of life's struggles and questions interrogating him.[8] Thus, his thought is always on the move, forced by the dynamic process of life to revise old concepts and positions by either updating or replacing them. In writing a book on Amaladoss's thought, the author must be conscious of this evolution, of the permanent contingency of Amaladoss's reflection. Readers must be conscious of the same. Amaladoss is not only an evolving thinker; he is also a fluid thinker in the sense of his comfort in accepting or rejecting ideas, including his own, in the course of a dialogue. He intends the dialogue to be a transformative process, a conversation in which an incessant mutual fecundation is at work, not a discussion based on given positions. For those who know their Panikkar well, Amaladoss resembles the Indo-Spanish thinker and his crisscrossing path, which renders his Western counterparts aware of their own Cartesian mindset. The same is true in a dialogue with Amaladoss: the more his positions reveal their contingent character, the more the Western reflective instinct is to ground, define, and clarify. I speak from experience.

The subject of this book is Amaladoss and his thought in the context of India and Indian theology. He considers himself an Indian who happens to be a theologian. He is an Indian theologian, as he proudly and consistently repeats, and India is his great love. For Amaladoss, Indian theology is the plastic representation in the domain of religious and theological reflection of the inexhaustible multiplicity of India. India is a country of immense diversity, disparate beliefs, and incredibly rich art. India is infinite in the sense that its diversity covers customs, legends, and mysteries. The country is a mixture of colors, music, and languages, including Sanskrit,

---

8   Michael Amaladoss, *Beyond Inculturation: Can the Many Be One?* (Delhi: Vidyajyoti Education and Welfare Society and ISPCK, 1998), xv.

6   MICHAEL AMALADOSS AND THE QUEST FOR INDIAN THEOLOGY

Pali, Prakrit, and Tamil, the regional languages from ancient times, Persian and Urdu from medieval times, and English from the modern period. Notes on his influence beyond India surface here and there in this book, but specific emphasis is given to the emotional and intellectual relationship that exists strictly between Amaladoss and his country.

Amaladoss's engagement with music is emblematic of his artistic mindset. Outside Tamil Nadu, the state where Amaladoss was born and now has returned, people may not know that Amaladoss is a gifted Carnatic musician.[9] When he was already a Jesuit, he enrolled in the Tamil Nadu Music College at Loyola College in Chennai (which was based in a building facing the Jesuit Residence where Amaladoss is hosted today). After two years of training, he received the title of Sangeetha Vidwan (scholar in music). He is very proud of his musical training and never fails to remember his musical production. What is important, however, is the use he made of that training. In the wake of the liturgical reforms inaugurated at the Second Vatican Council (or Vatican II or simply Council), Indian parishes needed hymns based on indigenous musical elements; this was in the early sixties when the Catholic liturgy moved from Latin to the vernacular. More specifically, Catholic devotional hymns were literal and straightforward translations of Gregorian and European hymns sung to Western tunes and melodies.[10] In those days, classical music and dance were still considered the sole marker of upper-caste Brahmins, but Amaladoss, who hails from a middle caste and more importantly is a Christian, saw an opportunity for the creative use of his musical knowledge. He composed music and asked for lyrics from talented lyricists to create hymns to be used in liturgical and paraliturgical services. Then he taught these hymns to the seminarists and scholastics, who in turn taught them to parish choirs wherever they went. His effort, however, did not stop here. He was asked to popularize these

---

9   The core of the story is told in M. A. Joe Antony, "Amal the Person," in *Seeking New Horizons: Festschrift in Honour of Dr. M. Amaladoss, S. J.*, ed. Leonard Fernando (Delhi: Vidyajyoti Education and Welfare Society & ISPCK, 2002), 3–4. The story has been integrated with further details that Amaladoss provided in conversations with the author of this book.

10   Selva J. Raj, "Being Catholic the Tamil Way," in *Vernacular Catholicism, Vernacular Saints: Selva J. Raj on "Being Catholic the Tamil Way,"* ed. Reid B. Locklin (Albany: State University of New York Press, 2017), 4.

hymns, so he started a periodical called *Isai Aruvi* (Cascade of Music). Published three times a year, each issue contained thirty to forty hymns that featured both Western and Carnatic notation for the hymns and provided priests and their choirs the material for the liturgy in transition from Latin to Tamil. Then, he expanded his audience to seminarists, nuns, and Catholic youth through booklets known by the title *Isai Elithu* (Music Is Easy), which presented the rudiments of Carnatic music and even offered illustrations.

Obviously, it is difficult to penetrate the core identity of an individual, particularly if the individual is a multilayered person, a remarkable thinker, and a priest. Without a doubt, Amaladoss is a "cosmic" person, an intellectual who lives in this eschatological time on this side of the eschaton with a remarkable absence of anxiety about the otherworldly horizon. His approach to theology is at once ambitious and unassuming: he has bold, original ideas about the destiny of Christianity in India, but he can easily set these ideas aside if a parish needs his help in some capacity. His primary inclination is to serve the people, then the Church, and finally metaphysics. Amaladoss is a committed man for others in the line of the purest Ignatian spirituality. As a theologian and a priest, he is at the service of people and the Church, but he is committed to persons first and then to principles; therefore, he is ultimately concerned with the practical existence of men and women.

Amaladoss shows a natural predisposition to serve that has been tested on several occasions, as this book reveals. He has paid his dues in educational, administrative, and advisory roles within the Society of Jesus while offering his wisdom to nuns, priests, bishops, and entire religious congregations. He considers himself lucky because, despite the numerous appointments and responsibilities he has accepted in his life, he has enjoyed extended periods in which he was left to reflect and write. Amaladoss is aware that in a highly clericalized world of Indian theology, where theologians are asked to serve as instructors and administrators in seminaries and other educational institutions, his duties have not been oppressively demanding; he always found the time to reflect and write about things that are crucial for the destiny of the Indian Church but may not be of immediate and practical concern.

The core of this study is Amaladoss's fundamental contribution to the construction of Indian theology as a well-articulated system. He believes the system is yet nonexistent, but that it is emerging.[11] Although his work as a Christian theologian has been dedicated to reading India with Christian eyes, his natural instinct is to do the opposite, that is, to read Christianity with Indian eyes. The scope of Amaladoss's theology is ambitious: to build a bridge between Christianity and India, but not in the sense that Western theologians would expect. For Amaladoss, it is not about operating a double hermeneutical process—one that goes from reality to the deep sources of Christian sacred tradition (henceforth Tradition) and another that goes in the opposite direction—so that the sources are reinterrogated with new questions, and the answer comes from the treasures of Tradition. He raises a series of questions and objections to this method because, he said, "I claim the freedom to reflect theologically in the Indian context."[12] There is no point in raising new questions and reflections if in the end they are filtered through a lens that is not Indian. The entire hermeneutical method needs to be rethought; the traditional hermeneutics, that is, the Western, Latin hermeneutics, needs to be rejected and replaced with another—namely, the hermeneutic of an experience built for a reality in which Indian theologians are at home. It is a monumental task, one that Amaladoss initially framed and has since pursued for decades.

ARGUMENT

Amaladoss is a recognized and renowned Asian theologian. He has spent most of his intellectual life dealing with ecumenical and interreligious dialogue and issues concerning the inculturation of the faith as an instructor, a scholar, an author, and finally one of the four general assistants to Father Peter-Hans Kolvenbach (1928–2016), superior general of the Society of Jesus from 1983 to 2008, in Rome. He is certainly one of the great

---

11 According to Amaladoss, "Although it is true that we do not have an Indian theology as a well-articulated system, I think that a framework is emerging." See Michael Amaladoss, "An Emerging Indian Theology: Some Exploratory Reflections," *VJTR* 58, no. 8 (1994): 473.

12 Michael Amaladoss, *Quest for God: Doing Theology in India* (Anand: Gujarat Sahitya Prakash, 2013), 12.

INTRODUCTION 9

postconciliar Asian theologians. In this book, I position Amal against the history of Indian theology, and I frame his contribution within the borders of a specific era of India and Indian theology. I argue that it is in that specific era that his contribution is particularly relevant. I make clear that Amaladoss is an influential but not controversial theologian, even though he briefly fell out of favor with the Vatican due to his views on the Kingdom and related issues. Like other giants of postconciliar theology—Hans Küng, Leonardo Boff, Dupuis, and Jon Sobrino—the Indian theologian also faced a Vatican investigation for allegedly espousing unorthodox beliefs, but he was cleared of any wrongdoing. As a matter of fact, his thinking is neither properly radical nor moderate, and it is not framed for challenging the Church's doctrinal imperatives.

The argument at the center of this book is that one must distinguish between Amaladoss's empirical and epistemic contributions to Indian theology. The empirical contribution is clear. For Amaladoss, Hinduism is not a religion but a pervading culture in which Christianity had grown up. The ubiquity and saturation of Hinduism have shaped, at least to some extent, Indian Christianity; consequently, Hinduism's inculturation of Indian Christianity has produced distinct forms and meanings of worship, sacredness, and popular religiosity. In the course of centuries, the two religious traditions—that is, Hindu and Christian—have mutually affected each other to the point that Christians have unconsciously imported intellectual frameworks, modes of worship, and forms of devotions exquisitely Hindu. Particularly in the South Indian religious context—the context in which Amaladoss grew up—both Christians and Hindus "draw from a shared religious worldview, a shared indigenous religious epistemology, a shared ritual data bank, and a shared grammar."[13] In an effort to describe the context in which Panikkar received Hinduism, Purushottama Bilimoria and Devasia Muruppath Antony crafted a splendid passage that can be used to describe the context in which Amaladoss grew up. Bilimoria and Antony say that in South India,

---

13   Selva J. Raj, "An Ethnographic Encounter with the Wondrous in a South Indian Catholic Shrine," in *Vernacular Catholicism, Vernacular Saints: Selva J. Raj on "Being Catholic the Tamil Way,"* ed. Reid B. Locklin (Albany: State University of New York Press, 2017), 137.

> In Kerala and Tamil Nadu, Christian, especially Catholic, practices reflect a mixture of unwitting assimilation of Hindu practices into a Christian context, intentional adaptation of Hindu practices to convey Christian messages, incorporation of Hindu practices despite their apparent contradiction to Christian messages, shared practices that convey polyvalent messages, and uniquely Christian practices that are authentically Indian.[14]

This is, in first approximation, Amaladoss's picture of Indian Christianity. Thus, the encounter of Christianity, including the case of the colonializing Catholicism of the last centuries, with a hinduized Indian culture is an opportunity for a deviation into the trajectory of Christianity; the opportunity exists to develop Indian Christianity autonomously from its European and North American counterparts.

This distinct interpretation of Indian Christianity pervades Amaladoss's work on inculturation. When he talks about inculturation, in fact, he means neither a translation of existing theological content into the Indian reality nor a fresh reframing of such content within the Indian conceptual and linguistic grid. What he means is the production of new content with little to no relationship with the Western one. Inculturation, for Amaladoss, is not the adoption of an equivalent vocabulary so that the concept, which originated in the West, is reformulated in Indian terms; it is another pattern of thinking that may (or may not) overlap to a certain degree with the Western one. For Amaladoss, inculturation may prove itself fruitful in theological reflection and concrete living conditions in India. The almost inevitable gap between the Western and Indian formulations that this position assumes is a necessary price to pay for a better inculturation; it is a reasonable price to pay for the construction of a true Indian Christianity. Amaladoss has built his reputation through the production of a chain of books—the most famous being *The Asian Jesus*—in which he takes a break from the Western line of thought and generates interpretations of Christian figures, events, and concepts that present both

---

14   Purushottama Bilimoria and Devasia Muruppath Antony, "Raimon Panikkar: A Peripatetic Hindu Hermes," *European Journal of Humanities and Social Sciences* 3, no. 2 (2019): 15.

similarities to and differences from their Western counterparts.[15] These formulations, although distant from their Western counterparts, are close to an Indian reality and totally meaningful in that context. Thus, the formulations of Tradition, almost fully developed in a realm of the Western world, are abandoned and replaced with formulations that make sense within the borders of India. In first approximation, this is Amaladoss's idea of inculturation.

Complementary to Amaladoss's notion of inculturation stands his specific understanding of religious dialogue. I already mentioned his idea of dialogue as mutual fecundation. But this definition is a poor approximation of Amaladoss's distinct understanding of religious dialogue. For him, the dialogue is not between two religions belonging to two different cultures but between two religions belonging to the same culture. He uses the Hindu metaphor of a river: religions are like rivers that merge into a single mainstream. But these rivers do not flow parallel to each other; they intersect, then diverge, only to reunite later. It is a mutual crisscrossing, a kind of dance that reveals the interdependence of religions. The dialogue, therefore, does not happen at the level of theologies or systems of beliefs; it cuts across personal conversations, communal rituals, and manifestations of popular religiosity. The dialogue is among the members of the same community or the same family. Selva Raj (1952–2008) ingeniously noted the following based on his impressive work on popular Catholicism in South India:

> A noteworthy feature of this popular Catholicism is that the usual distinctions between the Hindu, Muslim, primeval, and Christian traditions, as well as the normative boundaries between official and popular religion, become significantly blurred. The dynamic of Santal popular Catholic religious life, represented in its lifecycle ceremonies, life-crisis rituals, calendrical festivals, and magico-religious practices, provides a textbook case for this phenomenon of blurred boundaries.[16]

---

15   Michael Amaladoss, *The Asian Jesus* (Maryknoll, NY: Orbis, 2006; original edition: Delhi: ISPCK, 2005). All citations refer to the 2006 edition.

16   Raj, "Ethnographic Encounter," 45.

The dialogue is not between religions but between people who have already broken the boundaries between religions. It is dialogue on a profoundly existential level. To borrow another phrase from the late Selva Raj, one of the greatest contemporary scholars of Indian Christianity, dialogue is at the grassroots level: it is "dialogue on the ground" as an alternative to the "contrived, structured, institutional dialogical initiatives engineered and pursued by the religious elite."[17] This aligns with Amaladoss's idea of dialogue. Dialogue is not the expression of good intentions, as it may be seen in Europe, but is an inevitable consequence of the intertwining of the two religions in the very ordinary life of individuals and communities. It is also a necessity, as the intertwining can work both as an agent of unity and of conflict. Dialogue keeps communities in peace.

For Amaladoss, inculturation and religious dialogue constitute a unique conceptual block in which each element sustains and justifies the other, although he may afford more attention to one or the other on occasion. Behind this block lies Amaladoss's metaphysics. Given his idiosyncratic repudiation of all things metaphysical, he would not use this term. In a note he sent to me, he mentioned that his "dialogue with the Vatican Holy Office . . . has . . . led to a certain Christological reflection, not so much academic, but practical." I do not know what a practical Christology is and how it may differ from an academic Christology, but I assume Father Amal is referring to a framework that acts as a tool for promoting brotherhood rather than speculation. I think his Christology can be better characterized as pastoral. In fact, he turned his attention to the metaphysical architecture— Christology, soteriology, eschatology, ecclesiology, doctrine, and dogma— behind his theology when he was already an established theologian. This is not to say that for Amaladoss the metaphysical architecture does not count. By his own admission, after reflecting on the implicit metaphysical assumptions behind his theology, Amaladoss produced better, more refined, and rounded works, including his celebrated *The Asian Jesus*. The point is rather that Amaladoss's natural predisposition is experiential; his theology emerges

---

17   Selva J. Raj, "'Dialogue 'On the Ground': The Complicated Identities and the Complex Negotiations of Catholics and Hindus in South India," in *Vernacular Catholicism, Vernacular Saints: Selva J. Raj on "Being Catholic the Tamil Way,"* ed. Reid B. Locklin (Albany: State University of New York Press, 2017), 189.

as a response to the circumstances of life, or better yet, from his understanding of the slow and eventually troubling process of decolonization of India and related issues. Christianity should be a vehicle of peace and reconciliation for the people of India involved in this epochal transformation. Sensing that sometimes this is not the case, Amaladoss offers remedies. Thus, by natural inclination and for practical reasons, Amaladoss dedicated more time in the first decades of his intellectual work to defining the propositions and the limits of inculturation and religious dialogue. Then, the quality of his work and the stature of the responders forced him to pay more attention to the metaphysical assumptions behind his work.

These metaphysical assumptions are a bittersweet component of Amaladoss's reflection. They are sweet because they provide the needed depth to his work on inculturation and dialogue. His work on *The Asian Jesus*, for example, is surely sound because it benefits from a rigorous and profound Christology. These theological assumptions are bitter because they forced him to enter into territories he genuinely dislikes: religious dialogue at the theological level and the difficult relationship with European theology. The former, he believes, is dangerous territory, because it refers to truths of faith that are, by definition, incommensurable. When people of two different religions—say, Hindu and Islam—enter into dialogue at the level of metaphysics, they can hardly reach an agreement: the truths of the two faiths are mutually exclusive. The latter, unfortunately, places Indian theologians in relationship with the Western forms of Christian faith and the limits they pose on a true Indian theology. This is, in brief, Amaladoss's empirical contribution.

The epistemic contribution, however, is another matter: there is no doubt that the central point of his work as a professional theologian is an Indian Christian theology fully developed.[18] He is not content to be an Indian theologian; he aims to reorganize theology so that India has its own theological lineage, independent of the Western one. First, the emergence of an Indian theological lineage is related to the specific situation of Christians in India who are not only active in a daily relationship with the beliefs and practices of Hinduism and India's other great religious traditions but are often themselves—via family, communities, and ancestors—the partial result of such traditions. Second, the emergence has to do with the

---

18   Michael Amaladoss, *Lead Me On* (Chennai: Blink, 2016), 87.

14   MICHAEL AMALADOSS AND THE QUEST FOR INDIAN THEOLOGY

historical experience of Christianity as a wholly foreign import and with the practical remedies (inculturation, indigenization, and so on) for it. Indian theology grows as a result of this dual effort, that is, on one side, it framed its formulation through the assimilation of Indian religious and cultural heritage, and on the other, it maintains a certain degree of independence from Western-centric theology. In the end, this dual effort amounts to a specific approach to theologizing in India.[19]

The hermeneutical key to interpreting Amaladoss's peculiar position on the relationship between Western theology on one side and Indian theology on the other is his fundamental idea is that Indianness (Indian consciousness, identity) and Christianness (Christian consciousness, identity) are two traits of Indian Christianity that cannot be placed in reciprocal opposition. Amaladoss lacks the literary skills of W. E. B. Du Bois, but what he is trying to describe in his writings is Du Bois's idea of "double consciousness."[20] One can define *double consciousness* as the struggle Indian Christians face to remain true to Indian culture while conforming to a westernized Christianity. To paraphrase Du Bois, double consciousness is the peculiar sensation that Indian Christians experience—a sense of always looking at themselves through the eyes of a colonialist Western Christianity and measuring themselves by the means and forms of a Western Christianity that looks down in contempt.[21] It is no surprise that Amaladoss sees colonialism as a spiritual wound that afflicts Indian Christianity. The solution to this spiritual malaise is a truly indigenous Indian Christianity in which Indians are already Christians by proxy, without further teachings, approvals, or theoretical guidelines.

---

19   Michael Amaladoss, T. K. John, and G. Gispert-Sauch, eds., *Theologizing in India: Selection of Papers Presented at the Seminar Held in Poona on October 26–30, 1978* (Bangalore: Theological Publishers in India, 1981).

20   W. E. B. Du Bois, "Strivings of the Negro People," *The Atlantic*, August 1897, 194–98.

21   In 1903, the Black intellectual and political figure W. E. B. Du Bois finalized his concept of double consciousness in *The Souls of Black Folk*. Du Bois wrote, "It is a peculiar sensation, this double consciousness . . . one ever feels his two-ness, an American, a Negro; two souls, two thoughts, two un-reconciled strivings; two warring ideals in one dark body, whose dogged strength alone keeps it from being torn asunder." See *The Souls of Black Folk* (New York: Gramercy, 1994), 2.

INTRODUCTION   15

Christianity was indeed a colonialist force during the colonial interlude, which lasted nearly three centuries and during which Christianity was identified as the religion of the colonizers.[22] But Christianity is still today, almost a century postindependence, an agent of colonization because it imports to India modern forms of Western Christianity. Amaladoss briefly listed his concerns:

> Our Churches still have the distinct look of foreign architectural styles. Our institutions like schools are perceived as purveyors of western (English!) education. Our ministers—Bishops, Priests, Sisters—are largely identified by their foreign dress patterns. The rituals of our worship do not look Indian . . . our Seminaries and other centers are not in dialogue with the intellectual world of India. Their staff are foreign trained and seem to relate better to foreign groups of scholars.[23]

This condition resulted in Indian Christians being deemed a foreign presence by members of other religions. A more serious problem, however, is that Christianity is an agent of colonization because it imports to India the entire Western history of Christianity. Here is Amaladoss again:

> The "official" images and symbols of their worship are largely foreign and need a commentary to be understood. The worldview underlying the revealed biblical narratives is different. The ecclesial tradition which mediated the bible to them as was imposed as normative is also foreign . . . The texts of their official worship are a translation from sources in Latin or Syriac, so that even when the language is their own, the thought patters are foreign to them.[24]

This condition makes Indian Christians feel like foreigners in their own country. Amaladoss's quotes above are from a book published in 1998. Neither in his later works nor in his conversations with me can one infer

---

22   Amaladoss, *Beyond Inculturation*, 2.
23   Amaladoss, *Beyond Inculturation*, 2.
24   Amaladoss, *Beyond Inculturation*, 3.

that he ever changed his mind on the issue. On the contrary, one could hypothesize a certain fatigue after a lifetime of denunciation. As he told me, "Sometimes, I am tired of fighting. There is only so much one person can take."

To put it differently, colonialism is the myth behind the horizon of Amaladoss's thought. The term *myth* is not used as a synonym for a widely held but false belief or idea; it stands for the unconsciousness that lies behind the horizon (*cosmovision, doxa,* worldview).[25] Colonialism is the myth that provides the horizon of sense to Amaladoss's project of an Indian theology separated from the West. For Amaladoss, the West is not historically colonialist but essentially colonialist, so the experience of British colonialism in India is not a historical event of the past but the symbol of an enduring threat to India coming from the West. The myth of the colonialist West justifies a project of theological independence in view of an antihegemonic, anti-West-centric Christianity. Amaladoss's fundamental vision is that of a posthegemonic Christianity, a Christian order where the West is no longer hegemonic, and India is no longer a vassal.

Amaladoss's vision is not multipolar but bipolar. He does not see the new Christian order in terms of a multitude of local Churches in constant, mutual dialogue but rather as a confrontational relationship between West and East.[26] In his writings, he does not promote the pluralism of theologies but a challenge to the Western theological dominance. For Amaladoss, Asian theologies present a more equitable vision of Asian Christianity,

---

25   The myth embodies certain ontological assumptions about the status of reality, the place of humanity in the universe, and the role of the divine, if any. The myth is the subconscious that lies behind the unconscious structure of meaning. The horizon is the fundamental "syntax." Because this syntax does not hold a single meaning but an inseparable interweaving of meanings, it is a "structure," i.e., a logical-semantic complex consisting of the totality of determinations that must be present for people, things, and events to make sense. The horizon is the terrain where all ontological assumptions receive their proper meaning.

26   For example, see his contribution to the Forum for Liberation Theologies: "Against the official Church epistemology based on Greek traditions . . . we find Asian forms of thought. . . . Many Western Ontologies are dualistic and creationist . . . and [do] not need God anymore. Asian ontologies emphasize 'non-dualism,' where God is considered the form (not the efficient) cause." Michael Amaladoss, "Address to the Forum for Liberation Theologies," (November 30, 2011).

INTRODUCTION   17

which involves engaging with churches in the Global South as equal partners, as opposed to forcing them to enact a certain kind of ecclesial governance. The myth is based on a legacy of distrust. The preexisting perceptions of the West shape how Amaladoss decodes the messages coming from Rome and the West and those coming from Asia and the Global South. Although the horizon of Amaladoss's thought prioritizes the local over the global, it also shows an autonomist tendency, the aspiration for Indian Christians to get rid of external interference and take the future into their own hands. By framing anti-colonial narratives and articulating the message that the churches of the Global South can stand on their own feet, Amaladoss's theology becomes the vehicle of a specific vision: a better Christianity in Asia is possible only if Western interference can be diminished.

The position that Amaladoss openly assumes is that of the Indian theologian who thinks in the context of faith and wonders what the task of an Indian Christian thinker may be in the face of the future of Indian Christianity. The task, he believes, is not only the emancipation of Indian theology from current or recent Western forms of theology but from the ancient ones, too. He calls, in fact, for the circumvention of patristics. In a chapter he wrote for the Festschrift honoring the one hundred years of life of Father Josef Neuner, SJ, Amaladoss offered a much more ambitious definition of Indian theology.[27] He mentioned "the efforts of Indian (Asian) theologians to focus directly on God's self-revelation in the Bible and to respond to it in terms of the Indian context and culture, independently of the mediation of Greek culture and philosophy."[28] He then clarified, "We do not wish to ignore two thousand years of doctrinal and theological development. But a pole of dialogue is different from a norm."[29] Those passages contain much more than I want to disentangle here, but the implication is obvious enough: Amaladoss is in the business of building an Indian theology, distinct and eventually autonomous from the patristic

---

27   Michael Amaladoss, "Toward an Indian Theology," in *Theological Explorations: Centennial Festschrift in Honour of Josef Neuner SJ*, ed. Jakob Kavunkal (Delhi: ISPCK, 2008), 18–34.

28   Amaladoss, "Toward an Indian Theology."

29   Amaladoss, "Toward an Indian Theology," 19.

heritage. In fact, Indian theologians can correlate their experience to the gospel without the mediation of a Western theological system, which they see ultimately as a game of power and control.[30] More precisely, a Euro-American theological system is, for Amaladoss, a form of colonialism that either prevents or restrains Indian theologians from asserting their creative freedom.

In Amaladoss's opinion, Indian independence does not imply the assimilation and overcoming of colonialism but rather its rejection and eviction, as much as possible, from the Indian world. The traits of nationalism and self-determination that characterized the reaction to colonialism maintain their value in this current postcolonial era. Independence was a revolution, and postcolonialism is the continuation of that revolution: it is a process of expelling the remaining traces of colonialism from the Indian psyche; when the Indian psyche is liberated—and only then—can the revolution be considered completed. A stronger India will emerge when the last traces of the colonial contamination are purged. *Mutatis mutandis*, the same logic is applied to the relationship between Indian Christianity and Western Christianity. Amaladoss applies a sort of subtraction theory that suggests that the essential, pure core of Indian Christianity will be revealed once the needless foreign Western grip is stripped away.[31] This almost authentic Indian Christianity that Amaladoss has in mind is at once the starting point of his argument and the point of arrival of a theological and historical process in which Western influence loses ground. For Amaladoss, the emergence of a mature Indian Christianity is the only possibility that deserves his attention. The problem of colonialism in its ecclesial forms and the persistence of such colonialism, is, in his opinion, the essential problem to which Indian theology should respond.

Amaladoss's position on colonialism is not only a historical judgment; it also carries a moral implication. The reasoning is more or less this: colonialism is not a historical evil but an absolute evil—a kind of metaphysical evil. All those who have been colonized are consequently considered victims. They have remained victims even after independence,

---

30   Amaladoss, "My Pilgrimage in Mission," 24.

31   Amaladoss told me that he does not believe that a pure Indian Christianity is possible. The result of this operation of subtraction is destined to produce a hybrid.

INTRODUCTION 19

whenever the forces of reaction, secular as well as ecclesial, have opposed rightful attempts of emancipation. In this perspective, colonialism, both the colonialism of the past and the persistent forms of colonialism within postcolonialism, is the ultimate representation of evil. There is an implicit assumption at work here, a kind of dilemma between the manifestation of evil—that is, Western—and the elimination of evil—that is, Indian. But the real dilemma, I suggest, should be different: is evil a metaphysical entity and, as such, should it be investigated everywhere and every time because it is ubiquitous? Or is it only a historical event, a reality created by humans and by humans, maybe the same humans who produced it, possibly terminated it?

A certain idea of history lies behind this characterization of Catholicism as a confrontation between West and East, between colonialism and liberation. The idea is that two forces have been fighting in the last decades to either retain or take control of Catholicism: one is the force of Western conservatism; the other is Asian progressivism (here I use the terms with an ecclesiastic connotation). Even after the end of colonialism and Vatican II, the fight is ongoing because a reactionary, European-centric Church that acts like it can stop the emancipatory effort. The old Church of Rome is traditional and must be disengaged. The future of Indian Christianity is in this pattern of breaking with the past and starting over. India, Indian Christianity, and Indian theology are coming of age while authority, tradition, and the West are doomed to oblivion. To put it differently, the idea is that liberation is the subject of contemporary history.[32] Amaladoss is not a liberation theologian, but he is a liberationist to some degree when it comes to ecclesial matters. In *Life in Freedom*, Amaladoss crafted a decisive sentence in his efforts to "develop my own tradition in new directions by creatively integrating elements from other traditions. Such a process liberates me from the social, cultural and historical conditionings of my own religion—the liberation of faith and theology from the constraints of my own religious institutions."[33] He does not dare to liberate people from injustice; he is content

---

32   In his words, "Distributive justice and equality, then, become crucial issues in history." See Amaladoss, "Toward an Indian Theology," 20.

33   Michael Amaladoss, *Life in Freedom: Liberation Theologies from Asia* (Maryknoll, NY: Orbis, 1997), 134.

20   MICHAEL AMALADOSS AND THE QUEST FOR INDIAN THEOLOGY

to liberate Indian Catholicism from Rome. To some degree, the liberation of Indian Christianity is the theological continuation of the political autonomy movement that led to the liberation of India from the British Raj.

Amaladoss is a modern theologian, and not only because the antithesis between colonialism and India plays such an important role and frames several aspects of his thought. He is modern because this chain of polarities—modernity and tradition, progress and reaction, oppression and liberation, West and East—is an homage to modernity. Modern culture provides a decisive contribution to this bipolar reading of the world, namely, a conception of history as progress. Thus, a precise conception of history infuses Amaladoss's thought; that is, historical changes come from history itself. In the flux of history, people can grow and eventually become better Christians by the extension of their own degrees of freedom rather than with the help of God's grace. To put it differently, at the roots of Amaladoss's theology is a concept of history as a force of progress, as an irreversible force: what is gained cannot be lost. The emancipation of Indian Christianity progresses together with its estrangement from the West. This form of immanent eschatology is, in its simplicity, the organizing principle of Amaladoss's theology. In his own words: "The hope is also this-worldly, not merely other worldly. The focus is on the joy of being together as a community. . . . It is this movement that gives hope and dynamism to life."[34]

Gustave Flaubert is said to have claimed that "the artist must manage to make posterity believe that he never existed."[35] It is not the author that matters but their work. A legacy is precisely this chance for longevity. Will Amaladoss's work outlast its author? Amaladoss has always reached clarity, as a certain and indisputable datum, on the essential historicity of Christian revelation: Christianity is a historical event, not a system of thought or a matter of conscience, and therefore it has a political translation in the sense of becoming *civitas*, community, society. Part of his legacy depends on the endurance among Indian theologians of this crucial link between history and Christianity. The rest depends on the degree of decolonization of Indian theology, not in the sense of rejection of the

---

34   Michael Amaladoss and M. A. Antony, *The Joy of Living: Wisdom from the East and West* (Mumbai: St. Paul, 2004), 15–16.

35   Julian Barnes, *Flaubert's Parrot* (London: Picador, 1984), 95.

INTRODUCTION   21

Western influence but rather as exhaustion of the category of colonialism as hermeneutical key.

STRUCTURE

This book is organized into five chapters and framed by an introduction, conclusion, and post scriptum. The first two chapters build the context of Amaladoss's thought. In chapter 1 (The Man and the Theologian), I introduce Amaladoss to the reader. Although my concern in this study is with Amaladoss's texts rather than his life, an engagement with his life is necessary because life and work are interwoven. Thus, I offer a synthetic overview of his life and his self-perception. I also indulge in an investigation of his complex relationship with authority and with self-determination, which stands for the power over one's own identity. Before proceeding to the key themes of Amaladoss's theology, chapter 2 (Amaladoss and Indian Theology) is an attempt to situate his work in the context of the late-twentieth century and contemporary Indian theological circles. Here I do not read Indian theology through the lens of Amaladoss's theology; I do the opposite in hopes that the precise contours of his indigenization project and his work on religious dialogue are clarified and brought into sharper relief. I also frame a distinct schema to understand the different political approaches and theological currents and locate Amaladoss within such a schema.

Chapters 3, 4, and 5 focus on Amaladoss's empirical and epistemic contributions. Chapter 3 (Inculturation and Dialogue) is an investigation into the core of Amaladoss's theological work. His reflection on both inculturation and religious dialogue has followed a trajectory that I attempt to describe. The question of a theology that heals separations rather than builds walls is at the center of Amaladoss's writings. I show how inculturation and dialogue are linked to the Kingdom and social salvation. Finally, I synthetize his empirical contribution. Chapter 4 (Christology) addresses some delicate themes behind Amaladoss's work on inculturation and dialogue. He has developed precise positions regarding the uniqueness and universality of salvation in Jesus Christ, the Word and Jesus, the presence of the Spirit in other religions, the unity of God's plan and the role of other religions in it, and the relationship between the Church and the Kingdom of God. Each of these themes is investigated without further comment. I also discuss what I believe is an implicit assumption of Amaladoss's entire theological project: de-dogmatization. I compare his project of de-dogmatization with Rudolf Bultmann's famous scheme of demythologization. Chapter 5 (A True Indian Theology) reflects my investigation into Amaladoss's epistemic contribution. The chapter is concerned with the relationship between Amaladoss's thought and Magisterium, Tradition and Western theology. Specific space is dedicated to a couple of elements that sustain Amaladoss's theological enterprise: his vilification of hellenization as a corruption of Christianity—and by consequence, the eventual dehellenization—and his complicated relationship with modernity.

In the post scriptum, I raise a question about the Indian theologian as a hermeneutical key to bridging the epistemological distance between Amaladoss and the author of this study. Closing the gap requires exposing the underlying presuppositions of the work, which are not argued in the main body but instead simply taken for granted. It also requires some discussion of the politically engaged theology of Indian theologians who are in conflict with Western theologians. A mix of motives has forced me to raise the question of the Indian theologian, the most important motive being my desire to deliver a proficient interpretation of Amaladoss's writings. Among these motives is the increasing divide between Western and Indian theologians, which in turn is a derivate of the recent tendency on the side of Indian theologians to appropriate the capacity to represent themselves. The question of the Indian theologian is, ultimately, a problem of incommensurability between local theologies. If neither Western nor Indian theological patterns embrace the sense of their complementarity for their particular and inevitably culturally and philosophically conditioned and contingent formulations, Western and Indian theologians belong to different epistemic universes. If Western theologians keep considering their modes of theologizing normative, and Indian theologians frame the influence from Western theologians in terms of colonialism, how can the two groups understand each other?

TERMINOLOGY

In this study, I use terms such as *modernity, ideology, liberalism, socialism, nationalism, progressivism, radicalism, moderatism,* and *conservatism.* I use the word *modernity* to mean a theologico-philosophical, legal-political, and cultural-anthropological category to construct, codify, grasp, and experience the realm or reality of being modern and a worldview, which may be either consciously or unreflexively held. Modernity can refer, therefore, to historico-philosophical and normative-ideological projects, cultural programs, or epistemic knowledge regimes. An ideology represents a set of beliefs, opinions, values, and norms that guide an individual or a specific social group. I use the term as a neutral categorization to indicate whatever sufficiently coherent system of ideas and values aimed at directing social, economic, and political behaviors of individuals. Consequently, *ideology* is a generic term applicable to any political, social, and theological inclination supported by a theoretical framework. Liberalism hinges on the autonomous and self-sufficient value of the individual, promoting a society in which the state and market mutually negotiate their relationship. Socialism focuses on the necessity to suppress social privileges and promote total equality among social members. Nationalism promotes the exaltation and defense of the nation, which is considered the chief social value. Both progressivism and radicalism demand a process of change and question traditional institutions; the former, however, suggests a reform of the existing order, and the latter encourages projects to create perfect societies and replace current social orders. Another way to put it is this: progressivism and radicalism share the same theory of progress based on the belief that human development bears a progressive and unidirectional character. They differ in the nature and intensity of such progress: progressives accept modernity and a certain degree of innovation, and radicals embrace modernity and wish to lead it to the most extreme consequences. Both moderatism and conservatism are political philosophies that support tradition in its various representations—religion, culture, identity, beliefs, and customs—and that contrast all thrusts that encourage radical social change. Moderatism wishes to adapt to the present an order that has existed in the past. Conservatism is a radical ideology of those who challenge all forms of evolution and revolution to return to the principles of earlier times. In other words, moderates critically accept modernity, and conservatives challenge modernity and wish to turn back to the premodern sociotheological order.

In this book I constantly refer to Indian theology. One certainly cannot speak today of an Indian theology in the same way it could be talked about in the late-nineteenth century or the early twentieth century—the period of the Indian engagements with the gospel (Raja Ram Mohan Roy, K. C. Sen, Swami Vivekananda) and of the theological work of Hindu converts (Brahmabandhav Upadhyay, Nehemiah Goreh, Pandita Ramabai). It is also appropriate to distinguish between theology produced in India and Indian theology. Indian theology is only one part of the theology produced in India because another significant part of the theological production in India does not share the style of thinking that qualifies one theology as Indian but appears much more aligned with other traditions of thought, including Western traditions. Therefore, the expression "Indian theology" stands not for a hypothetical common denominator for all theological production in Indian but only for those—among the different traditions of thought recognizable among those produced in India—that speak to the present age. More specifically, Indian theology is a project directly related to the independence of the country from the British Raj and therefore to the cultural and political battle around the meaning to be attributed to the Indian identity of the just-constituted nation-state. Within that project, regardless of the variety of theological themes and approaches, it is possible to recognize a specific and unmistakable style of thinking that identifies Indian theology as such. In conclusion, the phrase "Indian theology" does not cover all theological production in India but only that particular style of thinking that, in the current national debate as well as in the international one, catalyzes greater critical attention and prominent interest.

I must signal a certain degree of ambiguity in Amaladoss's use of some terms. Amaladoss does not recognize the massive difference between the term *West* and the term *Europe*. In his writings, the adjectival terms *Western* and *European* are either used as synonyms or linked with the expression *Euro-American*. Readers should be aware that the subject requires careful examination.[36] Several Catholic thinkers—Augusto Del Noce and

---

36 The West is a geopolitical term; it was used in 1830 to articulate the political doctrine of President James Monroe (i.e., the Monroe Doctrine), which declared that the United States would oppose European colonialism in the Western Hemisphere. With the end of World War II, the Western Hemisphere

INTRODUCTION   25

Emmanuel Mounier, to mention a couple—and even pontiffs, including John Paul II, have resisted the assimilation of Europe within the West and the Americanization of European thought in the postwar period.[37] Thus, the phrase "European way of thinking" projects an idea of European identity that is lost in the phrase "Western way of thinking." Although I do not agree that Western and European are synonymous, I accommodate Amaladoss's view that the two terms can be used interchangeably. Sometimes Amaladoss substitutes the word Western for Latin as a synonym for Western Christianity.[38]

Amaladoss uses the expression "Western theology" as an umbrella term to cover the theology developed in the West by Western (mostly clerical) theologians, the theology of European theologians, the westernized doctrines of the Church, and the inherently westernized character of the official Catholic teaching (the Magisterium). Sometimes the context helps to identify the correct meaning of the term. In this study, I unpack Amaladoss's use of the expression in different circumstances. In his writings, the term *Greek* can stand for either Greek philosophy or the alliance of philosophy and Neo-scholasticism in the current official Catholic teaching.[39]

The same lack of accuracy can be found in Amaladoss's use of the words *globalization* and *capitalism*. For him, there is a substantial continuity between the past European globalization, namely imperialism or colonization, and the current form of neoliberal globalization, focused mostly

---

extended across the Atlantic and came to incorporate Europe. One might add that geopolitical terminology follows the winners. The Europeans have lost the Second World War and cannot expect to conserve the monopoly on geopolitics, including its terminology. The Americans won the war, and the West replaced Europe as the dominant concept that defines the Europeans. I must add that, in Amaladoss's writings, West and East stand for ontological entities.

37   Seth D. Armus, "The Eternal Enemy: Emmanuel Mounier's Esprit and French Anti-Americanism," *French Historical Studies* 24, no. 2 (Spring 2001): 271.

38   Amaladoss, *Quest for God*, 254.

39   Amaladoss stated, "The Fathers of the Church . . . used categories of Greek philosophy to understand the faith." See Amaladoss, *Peoples' Theology*, 2. See also Amaladoss, *Experiencing God in India* (Anand: Gujarat Sahitya Prakash, 2016), 5, where he stated, "The only system I can think of is the scholastic system based on Aristotelian philosophy."

on the exportation of capitalism and democracy. Readers should be aware that there is an undisputable difference between the nineteenth-century European globalization, that is, British Raj, and the most recent neoliberal globalization. Although Amaladoss qualifies capitalism as liberal, in his writings capitalism is often defined in neoliberal terms (that is, an economic reality with a small group of rich and many poor). He does not recognize capitalism as a means to decrease poverty, only to increase inequality.

Amaladoss is a Roman Catholic theologian, and his world of reference is, in large part, Roman Catholicism. Here I use *Catholicism* as short for Roman Catholicism. I also use Christian as a synonym for Catholic—for example, Indian Christian theology—not in the sense that Christianity can be identified with Catholicism, but rather that Catholicism belongs to Christianity. Of course, Indian Christianity is by far wider than Indian Catholicism.

For consistency, I did not apply the labels "Father Amal" or "Amal" throughout the book; primarily, I used only the name Amaladoss. The exception is limited to the initial sections of the book, the last section in chapter 3, and the post scriptum, where I recognize the human and therefore emotional bond that links the author with the subject of this book.

Catholic theology has its own rules, and one is to capitalize words like *Church*, *Tradition*, *Magisterium*, and *Kingdom* to signal that these terms are used with a specific meaning. Church is a pluri-dimensional entity: social, institutional, and mystical. From time to time, the context may emphasize one dimension or the other, but readers must remember that the Church in Catholicism is, in effect, multidimensional. Tradition is, together with Scripture, the so-called deposit of faith of Catholicism. Here, *Tradition* stands for sacred tradition, and *tradition* means a local line of thought (like Indian tradition), a belief, or a way of action that is neither necessarily inspired nor religious in character and is transmitted from one generation to another. Magisterium is the teaching function of the Church, and it teaches from both sources, Scripture and Tradition.

Inculturation is an abundantly known word in Catholicism, and I use it instead of the more common *enculturation*. The 1985 Second Extraordinary Assembly of Bishops defined inculturation as "the intimate transformation of authentic cultural values through their integration in Christianity and

the insertion of Christianity in the various cultures."[40] In brief, inculturation is a mutual mingling of Christianity and local culture. The Kingdom
of God is the manifestation and the realization of God's plan of salvation in
all its fullness. When, in this book, the pronoun refers to one of the three
persons of the Trinity, it is capped (He). Consequently, the Word and the
Spirit of God are capped, too. As usual, the Church is feminine (she, her).

METHOD

Although I am aware that a certain scholarship would require me to take an
etic (outsider-observer-objectivist) stance in this study on Amaladoss and
Indian theology, for reasons I explain in the post scriptum, I feel more at
home in an *emic* (insider-participant-empathic) methodological approach.
I believe that without participating in a certain cultural humus—from, as it
were, the inside—one has little hope of fully understanding and appreciating the essential elements molding the movements of Amaladoss's thought.
Although I am not Indian nor am I fully immersed in Indian culture, a
partially inside perspective might afford me a particular advantage over
certain cut-and-dried systematic theologians and textualists approaching
the same subject matter. If nothing else, that perspective is coherent with
the hypothesis that some Indian theologians maintain—namely that context counts.[41] More importantly, it allows readers to detect both my and
Amaladoss's voices. Of course, Amaladoss has found a way to make himself
heard through his publications. But it was important that his voice was
also heard in a book about him.

From the point of view of this book, I follow three simple rules. First,
I distinguish between doctrine and Western theology. I did not follow
Amaladoss in labeling the doctrine as Western. The doctrine is the doctrine. The Western theology, instead, is the nondoctrinal theology that is
generated by Western authors. Second, I provincialize, to borrow a word

---

40   1985 Extraordinary Synod, *The Final Report of the 1985 Extraordinary Synod*
(Rome, 1985), II: C, 6, https://tinyurl.com/26p2zeb2.

41   Amaladoss is one of those theologians. The original quote reads, "The context is a part of the theologizing process. Some even call it a source, besides
scripture and tradition." See Amaladoss, *Peoples' Theology in Asia*, 3.

from Dipesh Chakrabarty's influential *Provincializing Europe*, Western theology: I downsize it to the level of local theology.[42] I share the Indian concern that Western modes of thought are not universal, or put another way, that universal modes that happen to be born in the West are not universal at all. There is a difference between being Indian and theologizing in an Indian way that must be recognized and appreciated. I treat Amaladoss's theology in the same way I would treat the theology of Henri de Lubac or Hans Urs von Balthasar: by placing it in the contexts of its relevant, local theologies on one side and the universal Tradition on the other. I did not read Amaladoss through the lens of European theology, although I establish a parallel between European and Indian modes of theologizing where I found it appropriate.

Third, I distance myself and criticize the Occidentalist flavor that I detect in part of Indian theology.[43] Some Indian theologians, including Amaladoss, are committed to some degree to Occidentalism, or Orientalism in reverse, as an attempt to articulate a counterdiscourse to universalist narratives in relation to the local, inaccurate, and underdeveloped Indian phenomena. The main characteristic of the occidental narratives includes the binary opposition systems to describe the relationship between India and the West, in which the former is embraced quite uncritically and even idealistically, and the latter is exaggeratedly depicted as colonizing and exploitative. The standard strategy is to scrutinize and combat the residual effects of Western domination over the modes of Indian theology while developing the ability of the Indian theologians to speak for themselves outside the normative narrative of the Western theologians. This kind of narrative causes damage by creating a gulf between the West and India and leads readers to believe that the West is worse than it is.

A classical study of Orientalism is that of Edward Said, in which Said argued that the Orient and Orientalism are primarily Western constructs that reflect condescending demeanors and a primarily romanticized image

---

42   Dipesh Chakrabarty, *Provincializing Europe: Postcolonial Thought and Historical Difference* (Princeton: Princeton University Press, 2000).

43   I borrow the notions of "Occidentalism" and "Orientalism in reverse" from Sadiq Jala Al-Azm, "Orientalism and Orientalism in Reverse," *Khamsin, Journal of the Revolutionary Socialists of the Middle East* 8, no. 1 (1981): 6–25, 6.

of the East in contrast to the West. Said added that Western orientalists pretend to capture the essence of the East through the image of the mystical Orient.[44] Richard King, who authored a book on the impact of Orientalism on the Western view of Indian religions, adamantly rejected the emphasis often placed on the so-called "otherworldly" renouncing tendencies within Indian religion. "Indian religion," he argued, "is diverse and therefore not exclusively, or even essentially, mystical."[45] King explained that Orientalism is an exercise in self-reflectivity, in the sense that how the category of mysticism has been constructed in the West says something about how "this notion [of mysticism] has been projected onto Indian religious culture as a way of controlling, manipulating and managing the Orient."[46] But King also signaled the risk of the opposite form of essentialism, Occidentalism, a view of the West as affected by colonialist tendencies. There are several intellectuals (Western as well as non-Western) who believe that there exists a domain of knowledge called Occidentalism. The Chinese scholar Wang Ning believes that Occidentalism is an antagonistic form that strongly opposes Western hegemony and works as a "decolonizing" anti-colonialist strategy in Oriental and Third World (in his terms) countries.[47] The radical Syrian philosopher Sadiq Jalal Al-Azm enrolls Occidentalism in the post–World War II struggles of anti-colonial and anti-imperialist movements. When the old colonial empires collapsed and the former colonies became new nation-states, thinkers, artists, and political leaders came to dominate the narrative and imagery of their people with the rejection of previous conditions of subalternity. As a result, the West has been viewed as the Other.[48] Occidentalism consists of essentializing the West in the same way that Westerners used to do it with the Orient. Eastern occidentalist scholars objectify the Occident and construct stereotypes about the West. King remembers that "there are a multiplicity of 'Wests' hidden behind the

---

44   Edward W. Said, *Orientalism: Western Conceptions of the Orient* (New York: Vintage, 1978).

45   Richard King, *Orientalism and Religion: Postcolonial Theory, India and "the Mystic East"* (New York: Routledge, 1999), 5.

46   King, *Orientalism and Religion*, 6.

47   Wang Ning, "Orientalism versus Occidentalism?" *New Literary History* 28, no. 1 (1997): 63.

48   Al-Azm, "Orientalism and Orientalism in Reverse."

veil of a homogenizing and ahistorical essentialism (occluded by myths of cultural/natural homogeneity)."[49]

In this study on Amaladoss, I attempt to bring theology to life. I did not restrict myself to the grand-systems theology, but I reported personal experiences and sensations to bring to readers the voice of Amaladoss and his colleagues from the borderlands of India. The choice of balancing micronarratives with the main scholarly narrative came to me as a means to offer a colorful and vivid account of an Indian theologian. The idea, in other words, has never been to simply introduce a cornucopia of fresh materials and a compelling analysis of the theology of such a giant, but also to provide glimpses of Amaladoss's quotidian life and his varied and rich experiences. *David* by Michelangelo is the canon, perfection in art, but life and thought are less than perfect, including those of great theologians. The portrait of Amaladoss and his work offered in this study reflects this choice to dismiss perfection. Rather, I tried to make Amaladoss seem real and alive to readers. For this reason, I drew on a wide range of sources, including eyewitness accounts, interviews, and archival materials.

Wherever necessary, I mention in the footnotes the sources of quotes and other significant secondary contributions. When a source is not offered, it indicates that the content or reference originated either in the notes I took during conversations with Amaladoss or in emails we exchanged. It is also possible that the source is either an unpublished document or personal annotation he provided to me. Some of these materials are undated or are only tentatively dated. Notably, uncited sources as defined above (i.e., notes, emails, unpublished material) were double-checked with Amaladoss before submission of the manuscript for this book.

---

49   King, *Orientalism and Religion*, 3.

1

THE MAN AND THE THEOLOGIAN

PROFILE

Michael Amaladoss has been a scholar, an administrator, and an artist. His life has spanned the British Raj, through Independence, through the Second Vatican Council, through India's shift from socialism to economic liberalization in the early nineties, and up to the ascent of Hindu nationalism in the new century. He was born in Tamil Nadu (India) in 1936, and in 1953, he entered the Society of Jesus. During his novitiate, he met Father Ignatius Hirudayam (1910–1995), who was an expert in Indian culture and religion; notably, Amaladoss still considers Hirudayam his guru. In 1961, he completed a master of arts in Christian (Scholastic) philosophy after writing a thesis on C. G. Jung and Yoga. Then, between 1961 and 1963, he took the opportunity to complete a two-year diploma in South Indian classical music, specializing in singing, at a professional school in Chennai; the classes were hosted in a building that today faces the Jesuit Residence at Loyola College, which is where he currently resides. From 1969 to 1972, Amaladoss completed doctoral coursework at the Institut Catholique in Paris, where he graduated after defending a dissertation on sacramental theology that focused on the problems of inculturation, "Do Sacraments Change? Variable and Invariable Elements in Sacramental Rites." The content was later published as a book.[1] Back in India, he became a professor of theology, initially teaching at St. Paul's Seminary in Tiruchirappalli from

---

[1]   Michael Amaladoss, *Do Sacraments Change? Variable and Invariable Elements in Sacramental Rites* (Bangalore: Theological Publications in India, 1979).

1974 to 1979, then at Vidyajyoti College in Delhi from 1974 to 1983 and again between 1995 and 2012.

Amaladoss has spent his career between theology and administration, holding some of the most prestigious seats in India, Asia, and Rome. In his day, he acted as principal and rector of Vidyajyoti College (1976–1979); vice-provincial for Formation for South Asian Jesuits (1979–1983); president of Jnanadeepa Vidyapeeth, Pune (1983); special assistant to the superior general of the Jesuits, Rome (1983–1995); consultor to three Pontifical Councils, Rome, and to the Commission on World Mission and Evangelism of the World Council of Churches, Geneva (1983–1987); and president of the International Association of Mission Studies (1989–1993). He returned to Chennai in 2001 to transform Aikiya Alayam (Santhome High Road), an urban ashram established in 1967 by his guru, Father Hirudayam, into a research center called the Institute of Dialogue with Cultures and Religions (IDCR). Initially approved by the University of Madras, it moved to the Loyola College campus in 2005. Amaladoss has exercised—and still exercises—tremendous influence on the intellectual conversations within the Society of Jesus, the Indian theologians, and the Asian Churches. His network of contacts with institutions and people in Asia and beyond is unmatched.[2] Apart from that, he also arranged and eventually composed about 150 hymns in Tamil, of which about 90 have been recorded.[3]

Despite his relevant interests in administration and art, Amaladoss is primarily a theologian. The list of his publications (through December 2022) is overwhelming and amounts to thirty-six books in English—ten of which were translated into one or more other languages—and two in Tamil, as well as nine edited books and 504 articles in various languages. His main works are usually considered to be *Faith, Culture and*

---

2 See, for example, the number and level of people Amaladoss recognized in the first pages of his book *The Asian Jesus*, ix. See also *Vagdevi, Journal of Religious Reflection* 11 (2017). *Vagdevi* is the publication of Tulana, the Sri Lanka Jesuit Province Apostolate founded by celebrated theologian Father Marian Aloysius Reginald Pieris, SJ. The journal dedicated this commemorative issue to honor the eightieth birthday of Amaladoss, and the subjects of all the articles reflect concerns Amaladoss has dealt with in his life and work to date.

3 Biographical details were derived from Amaladoss's website, "Michael Amaladoss About Me," accessed May 22, 2020, https://michaelamaladoss.com.

THE MAN AND THE THEOLOGIAN   33

Inter-Religious Dialogue (1985); *Making All Things New: Dialogue, Pluralism, and Evangelization in Asia* (1990); *A Call to Community: The Caste System and Christian Responsibility* (1994); *Life in Freedom: Liberation Theologies from Asia* (1997); *Beyond Inculturation: Can the Many Be One?* (1998); *Making Harmony: Living in a Pluralist World* (2003); *The Dancing Cosmos: A Way to Harmony* (2003); and *The Asian Jesus* (2005).[4] Among his most recent books, *Quest for God: Doing Theology in India* (2013) is a sort of introduction of his thought, *Lead Me On* (2016) is his intellectual autobiography, *Interreligious Encounters: Opportunities and Challenges* (2017) is a compendium of his work on interreligious dialogue, and *Peoples' Theology in Asia* (2021) is a collection of lectures delivered to the East Asia Theological Encounter Program between 2006 and 2018.[5]

FURTHER DETAILS

The previous profile amounts to a preliminary, eventually dry introduction to the man behind the theologian; it offers little of the real Amaladoss. Fortunately, Amaladoss himself has provided abundant autobiographical material to bridge the gap. I refer, for example, to the video interview Amaladoss conceded to Lucette Verboven in 2000 and to an autobiographical article he drafted in 2007. He even penned an autobiography, published in 2016.[6] These sources can be used to learn about Amaladoss's life and work in more detail. One decisive event in his life was the meeting with his guru, Father Hirudayam. In his 2016 autobiography, Amaladoss described the circumstances of his encounter with Father Hirudayam, a fellow Jesuit.

---

4   Amaladoss, *Faith, Culture and Inter-Religious Dialogue*, Ideas for Action Series 2 (New Delhi: Indian Social Institute, 1985); *Making All Things New: Dialogue, Pluralism and Evangelization in Asia* (Maryknoll, NY: Orbis, 1990); *A Call to Community: The Caste System and Christian Responsibility* (Anand: Gujarat Sahitya Prakash, 1994); *Making Harmony: Living in a Pluralist World* (Delhi: ISPCK, 2003); *The Dancing Cosmos: A Way to Harmony* (Anand: Gujarat Sahitya Prakash, 2003).

5   Michael Amaladoss, *Interreligious Encounters: Opportunities and Challenges* (Maryknoll, NY: Orbis, 2017).

6   Michael Amaladoss, "Michael Amaladoss and Lucette Verboven," interview by Lucette Verboven, March 29, 2020, video, 30:38, https://tinyurl.com/4kw6vj7z. See also Amaladoss, *Lead Me On*, 13.

The only noteworthy event during these two years [1953–1955] was some sort of "field work" for a month. Two of us (myself and Fr. Chelladurai) were sent to a parish in Palayamkottai. We were supposed to teach religious doctrine to the children. But apart from a few classes we were mostly left alone. For the third and fourth week we went to another parish, Irudayakulam, close to the Papanasam dam, near Tirunelveli. God was leading me to my guru.[7]

Next, he elaborated his debt to Father Hirudayam:

Fr. Ignatius Hirudayam was very much interested in Indian culture, philosophy and religion. He had taught in the seminary in Trichy for a couple of years. Christianity had largely remained a foreign religion. Its main rituals of worship were in Latin. Philosophy and theology were taught in Latin. Younger people like Fr. Hirudayam wanted the Church to become more Indian. He was considered too "nationalist," at a time when India was just gaining independence, and was sent away to the farthest parish the Jesuits had in Tamilnadu. He was some years ahead of his time. The epoch-making Second Vatican Council of the Church came with its reforms eight years later (1962–1965). He was a self-made scholar in Hinduism, recognized as an expert in Saiva Siddhanta. He composed many beautiful hymns in Tamil and encouraged Indian music and dance. He had started to build a church with an Indian "gopura" in his parish, which was pulled down later by people who thought differently. His aim was to make Christianity Indian. Within fifteen days he introduced me to the elements of Karnatic music and to a love for things Indian—culture, philosophy and religion. Many seeds were then sown that produced fruit later. A creative discipleship started which was not without its ups and downs, as was inevitable between two intelligent and free humans, but from two different generations, at a time when history was moving fast in India. Much of what I have become goes back to that seminal moment of encounter with my guru and his inspiration.[8]

---

7   Amaladoss, *Lead Me On*, 16.

8   Amaladoss, *Lead Me On*, 16–17.

THE MAN AND THE THEOLOGIAN   35

The story reads this way: in the middle of a field research project, during the two-year period of novitiate, Amaladoss spent two weeks with Father Hirudayam. These two weeks became a decisive moment in his life because he found his guru, his mission, and his artistic passion. Some of the phrases and terms in the above quote recur in his writings, including the shift from Latin to Indian cultures and religions, Christianity perceived as a foreign religion, the possibility of an indigenous, that is, Indian stream of Catholicism, the goal of an Indian Church, the revolution of Vatican II, and Carnatic music; in other words, much of Amaladoss's subsequent theological agenda is summarized here. Surely, the meeting with Father Hirudayam was brief yet monumental in its consequences.

The fruits of this encounter would become evident during Amaladoss's pursuit of a master's degree in philosophy in Shenbaganur between 1958 and 1961. "The medium of instruction," he explains, "was Latin. I used to read a chapter of St. Thomas Aquinas per day. But the inspiration of Father Hirudayam made me take up privately a deeper study of Indian philosophy."[9] While he was studying Scholastic sources in Latin, he was privately reading Indian philosophy. Amaladoss met Hirudayam in 1954 and from him was inspired to turn his study to the riches of Indian art, philosophy, and spirituality. In his 2007 autobiographical article, Amaladoss provides an explanation about why he considers Father Hirudayam his guru:

> During my novitiate [at the Society of Jesus, 1953–1955] I spent about two weeks with Fr. Ignatius Hirudayam, who was an expert in Indian culture and religion and whom I still consider my guru. He planted the seeds of inculturation in my heart and spirit, which flowered much later under more favorable circumstances.[10]

Thus, Amaladoss gave credit to Father Hirudayam because, as Amaladoss explained, "He planted the seeds of inculturation in my heart and spirit, which flowered much later under more favorable circumstances." This

---

9   Amaladoss, *Lead Me On*, 18.
10   Amaladoss, "My Pilgrimage in Mission," 21.

"Indian turn" became the watershed of his adult life. From Hirudayam, Amaladoss learned to see the relationship between Christianity and India through different eyes, no longer as a religion that came to India as a foreigner but as one that flourishes in India in Indian forms.

The Indian turn severed Amaladoss's affiliation with European theology and its lineage. Amaladoss has often been connected to the work of another theologian, the Belgian Jesuit Dupuis, whose life intersected Amaladoss's on more than one occasion. Amaladoss studied under and then worked with Father Dupuis, yet Amaladoss barely mentions Dupuis in his autobiography. Dupuis, a celebrated and unfortunate Belgian theologian, contributed greatly to the development of the subfield of theology of religions with books such as *Toward a Christian Theology of Religious Pluralism* from 1997 and *Christianity and the Religions,* published in 2002.[11] He incurred the criticisms of the Congregation for the Doctrine of the Faith (or simply Congregation)—namely, the Vatican department responsible for enforcing orthodoxy—which opened an inquiry into his pioneering work, *Toward a Christian Theology of Religious Pluralism.*[12] The Congregation declined to discipline Dupuis but accused him of presenting ambiguities in his work.[13] The three years of contention with the Congregation left its mark on Father Dupuis's mental and physical health.[14] He died while the

---

11 Jacques Dupuis, *Toward a Christian Theology of Religious Pluralism* (Maryknoll, NY: Orbis, 1997); *Christianity and the Religions: From Confrontation to Dialogue*, trans. Robert Barr (Maryknoll, NY: Orbis, 2002).

12 Recently, Pope Francis replaced the Congregation with the Dicastery for the Doctrine of the Faith as a body within the Curia, with the responsibility of safeguarding the doctrine of faith and morals. See Pope Francis, *Praedicate evangelium* (Apostolic Constitution, March 19, 2022), art. 69–78, https://tinyurl.com/kv3wjka2.

13 Offices of the Congregation for the Doctrine of the Faith, "Notification on the Book *Toward a Christian Theology of Religious Pluralism* (Maryknoll, NY: Orbis, 1997) by Father Jacques Dupuis, SJ," January 24, 2001, https://tinyurl.com/3xtb24nz.

14 Gerard O'Connell, *Do Not Stifle the Spirit: Conversations with Jacques Dupuis* (Maryknoll, NY: Orbis, 2017), 250. Amaladoss wrote a sympathetic review of O'Connell's book on Dupuis. See Amaladoss, review of *Do Not Stifle the Spirit: Conversations with Jacques Dupuis*, by Gerard O'Connell, *Horizons* 46, no. 2 (2019): 413–15.

THE MAN AND THE THEOLOGIAN   37

Congregation was opening a second inquiry on his new book, *Christianity and the Religions*.[15]

Thirteen years older than Amaladoss, Dupuis was already a member of the faculty when Amaladoss joined Vidyajyoti College. In 1984, after thirty-six years in India, Dupuis was called to teach theology and non-Christian religions at the Gregorian University in Rome. He rapidly became director of the journal *Gregorianum* and was appointed consultor at the Pontifical Council for Interreligious Dialogue. Dupuis's seniority and his prominent status reached in the eighties and nineties in theological circles, both in Europe and Asia, have produced the impression that Amaladoss was a disciple of Dupuis. But Amaladoss reminded me during our conversations that Dupuis was a professor when Amal was principal and rector at Vidyajyoti College, and that Dupuis was the assistant editor of *VJTR* when Amaladoss was editor-in-chief of the journal; in fact, Dupuis took the position of editor-in-chief of the journal from Amaladoss, not the other way around. The point is that there was academic fellowship but not academic lineage between the two. Most importantly, there is no intellectual lineage. Dupuis was still working with Western categories of theologizing while Amaladoss was building a theology in dialogue with the Indian context.

Amaladoss's autobiographical material refers to his appreciation, so to speak, of the theological circles in Rome. In 1983, he moved to Rome as one of the counselors to the superior general of the Jesuits. There, he became a consultant to the Pontifical Council for Interreligious Dialogue and to the Pontifical Council for Culture, one of the seven Vatican representatives in the Commission on World Mission and Evangelism of the World Council of Churches, and a member of the executive committee of SEDOS, an organization that serves a group of religious congregations involved in mission. In his autobiography, however, he explained that he had to give up these roles after five years because the Vatican did not feel its position was represented. He adds, "I was speaking more as an Indian theologian" than

---

15   For an account of the dispute between the Congregation and Dupuis, see Bill Burrow, *Jacques Dupuis Faces the Inquisition* (Eugene: Wipf & Stock, 2012) and Gerald O'Collins, *On the Left Bank of the Tiber* (Leominster: Gracewing, 2013), 213–52.

a representative of the Holy Seat.[16] It is possible that Amaladoss's autonomy brought him into conflict with the Vatican Congregation for the first time. This period in Rome (1983–1995) gave him international exposure and elevated his profile. In the autobiographical article mentioned above, Amaladoss noted that his years in Rome were characterized by his shift to missiology and mission studies. In his autobiographical book, he recognized that "my time in Rome was a time of growth as a theologian."[17]

In our conversations, however, he indulged in more sad memories of alienation and perceived suspicion. In the years he spent in Rome, he said, he never introduced himself to the network of universities orbiting around the Vatican, including the famous Pontificial Gregorian University where Dupuis was teaching at that time. Amaladoss maintained some distance from the theologians based in Rome, and he believed that the feeling was mutual. Between his arrival and departure from Rome, he remembers, he was invited to present a lecture only once. It was a time when he could measure the remoteness, both intellectual and institutional, between the theology of the Roman School of Theology and his own. "Roman School" (Scuola Romana) stands for a conservative theological school that flourished at the pontifical universities in Rome (especially the Gregorian University and its predecessor, the Roman College, or Collegio Romano) in the first half of the nineteenth century and remained influential until the Council.[18] Although often associated with the Neo-scholasticism that became dominant after Leo XIII's encyclical *Aeterni Patris*, the theological method of the Roman Schools was fundamentally biblical-patristic in nature.[19] I borrow the term *lato sensu* to designate a stream of theology that can be both conservative and moderate and that remained influential in

---

16   Amaladoss, *Lead Me On*, 34–35.

17   Amaladoss, *Lead Me On*, 34.

18   Today, the Roman School remains prominent at the Pontifical Academy of Theology and at the Pontifical Academy of Saint Thomas Aquinas, and it makes its voice heard through the academic journals *Divinitas* and *Doctor Communis.*

19   Heribert Schauf coined the expression "Scuola Romana" in 1937 to identify the labors of four nineteenth-century Jesuit professors at the Roman College: Giovanni Perrone, Carlo Passaglia, Clemens Schrader, and Johann Baptist Franzelin. See Joseph Carola, "La metodologia patristica nella teologia preconciliare dell'Ottocento," *Gregorianum* 97, no. 3 (2016): 605.

the clerical circles around the Roman Curia during the pontificates of John Paul II and Benedict XVI.

Amaladoss's time in Rome was probably also a time of encounter with the European parochialisms in cosmopolitan Rome, which confirmed his notion that to find his place in the universal Church, he had to be, first and foremost, an Indian theologian. In other words, once he found himself at the center of global Catholicism, he proudly decided to emphasize, rather than play down, his national identity. He preferred to be the representative of his country within the universal Church rather than the opposite—that is, the representative of the universal Church to the different, local ecclesial realities. To paraphrase Robert Frost, he was placed in front of two diverging paths: the cosmopolitan and the nationalistic. He took the second "and that has made all the difference."[20] During his time in Rome, he concluded that universal Catholicism is not universal at all. There is no universal Catholicism; that would be impossible, Amaladoss noted, because religion is always culture-bound. Therefore, Catholicism is constituted by both regional and cultural Catholicism wherein the same gospel is proclaimed through various mediated cultural symbols.

AN INDIAN THEOLOGIAN

Reflecting on the decisive moments of his life in his 2007 autobiographical article, Amaladoss assessed his theological career, which by that time had spanned almost forty years (1969 marks when his first article published in an academic journal):

> The fact that I have not been tied to a faculty of theology may have enabled me to wander far and to be creative and free. I have not produced scholarly volumes that would delight specialists, a choice I do not regret. The attempt to create contextual theology in India may have also saved me from being a prisoner of Euro-American "systematic theology." Even now, we Asian (Indian) theologians resent the implication that our reflections are not systematic if

---

20 Robert Frost, "A Group of Poems," *The Atlantic*, August 1915, https://tinyurl.com/yrsnssex.

they are not a dialogue with the Euro-American "system." We are convinced that no serious Indian (Asian) theology will emerge as long as we are tied to the apron strings of a Euro-American system. We can correlate our experience to the Gospel without the mediation of a theological system, which we see ultimately as a game of power and control. Unfortunately, any reflections on the theme of the dialogue of the Gospel with cultures and religions are suspect today if they do not conform to the Euro-American system, which is thrust on us as normative. No one seems to imagine the damage this attitude is doing to the credibility and relevance of Christianity in Asia today. This issue may seem to be a special problem of the highly centralized Roman Catholic Church, but in fact is relevant to all Christian theology. Colonialism of all kinds dies hard. I am sure that Asian theologians will soon assert their creative freedom.[21]

This long quote is built around two main ideas: Amaladoss perceived himself as an Asian (Indian) theologian who is not organic to a faculty of theology and is in an adversarial relationship with the Western system of theology. First, I address the second idea; in the next section, I will focus on the first idea.

If one takes Amaladoss at face value, an Indian (Asian) theologian is someone who follows a distinct method of theologizing, namely, contextual theology, and who is autonomous from the Euro-American system. An Indian theologian, therefore, considers their reflections relevant precisely because they are elaborated outside the context of a Euro-American system. As a matter of fact, Amaladoss depicts himself as an Asian (Indian) theologian in opposition to Western theology because, "no serious Indian (Asian) theology will emerge as long as we (i.e., Indian theologians) are tied to the apron strings of a Euro-American system." Thus, serious Indian theology is a theology that refuses continuity with Euro-Western theology that, in turn, is characterized by being systematic. By systematic he means an exposition "of presumably a-temporal a-priori propositions" made by "most Western theologians" who claim that those propositions

---

21   Amaladoss, "My Pilgrimage in Mission," 24.

THE MAN AND THE THEOLOGIAN   41

are universal.[22] Thus, not only is the Indian method of theologizing autonomous from the Euro-American system, but it is also developing in opposition to it. At this point, however, a clarification of what the "Euro-American system" is for Amaladoss proves essential. Amaladoss has a precise idea of the purpose and character of Indian theology, but scholars may at first find his view of Western theology confusing. The lack of definition of terms in Amaladoss's writings may cause unnecessary misunderstandings.

As this study makes evident, Amaladoss knows the West, both in its European and North American realities. He earned his doctoral degree in Paris and spent twelve years in Rome. He has been invited several times to teach and give lectures in the United States, including in Cincinnati, Washington, and Berkeley. However, it is fair to say that he has intentionally developed his research outside the boundaries of Western thought. Not often in Amaladoss's writings will readers find mention of Western thinkers like Heidegger, Ricoeur, or Gadamer.[23] He does not distinguish between an analytical and a continental philosophical line of thought. He seems to miss the nuances of critical theory and hermeneutics, analytical and postmodern philosophy. But in Amaladoss's view, this is merely because he never studied philosophy. In his writings, he takes the high road and seems to have a dislike for philosophy tout court. In his *Quest for God: Doing Theology in India*, Amaladoss explicitly denied any positive role of philosophy—any philosophy, Western or Indian, ancient or modern; they are irrelevant to India.[24] He claims that "though traditionally philosophy is supposed to be the handmaid of theology, in practice, philosophy tends to structure and enslave theology."[25]

---

22   Michael Amaladoss, "The Mystery of Christ and Other Religions: An Indian Perspective," *VJTR* 63, no. 5 (1999): 327–38

23   There are exceptions, however. For example, he mentions the hermeneutics of Ricoeur and Gadamer as well as his discovery of Emmanuel Levinas's work in chapter 1 of his book *Quest for God*, 23–31. Despite these mentions, I am unsure whether Amaladoss is a safe guide to European philosophy. His first book, *Do Sacraments Change?* is a different thing. An elaboration of his doctoral dissertation, the book shows Amaladoss's easiness with both French and German modern philosophies. That book, however, represents a unicum in his production.

24   Amaladoss synthesized his argument in the foreword of his book *Experiencing*, 5.

25   Amaladoss, *Experiencing*, 5.

42   MICHAEL AMALADOSS AND THE QUEST FOR INDIAN THEOLOGY

It is equally fair to say that Amaladoss has been a stranger to European scholarly circuits. After the Second Vatican Council, the center of theological scholarship in the West shifted from the seminary to the university. At the beginning, the organization of the faculties of theology mirrored the disciplines inherited from seminary faculties—Scripture, history, ethics or practical theology, and systematic theology. Later, however, changing student demographics, shifting of interests in the new generations of theologians, and more importantly, the laicization of theology forced the faculties to abandon the older disciplines and embrace new ones, like religious studies, critical theory, and sociology. With fewer religious men and women and fewer clergy as faculty, the face of theological scholarship became decidedly less clerical and more diversified: young theologians definitively spend less time on Thomistic or manualist theology and more on biblical studies, ecumenism, and other religions. Today the problem is rather the opposite: the new generation of lay scholars lack training in the patristic authors and the ancient languages needed for studying the early sources of Christian theology. Scholars are encouraged to follow trends that currently prevail in the academy, like the members of other disciplines do, not to reconceive theology for the twenty-first century in continuity with Catholic theological traditions. These days, systematic theology in the Western sense is a marginal activity in the Western faculties of theology.

Amaladoss has a limited interest in academic theology in Europe and North America, the theology developed by laypeople in their academic careers. The rich plurality of voices of academic theology, the academic freedom that comes with pursuing scholarly research, and the commitment to scholarship for its own sake are absent in Amaladoss's evaluation of Euro-American theology. Although the theologians of the West produce, so to speak, a rich repertoire of blues and pop, rock and jazz, to Amaladoss's ear they all sound the same as classical music. In his view, the whole of Euro-American theology sings the same tune. His assessment is marked by a certain level of essentialism that leaves little room for theological traditions, streams and substreams, or variances and nuances. In the same fashion, he has little patience for the subtle but evident variations between the speculative European style and the pragmatic American style of writing theology. The work of Euro-American theologians is, in his view, always top-down, far from the living experience of people, systematic, and inherently self-referential.[26] European and American theologians produce Western theology, but they believe it is universal and therefore applicable to India and Asia. For this reason, Amaladoss concludes, they are colonialist in their approach, although they may fail to recognize it.

The Western audience can easily misunderstand Amaladoss's valuation of European and American theology as referring to Catholic lay theology. He is probably referring to the clerical theology that is promoted in the seminaries and pontifical universities with orthodox catechisms and under papal control. True, only quite rarely in his writings will readers catch a reference to theologians such as de Lubac, von Balthasar, or Rahner, to mention a few. He projects on the entire Western theology the more restrictive experience he might have with the theology of the Catholic circles of Rome, the academic reality I labeled in terms of the School of Rome. The latter, and only the latter, is under his evaluation. Amaladoss has been exposed, and he has exposed himself, to clerical theology; therefore, he has a vision of Western scholarship limited to its clerical-institutional component. As a result, his interaction with Western theology is more precisely an interaction with the official documents of the Magisterium and with the theologians who, like him, interact with those documents. And because the Magisterium, particularly during the decade in which Amaladoss was in Rome, showed a peculiarly diffident approach to non-Western forms of Catholic theology, Amaladoss maintains an unenthusiastic view of it.[27]

---

26   To prove the opposite, I cannot resist quoting this autobiographical note of one of the most decisive Western theologians of the twentieth century: "Almost everything I have written," de Lubac explained, "sprang from unforeseeable circumstances, without technical preparation. In vain would one look for a true, personal philosophical and theological synthesis in the ensemble of such diverse publications, whether to criticize or approve." See von Balthasar, *Theology of Henri de Lubac*, 10.

27   Nick Chui has written an interesting piece on the opposition of Amaladoss to what Chui calls the Roman theology, or the theology of the Catholic Magisterium. According to Chui, who is an educator based in Singapore, Amaladoss incorrectly identifies the current Roman theology with Neo-scholasticism. But, Chui protests, the Roman theology is marked by the *ressourcement* movement these days, not by Neo-scholasticism. *Ressourcement* theology is, lato sensu, the form of Neoplatonism of Monchanin, Abhishiktananda, and others.

Amaladoss has had "disagreements" (his word) with the Congregation over a period of thirty years.[28] The crux of the matter has been the positive role played in his theology by other religions in the economy of God's plan of salvation, as well as the unclear role of Jesus Christ and His Church in that plan. Amaladoss has been questioned three times by the Congregation regarding his orthodoxy. In the 1990s and between 2003 and 2006, the issue was easily resolved. From 2013 to 2015, however, Amaladoss was investigated, although not silenced or censured. A dialogue between Amaladoss, Father Adolfo Nicolás, the superior general of the Society of Jesus at that time, and Father Soosai Arockiasamy, SJ, who acted as theological advisor on one side and the theologians of the Congregation on the other, ultimately composed the matter. Amaladoss was cleared of any suspicion.[29]

Chui may have a point. In a recent book, Amaladoss wrote, "I am writing my book as a Catholic theologian and the only system I can think of is the scholastic system based on Aristotelian philosophy which is considered normative in the Church. This has been reiterated again by Pope Benedict XVI." Chui is correct in stating that Amaladoss confuses *ressourcement* theology with Neo-scholasticism. The scholastic system has been replaced by the so-called *ressourcement* theology that led to Vatican II. Benedict XVI is an Augustinian, not a Thomist. In the end, however, the confusion causes no harm because Amaladoss rejects any stream of Western theology. See Chui, "Is Roman Theology Neo-Scholastic? A Genealogical Reply to Michael Amaladoss," *Trinity Theological Journal* 21, no. 1 (2013): 43–60; and Amaladoss, *Experiencing*, 5. On the revival of Neoplatonism in twentieth-century French theology, see Wayne J. Hankey, "One Hundred Years of Neoplatonism in France: A Brief Philosophical History," in *Levinas and the Greek Heritage Followed by One Hundred Years of Neoplatonism in France: Brief Philosophical History*, eds. Jean-Marc Narbonne and Wayne J. Hankey (Leuven: Peeters, 2006), 97–248.

28 Amaladoss, *Lead Me On*, 96.

29 As far as I know, the available sources referring to these disagreements are the already-mentioned Amaladoss's autobiography, *Lead Me On*, 96–103, and Mong's comparative study of how the Congregation treated the theologies of two theologians. The theologies under consideration are the liberation theology of the Peruvian theologian Gustavo Gutiérrez and the liberation-inculturation theology of Amaladoss. See Ambrose Mong, *A Tale of Two Theologians: Treatment of Third World Theologies* (Cambridge: James Clarke, 2017), chapters 5–8. Moreover, a chapter included in a collection of "important (albeit hitherto inaccessible) papers and writings" of Amaladoss was

THE MAN AND THE THEOLOGIAN   45

Great theologians under investigation, like Dupuis, whom I already mentioned, even after being cleared of any wrongdoing pay a certain price, both physically and mentally, for the torture of suspicion and disapproval. Most of these intellectuals, a group that includes Maurice Blondel and de Lubac, emerged from the tunnel with a profound sense of insecurity, prepared to make concessions in their subsequent work. Others—Yves Congar comes to mind—became disillusioned with the institution and developed a poorly concealed irritation toward it. Amaladoss shows none of this: he writes prudently but remains unconcerned with potential consequences. He has no desire to wake the sleeping giant, so to speak, but he remains unafraid of it.

FREE THINKER

In his 2007 autobiographical article, Amaladoss framed himself as an Asian (Indian) theologian who is incompatible with a faculty of theology. In Amaladoss's opinion, the fact that he has not been tied to a faculty of theology may have enabled him to "wander far and to be creative and free." Amal identified the source of his creativity and freedom in the fact that he is not an academic theologian. He reiterated and expanded the same point in a statement he prepared for me in a preliminary phase of this project (I already quoted a couple of sections). The statement reveals much about his self-perception:

> Of course, I would consider myself an Indian Catholic theologian. Beyond that I would reject categories like Brahminical,

---

presented as his complete and unabridged response to the Conference. See Amaladoss, *Interreligious Encounters*, chapter 15. The quote on the "important papers" is on page xx. Father William Skudlarek has raised the question about how it is possible that chapter 15, which was originally published in 2008, can be read as a complete and unabridged response to the Conference, which, according to Amaladoss's religious superior, began its investigation on him in 2013. The answer is that the unbridged response refers to the investigation spanning from 2003 to 2005. Amaladoss provided me with a copy of his 2013 written response to the Congregation. See Skudlarek, review of *Interreligious Encounters: Opportunities and Challenges*, by Michael Amaladoss, *Dilatato Corde* 7, no. 2 (2017), https://tinyurl.com/4kcubjd6. For the above quote on "disagreements," see Amaladoss, *Lead Me On*, 96.

Dalit, etc. I am neither a Brahmin nor a Dalit. My theological reflection would be classified much more under the Asian triple dialogue of the Gospel with the poor, the cultures and the religions, though my own interests follow a reverse order: Dialogue with religions, Indian culture and the poor. I tackle questions as they come to me. I have not developed a system, nor do I belong to a school or a group. I have been in administration for fifteen years and more. I would consider myself a freelancer, though with a special interest in inter-religious dialogue and Indian theology. This special interest, which has been there from my study days, has been sharpened because of my "forced" dialogue with the Vatican Holy Office. It has also led to a certain Christological reflection, not so much academic, but practical. I have not been interested in systematic theology in the western sense, but a practical and dialogical theology in the Asian/Indian context. I have also had some interest in Indian Christian spirituality, but not of the ashram type, though I was a friend of Swami Abhishiktananda. I am not too involved with the poor and the Dalits, though I have written on the Caste system—not on the Dalits—and on Asian Liberation theologies. So I am an Indian theologian, but a generalist, not tied to any school or discipline. I am open to dialogue. But I would not like to be categorized. I do not belong to any group, though I have a couple of favorite students. I have not taught too long in any school. I have been a free—not a professional—theologian. By the way, I also have a diploma in Karnatic (South Indian) music and am a composer of more than 100 hymns in Tamil. This is where I stand.

This statement is a labyrinth of paths. Clearly, Amaladoss considers himself an Indian theologian who has been disinterested in systematic theology in the Western sense and is focused instead on a practical and dialogical theology in the Asian/Indian context. He is not an academic theologian but rather a free thinker. He does not side with the ashram movement and the Brahminical stream of Indian theology, nor does he side with Dalit theology, although he shows some interest in liberation theologies. He does not belong to a school or a group. He recognizes himself in the threefold

THE MAN AND THE THEOLOGIAN 47

dialogue with the religions, the cultures, and the poor. Whether his statement is accurate or rather the expression of an inner desire to be perceived in a certain way, it deserves scrutiny. I will return to this statement several times. Here I address his self-definition as an Indian and a free thinker, a nonacademic, and a nonsystematic theologian. In the next chapter, I situate Amaladoss's theology in the greater context of Indian theology.

In his autobiography, Amaladoss reiterated the same argument. He called himself "a theologian" but did not claim to be a systematic theologian: "I was not a systematic theologian in the traditional mode. . . . I was rather a 'wisdom writer,' exploring questions that rise out of experience."[30] Here he embraced the definition used by Father Kolvenbach: Amaladoss is a "wisdom writer." In Amaladoss's own autobiography, Father Kolvenbach's definition comes with a footnote: "*Saggista* in Italian." If I understand correctly, it means that the original definition was framed in Italian, i.e., "saggista," but "wisdom writer" is the English translation; whether the translation is Father Kolvenbach's or Amaladoss's, it is difficult to say. Whomever the translation belongs to, Amaladoss has made it his own. In the above quote, *saggista* is a term applied to someone who explores questions that arise out of experience. That is true: a saggista is someone who picks up a theme and explores related questions while seeking to answer them in the best possible way, even if that theme is not necessarily related to previous themes already discussed. This fits perfectly into the definition of a nonsystematic theologian. On the other hand, a saggista does not necessarily pick up a theme that arises from experience. The circumstance can be of personal interest, a public controversy or discussion, or an intellectual debate following the publication of an influential essay. Saggista is, more properly, someone who writes essays. Looking to France for inspiration, the term can mean "public intellectual," someone who enters a specific conversation to forge, or eventually disrupt, the public consensus on something.[31] In summary, a saggista is a public intellectual who does not

---

30   Amaladoss, *Lead Me On*, 86.

31   The public engagement of theology is a typical European given, being the result of a tradition that began with *les philosophes* in France at the end of the eighteenth century and with *les intellectuels* and the historical avant-gardes during the nineteenth-century political movements.

follow a methodical line of work. India has (and has had) public intellectuals, but it does not boast many religious intellectuals, even though there is, of course, a history of religious intellectuals active there; this kind of figure is no longer popular, probably because these days most people make the early calculation that they will not get far doing that. Amaladoss is a religious intellectual, more specifically, a Christian intellectual, who predominantly (but not exclusively) speaks to Christians. Christians are his constituency.

Now I turn to the phrase "wisdom writer." The meaning is straightforward: literally, an author who writes about wisdom. In the last fifty years, a genre commonly known as "wisdom literature" has risen to prominence in India as well as in Western countries, including the United States. Surely this is not what either Father Kolvenbach or Amaladoss intended. They meant the statements of the sage and the wise as mirrored in the Sapiential Books, or books of Wisdom (Job, Psalms, Proverbs, Song of Songs and Ecclesiastes, Wisdom, Sirach), included in the Hebrew Bible in the Septuagintal translation. So, Amaladoss writes as a sage does: on one hand, he picks up questions that emerge from his living experience; on the other hand, he attempts to write in a way that does not come exclusively from his mind but eventually springs from the very headwaters of Christianity, a higher source—a source that can perhaps be called Spirit. Lived experience and Spirit are, therefore, the ultimate sources of Amaladoss's writing, although I am sure he does not pretend that his writings are "inspired."

Some may find Amaladoss's long self-description both surprising and intriguing. There is no mention in it of his academic titles, thirty-six books written so far, or his 500 scholarly papers. Instead, he proudly mentions his hymns in Tamil. The core of the description is the term *freedom*, mentioned at least four times and two times explicitly: I do not belong to a school or a group; I rather consider myself a freelancer. I am not tied to any school or discipline, and I do not like to be categorized. I have been a free, not an academic, theologian. Here one has a scholar who is also a priest and a member of the Society of Jesus, a theologian who received his doctorate from the Institut Catholique in Paris and taught for fifteen years at Vidyajyoti College in Delhi. This is a man who spent twelve years in Rome as one of the counselors to the superior general of the Jesuits, took a variety of administrative roles, and gave lectures in the best universities of three continents. Still, this man calls himself a freelancer, a thinker with no belonging.

Amaladoss seems to be animated by the sense of rejection by the institution, whether the institution is academia, a scholarly discipline, or a school of thought. He senses an incompatibility between institution and personal freedom. He fears the risk of conformity and homologation. It is an interesting point: Amaladoss feels that personal freedom exists only outside the perimeter of an academic institution, theological school, or system of thinking. Behind the rejection of academic faculties, systematic theologies and theological systems, and schools and groups, as well as his proud claim of an intellectual freedom, is Amaladoss's determination to resist the process of institutionalization that comes with the assumption of certain roles inside an institution. Institutions transform people into organization people, that is, people of mainstream correctness who exhibit obedience, deference to authority, and conformity. Amaladoss is not part of the establishment and proudly so. Thus, resistance to the institution, or rather resistance to the almost inevitable effect of normalization that comes with being part of the institution, is behind his autobiographical notes. He perceives himself not as a member of an intellectual congregation but as a wandering, creative, free thinker. He has created for himself—and this is the message—a unique theological space in which he operates in accordance with his creative, namely artistic, orientation.

Amaladoss believes the condition of not being tied to a faculty of theology may have enabled him to "wander far and to be creative and free." Of course, Amaladoss has been tied to a faculty of theology—actually, to more than one. It is a fact that Amaladoss is an academic theologian: the reading of his autobiography provides evidence of his career as a professional theologian who spent a considerable amount of his adult life teaching, serving in academic roles, and writing articles. This is exactly what a scholar does. Yet, this is not how Amaladoss characterizes himself. Of course, Amaladoss is an academic, but what he wants to escape is the peril of approaching theology as a purely academic discipline; he aims to avoid the danger of academism. In themselves, titles and careers do not signal greatness in a theologian. If a theologian is truly great, they are finally a disciple of Jesus, which means that at base they will be a member of a community. Amaladoss is a great theologian, and behind his work as a theologian is a simple premise: theology must be conducted in the context of the community, and stripped of the community, Christian theology ceases to serve its purpose. Theology, including academic theology, is a service for the good of humanity, the Church, and the community; therefore, to borrow a phrase or two from Pope Francis, "true Christian wisdom can never be separated from mercy towards our neighbour."[32] The theologian who is not part of a community, "ends up sunk in the most disgusting narcissism," which the pontiff describes as "an ecclesiastical illness."[33]

Amaladoss's statements also reveal something about his distinct view of intellectual ministry. Free thinkers and nonacademic, nonsystematic, practical theologians are those who reject the traditional primacy of the speculative over the practical. For them, the speculative is at the service of the practical. A practical theologian is someone who has taken to heart the epigrammatic eleventh and final thesis of Karl Marx's *Theses on Feuerbach:* "Philosophers have hitherto only *interpreted* the world in various ways; the point is to *change* it."[34] I am saying neither that Amaladoss necessarily reads Marx nor that he adopts Marxian frames of reference. I am simply saying that he accepts a specific relationship between life and thought that is practical, not speculative. It is the preeminence of the praxis—a transliteration of an ancient Greek word for action, (πρᾶξις)—over reflection that moves the life of a theologian out of the classroom and onto the street. Praxis signals the unbreakable unity of active existence and thought that reflects an integration of theory and practice oriented toward transforming social relations. It is the subordination of speculation to praxis that transforms the work of a theologian from building a system to making a difference in the existence of a community.

Theology is a practical activity, built within the circumstances of life in the concrete context in which the theologian operates. Theology flows not from great books but from unpredictable circumstances of life. In this context, theology is not simply speculative reflection but also a social activity, and as such, it develops out of an active, continuous dialogue with the social reality that surrounds it. Ideas are not platonic entities coming from heaven; rather,

---

32 Pope Francis, *Gaudete Et Exsultate* (Apostolic Exhortation, Rome, March 19, 2018), no. 46.

33 Pope Francis, "Address to the Students of Gregorian University" (Rome, April 10, 2014).

34 This thesis is engraved on Marx's tomb. The emphasis was present in the original text.

they emerge from the interaction of the subject with the social context. It is in the praxis, namely in the reflective capacity of humankind to alter the social world, that the truths of a theological statement can be verified—not in a system of thought. For Amaladoss, theology is not speculation and therefore is not about building a system. This is why he does not consider himself a systematic theologian. It is because praxis is the reflective human capacity to alter the social world that for Amaladoss, theological problems are more precisely social problems abstractly conceived. Accordingly, theological remedies are ultimately social remedies. Here lies the nexus between reflection and social action: theologians solve social problems with their theological reflection, which in turn is more valuable if it solves problems rather than builds intellectual systems. To put it differently, theologians are, first and foremost, citizens of their own country. In Amaladoss's case, he is a citizen of the postcolonial India, on the road to greatness but still affected by social problems in the domains of religion, justice, and practical conditions of life. As a citizen of his country, he needs to stand up and act politically, which does not mean running for office but, more precisely, contributing to erect a *polis*, a plural and peaceful India free from colonial heritage and social injustices. Distinct from some of his more radical theological colleagues, Amaladoss's contribution focuses on ecclesial change, not social change. He works to reform the Church so that she becomes a force for peace, intercultural learning, and religious dialogue in India.

SELF-DETERMINATION

Some readers might think that in his self-descriptive statement, Amaladoss is only projecting a certain view of himself. I sense that behind Amaladoss's self-characterization there is more, like a commitment to self-determination, which stands for the power over one's own identity. In the words of Salman Rushdie, "Those who do not have power over the story of their lives, power to retell it, rethink it, deconstruct it, joke about it, and change it as times change, truly are powerless because they cannot think new thoughts."[35] This trait of self-determination takes different forms, some of them decidedly unique. For example, Amaladoss feels free to rewrite his own story. He did

---

35   Salman Rushdie, *One Thousand Days in a Balloon, in Imaginary Homelands: Essays and Criticism, 1981–1991* (New York: Penguin, 1992), 439.

it several times. This practice of writing and rewriting is functional to the projects of creating a line of resistance against institutions that come with their assigned identity and to building his own identity. I would synthesize Amaladoss's internal purpose for self-determination in the following terms: like many others, he grew up being told that Christianity is the way it is. It is like living in a defined world. And the life of a good Christian is to live a life in that defined world while trying not to bash into the walls too much. But one day, Amaladoss realized that everything around him—what is called Christianity—was made by people, and once he understood that, he tried to reach the limits of that world. He pushed and, amazingly, something popped up on the other side. He realized that Christianity is not to be accepted but molded. He did not settle, and this, I think, is his message: Christianity is a work in progress, and each of us is a craftsperson.

This approach is reflected in his autobiographical material. The story of his meeting with Father Hirudayam mirrors Amaladoss's belief that in the practical circumstances of life, and not in intellectual encounter with other scholars, life is oriented toward a certain direction. It is another way of stating that life precedes thought and proves itself capable of transforming human conditions into possibility. The story marks a shift from the intellectual realm to the conditions of life and incidentally casts a shadow on Amaladoss's intellectual sources. For the life and career of a man like Amaladoss, who is celebrated as one of the most prolific and profound theologians of his generation, it would seem at first glance quite indispensable to start with the philosophical and theological sources of his thought; from there, one might ask how far Amaladoss's own formal and conceptual innovations rested on the Indian milieu and enabled him to overcome the technical obstacles left unsolved by his contemporaries. That, one must say, would be the course to adopt in each case—that is, investigate the sources of Amaladoss's thought—in terms of the orthodox modes of academic inquiry, on the assumption that he worked as a professional theologian who happened to live in India. This is the implicit assumption of those who depict Amaladoss as a disciple of Dupuis. But an assumption of that sort may prove difficult for one simple reason: Amaladoss believes his sources are not other scholars but a series of decisive events that oriented his life in a certain direction. Thus, Amaladoss has no intellectual debt to pay to any thinker because his theology emerges from his interaction with life.

THE MAN AND THE THEOLOGIAN   53

Amaladoss started his 2007 autobiographical piece with a few words about his village:

> I was born on December 8, 1936, to Christian parents in Dindigul, Tamil Nadu, South India. My ancestors were Christians for about four generations. Both my father and my mother were teachers in government schools. Their jobs took them to various villages, largely Hindu. I grew up in a village of about one thousand families, only three of which were Christian. For worship on Sundays, we walked to a church that was three or four miles away. There was a popular temple of the goddess Mariyamman in the village. I grew up knowing more about Hinduism than Christianity. My friends and playmates were Hindus. It was a natural, human relationship, not hindered by ignorance or prejudice. My Christian identity was recognized and respected, as I respected their different identities. An open, easy relationship with other believers has its roots in these early experiences.[36]

The core of the story is the village. Amaladoss has repeated on several occasions the story of the Hindu village with three Christian families in which tolerance and respect reigned supreme to the point that the village is more than just a biographical note. To Amaladoss, the village is not simply the context of his life as a young man; it contains profound philosophical meaning. The village is reframed in terms of a *watan*, a homeland in which there is no space for Hindu or Christian because there is space for everyone. In his piece, the village—as a place, concept, and sense of self—is activated and reimagined as a force for forging a distinct Indian identity. The village of Dindigul, consisting of one thousand families, is the medium where an alternative political theology finds articulation. If I belonged to a small town in Italy or to a village in France, Amaladoss seemed to suggest, there would not be such diversity inside me. Being a Christian in India implies a self that is constitutively diverse, containing a plenitude, a subject formation only possible through the idea and lived experience in an almost totally Hindu village. His examination and articulation of a

---

36   Amaladoss, "My Pilgrimage in Mission," 21.

heterogeneity of the self comes not from his own experiences, but from the communitarian experiences of harmonious coexistence.

One can push this interpretation of Amaladoss even further in terms of self-determination, as if the trait reveals something about his distinct view of authority. Amaladoss did not reframe the parameters of the relationship between individual freedom and authority. There is an inevitable tension between the two poles; this tension can be experienced as the force that continuously questions and reframes the relationship. Amaladoss takes the high road: he rejects the authority and pursues a liberation from authority. In Amaladoss, a certain view of authority as repression is mirrored by an idea of freedom as resistance to repression and aspiration for emancipation. The interpretation of authority as power is, implicitly, the dismissal of a link between authority and metaphysics, namely, the primacy of being on becoming and therefore of the supernatural foundation of the authority. A totally historically based authority that is arbitrary and oppressive ("a game of power and control," he calls it) whose scope is primarily to dominate and limit individual potential can only be challenged for a higher level of freedom. In brief, Amaladoss interprets the authority as subjective and unnecessary, in the philosophical sense of the word. The rejection of the authority is, in fact, ultimately the rejection of the principle of necessity. Here, in this vision of a form of Christianity that is free from authority, his rejection of Tradition is hidden. For him, Tradition is a space to be relativized. The criticism of the authority is propaedeutic to the dismissal of Tradition. I do not suggest that all the theologians who reject Tradition reject authority as well. I am saying that in the case of Amaladoss, the personal drama becomes a hermeneutical key to a certain line of thought. I will return to this soon.

2

AMALADOSS AND INDIAN THEOLOGY

BETWEEN BRAHMINICAL AND DALIT THEOLOGIES

It is time to locate Amaladoss within the larger context of Indian theology. In his self-representation, he offers some elements to investigate:

> I would reject categories like Brahminical, Dalit, etc. I am neither a Brahmin nor a Dalit. . . . My theological reflection would be classified much more under the Asian triple dialogue of the Gospel with the poor, the cultures and the religions, though my own interests follow a reverse order: Dialogue with religions, Indian culture and the poor. . . . I have also had some interest in Indian Christian spirituality, but not of the ashram type, though I was a friend of Swami Abhishiktananda. I am not too involved with the poor and the Dalits, though I have written on the Caste system—not on the Dalits—and on Asian Liberation theologies.

The temptation, in effect, is to locate Amaladoss in either one or the other of the two main streams of Indian theology: the Brahminical or the Dalit, the textual or the social. Several elements combine to reach that conclusion. First, he often recognizes his friendship with the major representatives of the Brahminical stream, including Panikkar, Bede Griffiths, Sister Sara Grant, and the Benedictine monk Abhishiktananda (the Hindu name taken by French Christian Henri Le Saux). In his intellectual biography, *Lead Me On*, Amaladoss remembers long conversations with Panikkar, both in India and Rome, and meetings with Abhishiktananda.[1] He regarded both Panikkar and Abhishiktananda with passion and respect during his conversations with me. He attended regular meetings in Shantivanam ashram in Tamil Nadu. He shared experiences with monks and sannyasis during pilgrimages. He even wrote about joining an urban ashram in Chennai in 1967, but immediately remarked that it was not his vocation.[2] At the same time, his writings deal with the reality of social, cultural, and historical structures that oppress people and concrete forms of injustice, and he wrote a book about liberation theology.[3]

Biographically, Amaladoss could easily belong to either of the two streams. Born in 1936, Amaladoss entered academia in the early seventies when the Brahminical school was at its peak, after which he participated in the monumental efforts to define a proper Indian method of theologizing that severed Indian theologians from their Western counterparts. Then, he spent the next decades ascending to the pinnacle of Asian theology. When I explored with him this proposition of eventually being a bridge between the two Indian streams of theology, Amaladoss resolutely rejected it, and he has a point. The Brahminical school is more properly the Brahminical way of doing Indian-Christian theology; it celebrates the reciprocal impact of the Christian-Hindu (and Buddhist) dialogue on both sides, with an emphasis on the study of the foundational texts of both religions and doctrinal continuity. In the words of Panikkar, a mutual fecundation is at work between Christianity and India. This fecundation produces fruit: "It has Hinduized Indian Christianity; it has Christianized traditional Hinduism."[4] The writings of theologians draw upon ancient Christian and Indian sources, including the Vedas and Upanishads. A Brahminical-based Hindu-Christian theology tends to be identified with the study of the Hindu classical philosophy and religion. Dalit theology, instead, takes seriously the reality of the poor and marginalized condition of most Indian-Christians, including those who come from the Dalit

---

1   Amaladoss, *Lead Me On*, 23, 69.

2   Amaladoss, *Lead Me On*, 23.

3   See Amaladoss, *Life in Freedom*.

4   Raimon Panikkar, "The Dream of an Indian Ecclesiology," in *Searching for an Indian Ecclesiology*, ed. Gerwin van Leeuwen (Bangalore: Asian Trading Corporation, 1984), 37.

background. For Dalit theologians, the social problems and the gospel are indivisible. In their view, the Church is necessarily people centered, or more specifically, poverty centered: her concern is the liberation of God's people from any form of slavery or bondage. But the task of Christian theology, Dalit theologians believe, is not simply to liberate the oppressed, but more importantly, to transform the oppressing structures so that liberation is once and forever defeated. Thus, Dalit theology is not properly focused on liberating individuals but on making society more just and ultimately more Kingdom-like.

The criticism that Dalit (and liberation, tribal, feminist, and ecological) theologians have raised against the Brahminical school in the last decades is that it has identified Hinduism with the scriptural symbolic referents of upper-caste Hinduism. To put it another way, Christian theologians have wrongly associated one specific culture and religious tradition within India as the privileged way of Indianization or Hinduization of Christianity. Sathianathan Clarke, a theologian with scholarly roots in both India and the United States, elaborates his criticism of the Brahminical school in these terms:

> Indian-Christian theology by excluding and ignoring the voice of the majority, who testify to centuries of oppression and marginalization has been an ideological vehicle in the hands of the status quo. It could be said that theology sustained a process of hegemony by which the interests of the caste communities were espoused, strengthened and furthered in India. . . . The weaving of a meta-narrative, which combines together the Christian story with the tradition of caste Hindus, has tended to serve hegemonic purposes.[5]

Clarke believes that the Brahminical school considers the cultural and religious traditions of one dominant group of Hindu and elevates them to serve as the framework of reference in the school's engagement with Hinduism. Arvind Nirmal (1936–1995), who coined the phrase "Dalit

---

5   Sathianathan Clarke, *Dalits and Christianity: Subaltern Religion and Liberation Theology in India* (Delhi: Oxford University Press, 1998), 41.

theology," claimed thirty years ago that theologians should move from the "philosophical-propositional character of classical theologies" to the specific social context of the suffering of the Dalits in India.[6]

At stake in the debate between Dalit theology and the Brahminical school are questions related to the scope and the nature of the Church in India. The first question is whether Christianity should engage with, rather than withdraw from, the dramatic forms of injustice and discrimination that affect Indian society. The question, in other words, is whether the Indian Church should prioritize the social over the spiritual, the eradication of the social and economic disadvantages rather than the *entente cordiale* between Christianity and the other great religious traditions of India. Ultimately, the question is whether Christians are moved by socially ethical concerns or by the search for sanctity—whether the Church is a social or a spiritual force. From the viewpoint of Dalit theologians, the search for sanctity cannot be restricted to prayer and liturgy; it must be a matter of concern for the marginalized and the poor, too. From the viewpoint of the Brahminical school, an existential solidarity with the poor cannot extinguish the human journey of a faithful; it must also be a matter of entering into dialogue with the divine, the supernatural Presence.

The figure of Amaladoss emerged on the theological horizon in the early eighties. His work on religious dialogue and inculturation captured the imagination of the blossoming Indian theological community.[7] The time of his first major works coincided with a certain dissatisfaction with a Brahminical way of doing Indian-Christian theology and preceded the emergence of Dalit theology. In those days, theological education in India,

---

6   Arvind P. Nirmal, "Doing Theology from a Dalit Perspective," in *A Reader in Dalit Theology*, ed. Arvind P. Nirmal (Madras: Gurukul Lutheran Theological College & Research Institute, 1990), 140.

7   Of course, Amaladoss is not the only theologian involved in religious dialogue and inculturation. For a selected bibliography, see Chad Bauman, Arun W. Jones, Brian Pennington, Joseph Prabhakar Dayam, and Michelle Voss Roberts, "Hinduism and Christianity," *Oxford Bibliographies* (2012), http://dx.doi.org/10.1093/obo/9780195399318-0042. A list would include scholars like Francis X. Clooney, Catherine Cornille, Paul Knitter, and Michael Barnes in the West and Felix Wilfred, Sebastian Painadath, Paulachan Kochappilly, and Kurien Kunnumpuram in India.

namely seminaries, was moving from European modes to more indigenous modes of theologizing. Thus, a new impetus was born to make India theology really Indian. This impetus emerged in the Indian theological milieu against the background of certain interpretations of the Second Vatican Council ("the spirit of the Second Vatican Council") and recent attempts in non-European ecclesial realities to challenge mainstream ways of theologizing. In 1977, the Federation of Asian Bishops' Conferences (FABC), established only five years prior, advised the Asian Churches to discover their own identity or be ready to perish.[8] To build a true Indian theology, theologians aspired to use their own methods instead of using patronizing, Western theological methods, including those infusing the Brahminical approach. On one hand, Indian theologians were inspired to reject modes of theologizing that suggested their intellectual subordination to Western modes; on the other hand, they were busy building more suitable theological approaches. Indian theologians thus longed to revolutionize the hermeneutical foundations of Indian theology and encourage Indian Christians to reflect theologically on themselves.

The primary object of religious dialogue and inculturation is to reach peace among religious traditions and build an Indian Church that remains a minority presence among the great religions of Asia but no longer conserves her foreign face for the peoples of India. As a theological genre, it is responsible for important contributions in the fields of biblical studies and Christology; however, more work still needs to be done in certain fields, including pneumatology, namely, the person and the work of the Holy Spirit.[9] Amaladoss's theology is clearly not in opposition to the so-called

---

8   The original sentence reads, "If the Asian Churches do not discover their own identity, they will have no future." See "Asian Colloquium on Ministries in the Church 14" in *For All the Peoples of Asia: Federation of Asian Bishops' Conferences Documents from 1970 to 1991*, vol. 1, ed. Gaudencio Rosales and C. G. Arevalo (Quezon City: Claretian, 1997), 70.

9   Biblical interpretation in India has been flourishing for decades. George M. Soares-Prabhu, probably the most influential biblical scholar in India, explores the Bible from the standpoint of the poor, the victims, and the exploited. Gordon Matties, a professor emeritus of biblical studies and theology in Canada, prepared a selected bibliography; see "Biblical Interpretation in India" (unpublished manuscript, accessed March 2, 2021), https://tinyurl.com/bdewp2w7.

Brahminical approach in Christian theology in the same way Dalit theology is. Neither is Amaladoss's theology in opposition to liberation and Dalit theologies. More precisely, he proudly marks the differences between both. His theology, in fact, occupies a third space between the Brahminical school and Dalit theology. The space is filled with intercultural and interreligious concerns and refers to the concrete reality of the threefold dialogue with the cultures, the religions, and the poor of India in perfect alignment with the statement of the FABC, which reads, "The Asian bishops have understood evangelisation as the building up of the local church through a threefold dialogue with the cultures, the religions and the poor of Asia."[10] This statement and others issued by the FABC are evidence of a long and remarkable journey of the Asian bishops in the Asian Catholic consciousness. Moreover, they carry the weight of an ecclesiastical institution officially approved by Pope Paul VI on November 1, 1972. Amaladoss has mentioned the statement countless times in books and articles.[11] I remember the sense of reverence with which Amaladoss picked up the FABC documents from the shelves of his office in Chennai.

The FABC documents are an impressive body of work covering several themes that concern the Asian bishops; for the sake of this book, the matter of Asianness, that is, the FABC reflection on how to make the Asian Catholic Church more accessible to its people and more relevant to its own local contexts, is significant. In this theological historical work, Jukka Helle reconstructs the long journey that brought the FABC to articulate configurations of teaching, theology, and structure that are "truly Asian" while remaining "truly Catholic."[12] In Helle's opinion, the effort to become Asian (Asianness) has been the perennial theme throughout the existence of the FABC. Since its inception, the FABC has devoted much time and energy to amending the original sin of Christianity, namely, the foreignness of the Christian faith in Asia and the alliance between the Church and colonial empires. At the same time, Asianness should not be seen as a polar

---

10   Theological Advisory Commission of the Federation of Asian Bishops' Conferences, "Theses on Interreligious Dialogue: An Essay in Pastoral Theological Reflection," *FABC Papers* 48 (1987): art. 6.4.

11   See, for example, Amaladoss, *Peoples' Theology*, 8, 35.

12   For a historical and theological review of the FABC documents, see Jukka Helle, *Towards a Truly Catholic and a Truly Asian Church* (Boston: Brill, 2022).

opposite to Westernness, although Helle detects this risk: "In their attempt to decolonise theology from its western vestiges and perceived foreign structures, the Federation ends up creating another category in which 'Asia' and Asianness becomes the decisive framework for an Asian compatible contextual theology."[13] Like others, Amaladoss was attracted to the novelty of this new category; it perfectly fit his concern for a truly Indian theology. He was naturally diffident about doctrinal or dogmatic systems and rather craved new theological explorations. He aimed to use Indian categories of thought and to give expression to the Indian experience of the divine. To put it differently, his theology aspired and still aspires to manifest the Indian experience of the divine in Indian modes of expression. In that sense, Amaladoss's theology tends to be a theology of self (namely Indian) narration.

When Dalit and other liberation (tribal, feminist, ecological) theologies arose, some critics pointed out the limits of dialogue and inculturation theology. Dialogue and inculturation certainly aim to make India a more harmonious and tolerant society, it was said, but they risk being a passive instead of transformative theology. Amaladoss is not, by his own admission, a liberation theologian. One of his goals, however, is to free Indian theology from Western captivity, that is, Western styles, approaches, and modes of theologizing. Like many of his generation, Amaladoss was a kind of witness to the creation of an indigenous Christianity in his country. His purpose was and still is not fueled by the promptings of social justice but by the yearnings of a nation-state seeking to free itself from the vestiges of a Western colonial power and, in the process, to develop its own composite Christian-Indian identity.

BETWEEN MODERATES AND PROGRESSIVES

In his defense document submitted to the Congregation, Amaladoss positioned himself in the grand scheme of Indian theology. He explicitly mentioned "that Jose Kuttianimattathil in an elaborate study on the theology of dialogue in India counts me among the moderates." Then he continued, "I have consciously tried to hold to a middle position between two extreme

---

13   Helle, *Towards a Truly Catholic*, 46.

views: a relativising pluralism and an inclusivism that is, in practice, exclusivistic." The mentioned study was originally presented as a doctoral dissertation to the faculty of the Pontifical Gregorian University in Rome. The author, Father Jose Kuttianimattathil, SDB, wrote his dissertation under the supervision of Father Dupuis.[14] Thus, Amaladoss takes his own position on theology of religions as paradigmatic of his more general place among the different streams within Indian theology: he is a moderate, or at least he occupies a third, central space between radicals on the right and conservatives on the left. Of course, definitions depend on the context.[15]

Amaladoss is an Indian theologian. This phrase can mean, putting emphasis on the noun, that he is a Catholic theologian who extends to India the principles and frameworks of Catholic theology. Putting emphasis on the adjective, he is an Indian theologian who develops an Indian path within Catholic theology. This second interpretation can be further elaborated upon: if the Indian path is understood primarily in terms of social and economic liberation, one has a more radical type of Indian theologian. If the Indian path is instead appreciated as liberation from the Western ecclesiastical forms and ultimately as a mandate for the Indianization of the Church,

---

14   Jose Kuttianimattathil, *Practice and Theology of Interreligious Dialogue. A Critical Study of the Indian Christian Attempts Since Vatican II* (Bangalore: Kristu Jyoti, 1995), 231–394.

15   One common framework is to summarize the position of individuals in terms of center, left, and right. In his book on Pope Francis, Massimo Borghesi, a professor of moral philosophy at the University of Perugia, framed the Pope as having outlined a "third position" different from both the conservative and the progressive one. See Borghesi, *The Mind of Pope Francis: Jorge Mario Bergoglio's Intellectual Journey* (Collegeville, MN: Liturgical, 2018). My inspiration is instead Shaun Blanchard and Stephen Bullivant, *Vatican II: A Very Short Introduction* (Oxford: Oxford University Press, 2023). In their analysis of the Vatican II, Blanchard and Bullivant elaborated a fourfold schema to understand the different interpretations of the Council: the "Traditionalist Paradigm," characterized by "suspicion or rejection of the Council, or marginalization of it as exclusively 'pastoral;'" the "Text-Continuity Paradigm," which celebrates the Council, with an emphasis on the final texts and doctrinal continuity; the "Spirit-Event Paradigm," which also accepts Vatican II, but emphasizes the spirit of the Council and insists on doctrinal change and innovation; and the "Failure Paradigm" that complains that the Council ultimately failed to reform the Church.

one has a more progressive, eventually reformist type of Indian theologian. Moderate theologians work to recenter the Church on liturgy and encourage a genuine encounter with transcendence. Finally, conservatives simply apply with enthusiasm the guidelines from the Magisterium to the Indian Church. I doubt Amaladoss can be defined as a moderate under either Indian or Western standards. I agree that he holds a third position, not between conservatism and radicalism but between moderatism and radicalism.[16]

When I say that Amaladoss is a progressive, I have a precise picture of the recent history of Indian Christianity in mind.[17] The literature on the standing of Indian Christians during the pre-Independence nationalist movement is scarce. A recent publication, however, sheds some light on the topic.[18] The nationalist movement was a conglomerate of different ideologies.[19] There was the universalistic ideology of Gandhi and Tagore, who believed that Indian civilization, not Indian nationalism, was the future of the country. The more proper nationalistic leadership was divided between

---

16   Amaladoss defines himself theologically as somebody who is left of center. See Amaladoss, *Lead Me On*, 88. He calls for a form of Asian participative social democracy over the dominant North American liberal democracy in *Making Harmony: Living in a Pluralistic World* (Delhi: Indian Institute for Promoting Christian Knowledge, 2003). His profound appreciation of Indian culture, which he contrasted with a rationalist trait of Western civilization, and his propensity to think of society in terms of groups rather than individuals, make him an improbable candidate for liberalism, including social liberalism. He is probably better identified as a liberal socialist.

17   I consider Amaladoss a Christian socialist who urges the correction of injustices without embracing Marxism.

18   Mary John, *Indian Catholic Christians and Nationalism* (Delhi: ISPCK, 2017).

19   On the nationalist movement, see Jabez T. Sunderland, "The New Nationalist Movement in India," *The Atlantic*, October 1908, 518, https://tinyurl.com/bdh9u8wh. The article begins with the interesting distinction between colonies and dependencies. Sunderland explains that "colonies, like Canada and Australia, though nominally governed by the mother country, are really self-ruling in everything except their relations to foreign powers. Not so with dependencies like India. These are granted no self-government, no representation; they are ruled absolutely by Great Britain, which is not their 'mother' country, but their conqueror and master." It was against this situation of dependency that the nationalistic movement in India was born.

those who tended to look back to a past that aligned with the Hindu and those who identified the axis of the nation in its social, religious, and cultural pluralism. The revivalist stream of Indian nationalism provided religious nationalism its ideological foundation; the eclectic stream instead gave birth to secular nationalism.[20] After independence, secular nationalism established itself as a center of gravity of the nation.

In the aftermath of independence in India, Christians positioned themselves along different political and theological traditions. The Nehruvian India appeased the preoccupations of Indian Catholics who found their place in a pluralistic India shaped by the Indian National Congress. The long period of Indian history dominated by the Indian National Congress favored the acceptance of the Catholics of the revolution who freed the country from the British Raj. This acceptance of the revolution, however, took different forms: radicalism saw the Indian revolution as an extension of the anti-colonialist movement, the struggle against Western rule in colonized countries that dominated the history of the twentieth century. This position was a constant invitation to bring the revolution to its ultimate end and achieve liberation for all. When it became clear that the Indian National Congress was unwilling to do so, the radical position became a lament that the aspirations of the nationalist movement had been ultimately betrayed. Progressives instead found their home in the democratic, socialist, secular Nehruvian India, and finally, moderate Catholics maintained their link with the West. Conservativism in Catholic India is surviving in the government of the Indian Church.

Nobody can underestimate the impact that the Second Vatican Council had on Catholicism in Europe and South Asia. In Europe, the Council has been interpreted as an enormous and felicitous effort to reverse the attitudes and strategies with which the Catholic Church had consistently opposed the modern world, created by the political, philosophical, and scientific revolutions of the previous centuries. This is at least one interpretation of the Council, and it is an interpretation with which many agree. In South Asia, however,

---

20   K. N. Panikkar, "Alternative Historiographies: Changing Paradigms of Power," in *The Struggle for the Past: Historiography Today*, eds. Felix Wilfred and Jose D. Maliekal (Chennai: Department of Christian Studies, University of Madras, 2002), 14.

the Council has been interpreted mostly in terms of openness to the complex and pluralistic reality of the world.[21] The interreligious and intercultural dialogue, the theology of religions, the sociopolitical mission of the Church, the preferential option for the poor, and the liberation theologies are only some of the implications of the notion that Vatican II was not about changing sacred doctrine but reorienting the Church far from walls and barriers and reconciling her with the Asian world in the light of the gospel. The celebrated divergence on the hermeneutic of the Council—whether it should be considered in terms of continuity with the earlier sacred tradition or rather a far greater break from the preconciliar Church—has monopolized the reception of the Council in Europe. Regarding the first option, hermeneutic of continuity, the Council is an event to be placed in the long history of the Church; regarding the second, hermeneutic of discontinuity (sometimes referred to as the hermeneutic of rupture), the Council is instead the primary judgment criteria of that history. For the supporters of the hermeneutic of continuity, the theological arc designed by the conciliar Fathers resulted in a reform, a re-form (a new form) of the sacred tradition; for those sympathizing with the hermeneutic of rupture, the conciliar Fathers moved sacred tradition into new territories.

Vatican II was received almost unanimously in India in terms of the "spirit of Vatican II," namely, an interpretation of Vatican II in terms of doctrinal change and the idea that the Council was a historical event that moved Catholicism away from its European roots. The spirit of Vatican II is not just an expression but has become the label of an entire approach to interpreting the Council. It is generally understood to signify that, unlike the other ecumenical councils, the Council is not an event to be placed in the long history of the Church; the Council is instead the primary judgment criteria of that history. It is normally considered to mean that, differently from the other ecumenical councils, the definitive significance of the Council resides not in the magisterial documents it produced but in the impulse for change and reform the event inspired, even if they appear

---

21   One may say that the Asian reflection on the Council is far more limited than the Western. In his article on the reception of the Council in the period 2016–2019, Massimo Faggioli identified only two writings in Asia against hundreds in the West. It is also possible, however, that Faggioli privileges Western sources. See Faggioli, "Vatican II: Bibliographical Survey 2016–2019," *Cristianesimo nella Storia* 40, no. 3 (2019): 713–38.

to overcome established Church teachings. Thus, the spirit of Vatican II stands for the belief that the Holy Spirit protects the texts of the Council from errors that would contradict the Church's essential doctrines. Consequently, the doctrines are interpreted in light of the conciliar texts rather than the other way around. From the perspective of the spirit of the Second Vatican Council, the Council was a theological revolution in the sense that the conciliar Fathers moved sacred tradition into new territories.

The almost undivided reception of the Council in terms of the spirit of Vatican II and the correspondent irrelevance of the hermeneutic of continuity has produced massive effects on the postconciliar theological reflection in India. The first effect has been the decline of the intellectual influence of moderates. In India, Catholic moderates appreciated the Council with reference to recentering the Church on liturgy and encouraged a genuine encounter with transcendence. They celebrated the Council with an emphasis on the final texts and doctrinal continuity. Today, moderation has no voice in the Indian theological circles. The theology of the French priest Jules Monchanin (1895–1957), the founder of a Benedict ashram in Tamil Nadu, is so sophisticated that Pierre Emmanuel kneels down "devant l'abstraction de cette pensée souverainement elliptique" (before the abstraction of this supremely elliptical thought).[22] But Monchanin's writings attract a small congeries of spiritual seekers and expatriate priests in India these days. Abhishiktananda is probably the closest to a mystic the Indian Church can celebrate. Yet, Indian theologians declined to dedicate one of their annual conferences to the heritage of Abhishiktananda. The lineage that has in Monchanin and Abhishiktananda two of its progenitors is not extinguished. For example, Father Yann Vagneux, a French missionary priest who lives between Varanasi and Kathmandu, seeks to exist in the twenty-first century and reflect on the ideals of the pioneers of the previous generations.[23] The lineage, however, is out of

---

22   Jules Monchanin, *Théologie et spiritualité missionnaires*, eds. Edouard Duperray and Jacques Gadille (Paris: Beauchesne, 1985), iv.

23   See, for example, Yann Vagneux, *Indian Portraits: Eight Christian Encounters with Hinduism* (New Delhi: Nirala Publications, 2021); *A Priest in Banaras*, trans. Roderick Campbell Guion (Varanasi: ATC Publishers, 2020); "A Marriage with Hinduism," trans. Roderick Campbell Guion, *Dilatato Corde* 10, no. 1 (January–June 2020), https://tinyurl.com/tbu6zk67; "Abhishiktananda: A Priesthood in

sync with the present theological debate.[24] In the words of Roy Lazar, a priest and pastoral theologian at the University of Madras, "the attempts to incorporate the spirituality of the Advaita into Christian contemplation through ashram movement or adaptation of Hindu symbols mostly from Brahminical culture were shunned off as a Sanskritisation process. Such attempts of Indianization were rejected both by the Hindus as well as by the majority Catholics who were victims of marginalization of Vedic Hinduism."[25] The Spanish priest Raimon Panikkar, the son of a Hindu father and a Catholic mother, made his name through a book written in India about Hindu-Christian dialogue and reached celebrity status inside and outside the narrow boundaries of professional scholarship. His efforts to Indianize Catholic thought through an encounter with the Indic and, more specifically, the Buddhist and the Hindu, are unquestionable. And yet, his highly philosophizing theology poses little to no interest for a generation of theologians concerned with the practical conditions of the marginalized. Despite his celebrity status and genuine attachment to India, Panikkar's influence on Indian theology is minimal these days. In Amaladoss's words, "only a few students read Panikkar in Indian seminaries."[26]

---

the Spirit," *VJTR* 83, no. 8 (2019): 625–38; *Co-esse: Le mystère trinitaire dans la pensée de Jules Monchanin (1895–1957)* (Paris: Desclée de Brouwer, 2015); "'The One in Greece and the Indies': An Unpublished Work by Jules Monchanin," *Revue des sciences philosophiques et théologiques* 96, no. 3 (2012): 514–56.

24   Generalizations need to be approached with caution. It is true that in recent years, there has been a growing interest within religious studies and theology in issues related to social justice, activism, and community engagement. This shift in focus has been driven in part by broader cultural and political trends, as well as by changing attitudes within academia about the role of scholarship in promoting social change. However, it is important to note that this shift in focus does not necessarily mean that the study of religious texts and ideas has become less relevant or less important. Rather, it reflects a growing recognition that religious beliefs and practices are deeply embedded within social and political contexts and that understanding these contexts is crucial for fully appreciating and engaging with religious traditions.

25   Roy Lazar, "Five Years of Pope Francis—Insights for Indian Christians" (unpublished paper, 2018), 4.

26   Once again, all generalizations need to be taken with a grain of salt. It is difficult to generalize about the extent to which Panikkar's work is studied

The second effect of a certain interpretation of the Council in India has been to leave the intellectual leadership of Indian theology in the hands of progressivism and radicalism. According to those lines of thought, the Council abandoned the past and pushed Catholicism into a post-Western order. Almost unanimously, the Council was also framed as a historical event that marked the exit of Catholicism from Christendom. At first approximation, Christendom is Christian civilization, the civilization that Christianity embedded during the European Middle Ages. The Council was the exit of Catholicism from Christendom, an exit that (and Pope Francis would agree with this) is ongoing.[27] The exit from Christendom, however, can be seen as either a return to a new Christendom or a passage to a post-Christendom order. That return to a new Christendom means a reform—a re-form or a new form of Christendom; this is, in brief, the position of moderates like Pope Benedict XVI. When Panikkar mentioned Christianness, it was the exit from Christendom that he had in mind; when

---

or appreciated within Indian seminaries, as there is likely to be considerable variation depending on the specific institution and the particular academic programs or departments involved. That being said, there are a few possible reasons why Panikkar's work may not be as widely studied in Indian seminaries as one might expect given his background and interests. One possible factor is that many Indian seminaries are focused primarily on the study of Christian theology and doctrine and may not have as much of a focus on interreligious dialogue or comparative theology, which are areas where Panikkar's work has been particularly influential. Additionally, Panikkar's ideas and terminology may be seen as difficult to integrate within more traditional Christian theological frameworks, which could limit his appeal for some scholars and students in Christian seminaries. It is also worth noting that the study of religion and theology in India is a complex and multifaceted field, with many different approaches, perspectives, and traditions represented. Although Panikkar's work may not be widely studied within some Christian seminaries, it is possible that it is more appreciated within other academic contexts like departments of comparative religion or Indian philosophy. Ultimately, the degree to which Panikkar's work is studied and valued within Indian seminaries is likely to vary depending on a range of factors, including the specific institution, the academic focus of the program, and the interests and perspectives of individual scholars and students.

27 Pope Francis, "Ma il Cammino è ancora lungo," *La Repubblica*, October 2, 2022, 37.

Abhishiktananda criticized the Church for still being too neolithic, what he had in mind was the passage from Christendom to something else.[28] However, their primary idea was the return to a pre-Christendom Christianity, and therefore, a re-formed form of Catholicism. Their aim was to reform the Church to make it more transcendental.

A post-Christendom order, instead, refers to an exit from Christendom that is not propaedeutic to a return to a purified, reformed Christendom but to progress toward a Christian order that has nothing to do with Christendom. This is the position of an intellectual stream within Catholicism that, in the course of history, has been associated with progressive and radical Catholics. In South Asia, the past is the colonial era and the westernized attitude of the Church. Both progressives and radicals in India, therefore, read the exit from Christendom as a revolutionary movement beyond colonialism, either ecclesiastical or political. With the collapse of the colonial empires and the indigenization of the Church, Catholicism focuses on transformative social action, namely, making Christianity more Indian (progressivism) or India more just (radicalism). The exit is an Indian Christianity that ultimately identifies itself in a post-Western Christianity. The unifying principle of progressivism and radicalism is the possibility of a new Christianity away from Western Christianity, a postcolonial Christianity with an Asian face. Where they differ is in the scope of the change: for progressivism, Christianity must change to adjust to the pluralistic, Asian (non-Western) society of India. For radicalism, Christianity is a social force to structurally change India for the good.

It is this twofold hermeneutic of the spirit of Vatican II and the postcolonial order that informs Amaladoss's progressivism and his view of a post-Western Christianity in India. He is not a moderate. The difference between moderates and progressives can also be investigated regarding the conciliation between Christianity and the complex and plural reality of India. For moderates, the conciliation happens in metaphysics and for progressives, in praxis. Instead, at the core of progressives like Amaladoss, there is a peculiar understanding of history, an understanding that

---

28   Raimon Panikkar, *Christianity*, in Opera Omnia, vol. 3, no. 2 (Maryknoll, NY: Orbis, 2016), 29; Abhishiktananda, *Ascent to the Depth of the Heart: The Spiritual Diary (1948–1973) of Swami Abhishiktananda* (Delhi: ISPCK, 1998), 140–41.

70   MICHAEL AMALADOSS AND THE QUEST FOR INDIAN THEOLOGY

has both a philosophical and a political ingredient, and the two cannot be separated. Or, to borrow a sentence from Antonio Gramsci, "It is a philosophy that is also a politics, and a politics that is also a philosophy."[29] At the theoretical level, the argument is embedded in a larger aim to recognize attempts within Indian theology to articulate a distinct trajectory that does not simply accept the tale of a singular path to an Indian Church based on the Western model but instead tries to articulate an alternative vision of the Church grounded within an Indian perspective. History becomes an irreversible force—one of progress and of liberation. It is in history and through history that people, including Christians, and even the Church are redeemed. Therefore, it is in praxis, in the realm of experience and in the concrete circumstances of life that the truths of philosophies, theologies, and even doctrines are verified. The nature of these truths is modified: they are historically built frameworks that are experimentally verified in the reality of human affairs. In praxis, one is concerned with the primacy of the historical over the philosophical. Philosophies, theologies, and even doctrines are intertwined with history, the latter enjoying primacy over the former. In this view, praxis is elevated upon speculation; therefore, theology of experience is placed above systematic and doctrinal theology. It is in the immanent realm of experience that the truths of Catholicism are judged.

INCULTURATION AND RELIGIOUS DIALOGUE

Amaladoss's India is neither the India of the moderate theologians of the Brahminical school nor that of the radical theologians. His peculiarity is embedded not only in his theological style but also in the language used in his writings to describe the reality of India. In an interview given in German, Panikkar described his first encounter with India, the land of his father, in 1954: "I did not go to India, my land of origin, as a teacher, but as a student; not as someone who is already a scholar, but as a seeker. I sat without any difficulty at the feet of the master, learned the language of the people and was one among them. It was not preplanned. It was my *karma*."[30]

---

29   Antonio Gramsci, *Quaderni dal Carcere*, vol. 3 (Torino: Einaudi, 1975), 1860. The translation is my own.

30   "Ich ging nicht als Lehrer nach Indien, meninem Herkunftsland, sondern als Schüler, nicht als jemand, der schon einiges studiert hatte, sondern als

AMALADOSS AND INDIAN THEOLOGY 71

One can notice the change in tone and style from Panikkar to Amaladoss in this passage in which Amaladoss offers a portrayal of himself as a child: "I grew up in a largely Hindu village, Samayapuram, near Trichy. . . . Growing up in a Jesuit-run boarding school, I also became deeply Catholic. At the Novitiate, Fr. Ignatius Hirudayam opened my eyes to the riches of Indian cultures and religions. When I was doing my philosophy, I was privately immersing myself in Indian culture, philosophy, and religion."[31]

In reading the two passages, one experiences the feeling of a return from solitude to society, from spiritual to physical, from concepts to issues, and from lyrism to pragmatism. The reader notices how the mysterious, boundless, and sublime image of India as the master (or the guru) in Panikkar becomes in Amaladoss a series of events in the ordinary life of an Indian Catholic boy. The two descriptions of the encounter with Indian culture, philosophy, and religion contain the most distinguishing elements of the two streams of Indian theology. To begin with, note how Panikkar views his encounter with India as the meeting with a metaphysical entity and an ancient wisdom. And see how Amaladoss views the same encounter as practical, social, and geographical. For Panikkar, India is something general, absolute, and abstract, a sort of concept; for Amaladoss, India becomes concrete, particular, and specific, a real identifiable location. Further, consider how Panikkar's description is expressed in a rather literary language using even religious terms (*karma*), but Amaladoss's style is more informal and offers a detailed picture of living events and people. India no longer represents the mystery of the eternal presence but rather the physical and social places where events happen and people experience happiness and troubles. The transcendent India has become the immanent India.

Just as philosophy is the predominant mode of investigation in the Brahminical stream, so is social theory in Amaladoss's contextualized theology. And just as Sanskrit is the door into the mystical heart of India, culture is the perfect gateway to approach the pluralistic reality of South Asia.

Suchender, als jemand, der ohne Schwierigkeiten zu Füßen eines Meisters saß, die Sprache der Einheimischen lernte (und das schlect) und einfach einer unter vielen war. Das war ganz offensichtlich keine Taktik, ich hatte es auch nicht vornherein so geplant. Es war mein Karma." Pinchas E. Lapide und Raimon Panikkar, *Meinen Wir denselben Gott?* (München: Kösel Verlag, 1994), 177.

31 Amaladoss, *Lead Me On*, 65–66.

Accordingly, the spiritual journeys of the gurus are replaced with the stories of the religious encounters in the pluralistic Indian society. The imaginative contemplation of the spiritual world is substituted with the description of issues, situations, stories, and, more importantly, an urgency for the Church to inculturate once and forever in the practical reality of India. The passage from Panikkar's Brahminical to Amaladoss's *inculturationism* is a kind of return from a romantic exile. The boundless and mysterious world of the spiritual is left behind in favor of the real society and the ordinary life of a billion and a half people marked by religious controversies and pacific coexistence, cultural tensions, and overall harmony.

Amaladoss's India indeed differs from that of theologians of the Brahminical school, but it also diverges from the India of radical theologians. Modernity has many faces, including the passage from the community life of the rural society to the new, modern, urban civilization. Yet not all theologians address the same side of modernity: some capture the withdrawal from the village, and others face the flowering of the urban context. Some theologians have a very limited interest in the effects of modernity on the threefold dialogue with the cultures, the religions, and the poor and prefer to work on the inimical challenge that modernity poses to the masses. One example of the two theological sensibilities is offered through a brief comparative analysis of Amaladoss and Father Sebastian Kappen, SJ (1924–1993). Amaladoss completed his doctoral studies at the Institut Catholique in Paris with a thesis on sacramental theology that focused on the problems of inculturation. Kappen did his doctoral studies in Rome at the Pontificial Gregorian University, writing a dissertation titled "Praxis and Religious Alienation According to the Economic and Philosophical Manuscripts of Karl Marx." Amaladoss discovered in the social sciences an extension of his philosophical and theological studies, and Kappen found in Marxism the tools of social analysis he needed to understand the people's alienation from freedom. Here is an example of Amaladoss's work on sacraments:

> The seven sacraments of the Catholic Church, for instance, mark some moments of the lifecycle of persons in community, not all of them. They ignore totally the agricultural and seasonal cycles. Besides, many of the rituals of cosmic religions also aim at

celebrating and stabilizing the social order in addition to religious faith. The rituals around birth, initiation, marriage, and death spell out mutual relationships and responsibilities of different people in the wider family and in the village. This is the reason that the official rituals of the church do not totally satisfy the people. They complete them with many other rituals taken from their own culture and cosmic religion. Since cosmic religion refers to this world, it need not contradict the metacosmic insistence on the other world.[32]

To follow is an example of Kappen's writings on alienation:

> Today, more than ever, there is a need to take a critical view of the productive forces of capitalism to draw from it the right theoretical and practical conclusions: all the more so, since contemporary capitalism is far different from the one that existed in nineteenth-century England . . . the gravity of the problem will become clear when we remember that 65 percent of the corporate investments in the western world are for "rationalization" and technical innovation, calculated to deform and denature the masses by reducing them to consumers of useless and even harmful goods or to fashion instruments of mass murder and collective extermination . . . the dominant trend in contemporary India is one of progressive estrangement. The value shaping the everyday life of the bourgeoisie, the urban petty bourgeoise, and youth are largely those of capitalism. . . . This alien culture is steadily percolating down to even the lowest strata of society.[33]

Both Amaladoss and Kappen reflected on the transition from the agrarian, traditional way of life to the industrial, modern order. But they approached the transition from different perspectives. Amaladoss's major concern is not the city but the village that is on the verge of erasure at the hands of

---

32   Amaladoss, *Interreligious Encounters*, 201.

33   Sebastian Vattamattam, ed., *Hindutva and Indian Religious Traditions*, vol. 5 of *Collected Works of Sebastian Kappen* (Delhi: ISPCK, 2021), 132, 150.

modernity. People find themselves cut off from their native communities to become part of a much larger society. In Amaladoss's words,

> One of the tools that Gandhi used for promoting interreligious harmony was interreligious prayer meetings. At such meetings passages from different scriptures were read and devotional songs from different religious traditions were sung, concluded by an exhortation to promote interreligious peace and harmony. The aim of these meetings was to show that all religions were for peace. If we all believe in one God and we have mutual respect for and acceptance of one another, then praying together for our country and community will be a welcome religious practice. . . . One could also suggest the celebration of festivals, which could become occasions for sharing one's joy with one's neighbors of other religions. This happens even today in villages. In reality, at the popular level there are instances of greater involvement in the celebration of festivals and pilgrimages. However, it is unfortunate that such traditional practices are being given up in some places under pressure from fundamentalist groups.[34]

Kappen's main preoccupation is the incumbent prospect of social annihilation under the threat of rationalism and technology. They studied the same historical passage, but Amaladoss focused on what was left behind and Kappen on what must be embraced. The theme in Amaladoss is the journey from community to society, from village to city; the theme in Kappen is instead the journey from humanism to Darwinism, from humanity to machinery. The difference is also in style: in Amaladoss, the communities are still the makers of their own destiny, not creations of the environment. The humanity portrayed in his writings is self-reliant, shows a strong sense of moral responsibility for their actions, and subjects events and things to rational explanation. Life is still governed by commonly accepted and mutually respected values, in which some positive and negative ties are still considered

---

34   Amaladoss, *Interreligious Encounters*, 66. The same story is offered, with small changes, in Michael Amaladoss, *The Challenges of Fundamentalism* (Chennai: IDCR Publications, 2009), 61–62.

valid. In Amaladoss, character and faith take precedence over circumstances and settings; in Kappen, the mass of individuals struggles to maintain self-direction in a world framed by utilitarianism. Kappen's world is made of production, prices that fall or rise, and individuals who are interchangeable economic units that can be dispersed and reassembled into new groups by the pressure of capitalism's laws of wage and profit. It is no surprise that he invites theologians to be more vocal about "the need for a reinterpretation of the Gospel in tune with the requirements of radical social action."[35]

The comparison between Amaladoss and Kappen, like the previous one between Amaladoss and Panikkar, serves a limited but well-defined scope: to place Amaladoss's theology in the larger context of contemporary Indian theology. His work belongs to neither the Brahminical current of Indian theology nor the more radical ramifications of the social stream of Indian theology. Of course, he is troubled by the contrary interests of economic growth, justice, democracy, and discrimination that still affect modern India. However, the subjugation of the poor, the inherent injustice of castes, and the liberation from predicament are not the reasons for his primary disquietude. In his writings, he addresses social institutions such as capitalism, globalization, and religious fundamentalism, but these institutions work as the firmament of his theological analysis, not as the target of polemical vehemence and scholarly aggressiveness as it occurs in Kappen. Amaladoss's target is the Church and her stubborn resistance to change and to becoming totally Indian, but his concern is the peaceful coexistence of Christians in a pluralistic country.

BUILDING OUR OWN CHRISTIANITY

The three streams of Indian theology—namely Brahminical, dialogue and inculturation, and liberation and Dalit—can be seen as competitive approaches, but more correctly, they belong to different ages or periods in the development of Indian theology.[36] They should be evaluated in reference

---

35   Sebastian Kappen, ed., *Jesus Today* (Madras: All India Catholic University Federation, 1985), ii.

36   For historical reconstruction of the different phases of Indian theology in the Catholic realm, see Xavier Gravend-Tirole, "An Examination of the

to the spirit of their age—the zeitgeist. In the seventies and eighties, religious dialogue and inculturation in India slowly but decisively replaced the Catholic ashram movement and more generally the Brahminical school as the most powerful theological stream in India. In the following decades, Dalit theology and more generally the school of social transformation took the place of inculturationism and religious dialogue as the leading force in Indian theology. Somehow, the theology of social transformation gained momentum and came to be seen as the new theological vanguard. New generations of theologians became accustomed to a form of theology that is inherently Indian (or, in the words of Nirmal, "authentically Indian") without the obligation of translation from the Western sources.[37] By the late eighties, Dalits began entering religious orders, particularly the Society of Jesus, in greater numbers, and their liberationist, subaltern, social justice concerns displaced those of the previous generation.[38] In this context, intercultural and interreligious initiatives began to languish and lose energy, it seems, while these newer, innovative theological movements took the initiative. Amaladoss himself has been seen from some of these younger and more radical theologians as belonging to a past era.

When I asked Amaladoss whether there is an Indian theologian he feels to be close in terms of theological style and interest, he named Jesuit

---

Indigenisation/Inculturation Trend within the Indian Catholic Church," in *Constructing Indian Christianities: Culture, Conversion and Caste*, eds. Chad M. Bauman and Richard Ford Young (New Delhi: Routledge India, 2014), 110–37; "Towards a Theology of Religions: An Indian Christian Perspective," statement of the twelfth meeting of the Indian Theological Association, in *Religious Pluralism: An Indian Perspective*, ed. Kunchria Pathil (Delhi: South Asia Books, 1991), 324–37; David J. Bosch, *Transforming Mission: Paradigm Shifts in Theology of Mission* (Maryknoll, NY: Orbis, 1991); J. Russel Chandran, "Methods and Ways of Doing Theology" in *Readings in Indian Christian Theology*, vol. 1, eds. R. S. Sugirtharajah and Cecil Hargreaves (Delhi: SPCK, 1993), 4–13.

37   Arvind Nirmal, "Towards a Christian Dalit Theology," in *Readings in Indian Christian Theology*, vol. 1, eds. R. S. Sugirtharajah and Cecil Hargreaves (Delhi: SPCK, 1993), 57.

38   Kerry P. C. San Chirico, "The Grace of God and the Travails of Contemporary Indian Catholicism," *Journal of Global Catholicism* 1, no. 1 (2016): 58. Today, some 80 percent of India's Catholics hail from Dalit and low-caste backgrounds. This percentage is higher in northern India.

theologian and longtime friend T. K. John. Another name that he mentioned, although not to signal the same degree of intellectual proximity he feels for John, was Duraiswami Simon Amalorpavadass, a diocesan priest who, like Amaladoss, earned his doctorate at the Institut Catholique in Paris. Amaladoss did not mention those names as sources of his thought, but rather in terms of intellectual brotherhood. What makes Amaladoss so close to Father John is probably the fact that for both, theological work is instrumental to "build our own Christianity," that is, an Indian Christianity that is intellectually, liturgically, and normatively autonomous from the Western influences of the Church of Rome. To put it differently, their theological writings are an attempt—to borrow a line from Amaladoss—"to remain Indian without becoming someone else." An Indian Christianity would allow Amaladoss and others to remain Indian and be Christian without passing through a transformation. I mention transformation because then-cardinal Ratzinger described "becoming Christian" as an exodus and transformation: "Conversion does not destroy the religions and cultures but transforms them."[39] Amaladoss does not want to be transformed in becoming Christian. He feels he is both Indian and Christian, and the two sides of his identity do not require adjustments. Of course, the crux of the matter is a certain interpretation of the relation between the universal culture of the Church and the local culture of India. If the former comes to India, transformation is inevitable. When the former is prioritized over the latter, transformation is once again inevitable. For some, the Church's official documents carry the urgency of protecting the integrity of the gospel against theological approaches favoring cultural diversity.[40] A case in point is the Council document *Gaudium et Spes* (Pastoral Constitution of the Church in the Modern World), in which the term *culture* is believed to represent both a universally human phenomenon and a variety of diverse cultures. Thus, the pluralistic character of human cultures is subordinated to the universal character of the human culture (as a human

---

39   Joseph Cardinal Ratzinger, "Christ, Faith and the Challenge of Cultures." *FABC Papers* 78 (1993): 16.

40   See Congregation for the Doctrine of the Faith, "Doctrinal Note on Some Aspects of Evangelization" (Rome, December 14, 2007), 6.2, where it is said that the gospel is "independent from any culture."

phenomenon), which in turn is subordinate to the gospel.[41] For Amaladoss, the local culture is instead emphasized over the Church's own universal culture. In his mind, the gospel is embedded in culture, as cultures and religions are intertwined, mutually informing and reinforcing each other.

All in all, Amaladoss has maintained a commanding presence in the theological conversation for decades, extending his reach to territories outside India. Good theology is theology that makes changes. Although not implemented in the same radical way of Dalit theology, Amaladoss's theology is based on the unity of thought and action. His mode of theologizing aims to counter neither the Brahminical nor the liberation modes. Rather, he explores alternative approaches that attempt to break new ground. A closer look at the theological reasoning behind his work suggests that he resorts to a reader-centered approach. Amaladoss's hermeneutics is based on reading the Christian text from an Indian perspective and particularly from the perspective of religious dialogue and inculturation.

---

41 Pope Paul VI, *Gaudium et Spes* (Pastoral Constitution on the Church in the Modern World, Rome, December 7, 1965), no. 53.

3

INCULTURATION AND DIALOGUE

THEOLOGY IN CONTEXT

Michael Amaladoss is known for his work on inculturation and religious dialogue. However, he would probably reframe his work as a movement outside the temple, that is, outside the comfort of a theological system and the security of an established tradition. By leaving the temple behind, so to speak, he ventures into the unknown territories of the encounter with the Other. The Other is both the divine nature and the human nature of Jesus Christ. The Other is the mystery that pervades everything and everyone around. Moving outside the temple, then, equates to discovering "the challenging presence of the divine in the context of life," as Jacob Parappally defined the distinct Indian way of theologizing.[1] The movement is the challenging and yet rewarding process of recognizing the Presence in the ordinary, practical circumstances of human life. Because Christians believe that God is the creator of all things and seeking Him is the goal of all people, they must recognize His action everywhere.[2] His presence and work

---

1   Jacob Parappally, "Theologizing in Context," in *Theologizing in Context: Statements of the Indian Theological Association*, ed. Jacob Parappally (Bangalore: Dharmaram, 2002), 23.

2   Amaladoss noted that Pope John Paul II recognizes the Spirit being present in every prayer that was authentic. See John Paul II, "Christmas Address to the Roman Curia," *Bulletin of the Secretariats for Non-Christians* 64 (1987): 54–62. Amaladoss added, "The fact that the prayers of the believers of other religions according to their own rites were considered effective gives a positive value to other religions as mediations of divine-human encounter. It must be emphasized, however, that this positive appreciation of other religions IS developed in

can be appreciated through the "fruits of holiness" that Christians can see all around.[3] The gift of the Spirit, Amaladoss notes, is not for individuals but for the community (1 Cor 12).[4] One may say, with Father Samuel Rayan, SJ (1920-2019), that every person is the temple.[5] Amaladoss's perspective, however, is different: he laments that the merchants have occupied the temple and God can be found outside of it (Matt 21:12).

For Amaladoss, the context of life is defined with the threefold dialogue of the gospel with the poor, the cultures, and the religions, in accordance with the guidelines of the Asian bishops. India is not a poor country; the problem is that the distribution of wealth is unfair. The top 10 percent of the people hold over 70 percent of the country's wealth. The bottom 20 percent must be content with less than 2 percent of the country's wealth. The causes of this unjust distribution are numerous: the colonial rule of the past, a lack of education and access to health care, the exploitation of the poor by the ruling classes, and corruption in administration.[6] Conversely, India is rich in cultures and religions. South Asia is a subcontinent of a multiplicity of cultures. It hosts 325 functioning languages with twenty-five different scripts. It boasts four morphological types and contains all the genetic types that can be found anywhere in the world. It has 4,693 communities and 4,500 endogamous groups, sometimes called castes. India had a succession of migrants who came and merged with the local population in some way. Indian culture is a mixture of a vast variety of cultures that have been in constant interaction: the Indigenous peoples, the Dravidians, the Aryans, the Mongoloids, the Muslims from Persia and Arabia, and the British. This plurality of cultures withstood the impact of the colonial period and the European impact and survived the thrust of scientific and

---

the context of the universal though 'hidden' presence and action of Christ and the Spirit affirmed by *Gaudium et Spes*." See Amaladoss, "Freedom in the Spirit and Interreligious Dialogue," *Studies in Interreligious Dialogue* 8, no. 1 (1998): 10.

3   Michael Amaladoss, *Beyond Dialogue: Pilgrims to the Absolute* (Bangalore: Asian Trading Corporation, 2008), 208.

4   Amaladoss, "Freedom in the Spirit," 6.

5   Samuel Rayan, "Doing Theology in India," in *Theologizing in Context: Statements of the Indian Theological Association*, ed. Jacob Parappally (Bangalore: Dharmaram, 2002), 12.

6   Parappally, "Theologizing in Context," 31–32.

INCULTURATION AND DIALOGUE   81

technological modernity while adapting to it. A cultural revival across India as a means of discovering and affirming one's self-identity is underway, so any attempt to impose uniformity by foreign and local hegemonic forces is destined to fail.[7]

Religiously, India has never featured a singular pursuit. There must have been many different cults in India in the early period. Vedic Hinduism was one of them. The period of philosophic Hinduism with the Upanishads coincided with the emergence of Shramanism represented by Buddhism and Jainism, which opposed Brahminism, consisting of Vedic ritual and the Dharmasastras. The Jews may have come as traders more than two thousand years ago to the West coast. The Christians came about two thousand years ago. The Muslims were there 1,200 years ago, and so on. Hinduism must have acquired a common face only progressively and only after the Gupta period. India is a nation made up of the people who happen to live within its boundaries. The identity of this people (and the nation) is multiethnic, multicultural, and multireligious.[8] This is the India that Amaladoss has in mind. This is the context in which he conducts his theological work.

This context is not only a phenomenological reality. God is, in fact, reaching out to all people through the Word and the Spirit in various ways, at various times, and through the different religions. This ongoing divine-human encounter is, to some extent, salvific. However, God's plan is not merely to save individual souls but to gather together all things in heaven and on earth. Amaladoss argued the following:

> God is working out this plan in history through various sages and prophets at various stages. First of all, there is the mission of God in history, also in other religions, through the Word and the Spirit. This is followed by the mission of Jesus, who "visibilizes" and humanizes the presence and action of God in history. It is a kenotic manifestation of the Word as a servant (cf. Phil 2:6–13).[9]

---

7   Amaladoss, "Together Toward the Kingdom: An Emerging Asian Theology." 2005–2008 INSeCT Project, 3.

8   Amaladoss, *Challenges of Fundamentalism*, 42.

9   Amaladoss, *Peoples' Theology*, 35.

Jesus's resurrection emphasizes that His and God's commitment to the liberation of humanity will be fulfilled in history at the eschaton. The mission of Jesus is continued by the mission of the Church, as a community of witnesses at the service of the cosmic reconciliation as planned by God, manifested definitively and started in Jesus Christ. The Church becomes the symbol and servant of the Kingdom of God. In this context, it can be said that baptism is not a safe conduct to salvation but a call to mission.[10]

In a fascinating note, Amaladoss criticized the social contract that is at the root of modern states. He thinks that the state, and more specifically, the institutional structure of the state, has been superimposed over a multiplicity of communities, groups, and castes. The primary loyalty, he claimed, is not to the state but to the community. Amaladoss believes that a nation is a "community of communities"; accordingly, individuals are not the basic element of the state, and citizenship is not their only status. Communities are the building blocks of the state, and being part of a community, or community-ship, is crucial, too.[11] He may have a point. Almost two thousand years ago, in the twenty-fourth ode of his third book, the Roman poet Horace asked, *Quid leges sine moribus proficient?*, which translates to "What use are all these empty laws without [good] morals?" The general idea is that the polis, the way people stay together, is not a top-down construction led by law but the result of passion, moral behavior, shared values, closeness, and binding relations among the members of a community.

Amaladoss also revealed his reservations about representative democracy because he finds the rule of majority unfair; he is inclined toward a participatory democracy, a deep democracy in which individuals participate directly and without any mediation of the government in their (local) affairs.[12] For Amaladoss, there should be a clear separation of powers between the state (the institution) and the people: the first should limit its jurisdiction to enforce the law and deliver justice. To the second should be assigned the responsibility of peace and reconciliation.[13] It is an interesting

---

10 Amaladoss, *Peoples' Theology*, 35.

11 Amaladoss, *Beyond Dialogue*, 28.

12 Amaladoss, *Beyond Dialogue*, 29–30.

13 Amaladoss, *Beyond Dialogue*, 32.

INCULTURATION AND DIALOGUE 83

point: Western political theorists such as Thomas Hobbes, John Locke, and Jean-Jacques Rousseau envisioned (different forms of) social contract precisely for ensuring peace among the members of a community who would limit in some degree their individual freedom for state protection and justice. But Amaladoss believes that, in a polis of communities, the role of the state should be restricted, and peace should no longer be an exclusive prerogative of sovereignty.

Amaladoss's statement can be read in two ways: the first reading assumes that religions exercise their power by administrating the state of affairs in India so the country remains in peace. This would equate to the religions trespassing in the domain of the government of the country. This is definitely not the correct interpretation of Amaladoss's statement. The second reading assumes that the religions have authority to speak about peace, either for maintaining and defending order in the country or to contest such an order, whatever brings peace. This is the correct interpretation of Amaladoss's statement. In brief, Amaladoss has in mind countercultural communities that are not based on personal profit or abstract principles but on "the power of the Spirit and in their [i.e., the communities] own call to serve."[14] These communities are agents of cultural transformation, that is, they promote the "change of people's" worldviews and systems of values."[15] The engine of this transformation is a distinct form of spirituality that is human—in the sense that it is common to all human beings—and crosses religious boundaries. This spirituality "motivates, inspires, and enables people to search for a fuller life for all."[16] The world is struggling to offer meaning to the people who live through cultural crises. "Our mission," he claimed, is "to offer an alternative way of living in the world."[17]

In one early work, Amaladoss referred to "the failure of the Church" of India, although the phrase is more of an admonition to the Church to do more than a real critique.[18] Amaladoss, however, reserves his main doubts not for the Church but for the state as an institution that constrains rather

---

14   Michael Amaladoss, "Mission in a Post-Modern World," *Mission Studies* 13, no. 1 (1996): 68–79, 68.

15   Amaladoss, "Mission in a Post-Modern World," 68–69.

16   Amaladoss, "Mission in a Post-Modern World," 68–69.

17   Amaladoss, "Mission in a Post-Modern World," 72.

18   Amaladoss, *Making All Things New,* 5.

84   MICHAEL AMALADOSS AND THE QUEST FOR INDIAN THEOLOGY

than empowers a large part of the population. Too many people in India are still marginalized; too far is the integration of all in the Great Tradition (Amaladoss's term) of India.[19] In simple terms, Amaladoss believes that the *theologicus locus* of Christ in India can be found within the Great Tradition, namely, "the Vedas and the Upanishads, the Bhakti traditions and the Epics, the Architecture and the Arts."[20] The Grand Tradition plays in India, per Amaladoss's logic, the same role that the Early Fathers played in the Mediterranean milieu. In his more recent books, Amaladoss reframed and extended this Great Tradition to the point that it becomes a complex cultural and religious tapestry.

This cultural and religious tapestry is the background of Amaladoss's way of theologizing. Life and faith are in dialogue in the very context of India, and theology is the name of their relationship. Thus, theology is not theological reflection on systems and traditions but on the ever-changing encounter of life and faith. Theology is not a profession and is not pursued for the sake of academic acumen. Kurien Kunnumpurum, who presented a paper at the seminar on theologizing in India during the 1978 conference of the Indian Theological Association, set the guidelines for the Indian paradigm of theologizing that has since been followed by Indian theologians. He claimed that the method of Indian theologians must be experience based, praxis oriented, dialogical, and interdisciplinary.[21] Theology cannot be confined to sterile and abstract reflections within university classrooms; it is a matter of challenging and healing the harsh reality of life. An analysis of the socioeconomic and sociocultural context is considered propaedeutic to the development of a truly Indian theology. The poor, the marginalized, the oppressed on one hand, and on the other, the richness and diversified reality of India constitute the mandatory background of any meaningless act of theologizing. Theology is an enabler of the community in the sense that theology makes the gospel alive in and to the community; at the same time, the community reveals the gospel.

---

19   Amaladoss, *Making All Things New*, 7.

20   Amaladoss, *Making All Things New*, 7.

21   Kurien Kunnumpurum, "Theology in India at the Cross-Road," in *Theologizing in India Today*, eds. Michael Amaladoss, T. K. John, and G. Gispert-Sauch (Bangalore: Theological Publications in India, 1981): 208–16, 212.

INCULTURATION AND DIALOGUE   85

Therefore, theology cannot be an individual, solitary, self-centered activity: it is a social activity done together with others. In the very first meeting of the Indian Theological Association in 1976, Bede Griffiths complained about the inherently Western character of theology:

> The Indian Church, he said, has inherited a tradition of ritual and doctrine, which was developed in Western Europe and has little or no contact with the cultural tradition of India. This has meant that the Indian Church has become incapable either to awakening any mystical experience or of working any social transformation.[22]

In the same period, the Asian Bishop identified the antidote to this condition of alienation. What Asia (India) needs is a local Church as "a Church incarnate in a people, a Church indigenous and inculturated."[23] Theology may have its roots in the incarnation. But a totally local Church is still a work in progress both in Asia and in India, and the work of theologians is to facilitate the migration, clearing the way of obstacles and empowering the communities through inculturation and dialogue.

Although the bishops adopted the concept of incarnation to legitimize their project of inculturation, Amaladoss remains suspicious of this concept. He believes that it carries a certain degree of ambiguity. For example, incarnation can imply a pure and simple adaption of the Word from the center to the periphery of the world: think of inculturation in terms of indigenization of the theological, liturgical, and administrative of Christian faith and life. This triumphalist understanding of incarnation, Amaladoss argued, is not useful. Incarnation, he claimed, is "the wrong paradigm to seek to understand the process of gospel-culture encounter."[24] He prefers to look at the image of the baptism of Jesus: a dying and rising, a new beginning.[25] The Church has to renounce her previous historical

---

22   Bede Griffiths, "The Mystical Dimension in Theology," *Report of the First Annual Meeting of Indian Theological Association* 14 (1977): 229–46.

23   "First Plenary Assembly: Statement and Recommendations" (Federation of Asian Bishops' Conferences, Taipei, Taiwan, April 22–27, 1974), no. 12.

24   Amaladoss, *Beyond Inculturation*, 16.

25   Michael Amaladoss, "Dialogue and Mission, Conflict or Convergence," *VJTR* 48, no. 2 (1986): 79.

embodiments as well as the cultural and intellectual baggage that comes with them and walk a kenotic path.

There is no global ecclesiastical governance in Amaladoss's vision but a world system where local churches may interact according to the West-East logic of mutual opposition. In other words, he envisions an anarchic governance of the global Church with no overarching central authority and sovereignty: a multiplicity of local churches, each identified with a community, in which local theologies are developed in the ordinary circumstances of life. These churches are not institutionally defined, as I will show, but rather blended into other religions within the community. The role that Amaladoss envisions for the Church in the Indian environment is ambitious: she is not devoted to her own development and preservation but to the empowerment of the whole people of India. She is the seed of the growth of the entire community (Matt 4:26–32), not in the sense of Christianizing the culture of that community but in contributing to building a better world.[26] The local Church, in fact, is at the service of the Kingdom of God and received from it her justification. And it is in serving the Kingdom, that is, involving herself in the concrete condition of human existence, that the Church becomes local. In that sense, Amaladoss envisions the local Church as both a symbol and the servant of the Kingdom.

INCULTURATION

In 1998, Amaladoss wrote a book titled *Beyond Inculturation*. For him, the term *inculturation* delivers a false sense of familiarity. He believes that, as a theological paradigm, inculturation carries a distinct top-down inclination, the celebrated image of the missionary who brings the gospel to the natives. Inculturation, then, is the process of making the gospel intelligible within the new cultural situation. But, Amaladoss complained, inculturation does not mean the translation of a religion and its vocabulary, worship, or even doctrines into a new culture. Translation, so to speak, is more precisely a transformation, as it always comes with a difference that is also a creative contribution. Thus, inculturation stands for a mutual transformation of the religion and the culture: the religion may be placed

---

26   Amaladoss, *Making All Things New*, 15–44.

in a new perspective; the culture may receive a new dimension.[27] The agent of inculturation is not the missionary but the local community itself that interprets the gospel and proceeds into a conversion that ultimately changes the culture of reference and extracts new meaning from the gospel. Transformation is not limited to individuals and their choices in life but involves the institutions, rituals, and intellectual frameworks. Inculturation is another word for a theology of difference. In an article written in 1985 while he was in Rome, Amaladoss described his personal journey from inculturation as a theological paradigm to a life experience:

> Twenty-five years ago, I was busy studying Tamil language and culture in order to translate and adapt the gospel and Christian theology into linguistic and cultural categories that would be familiar to those to whom I was going to proclaim Christian truth. But the study of Indian, largely Hindu, religion and culture and contact with practising Hindus led me to discover many good and inspiring things in their tradition that I wished to integrate into my own Christian tradition. In the course of that effort, I realized that what I was really looking for was an Indian Christian spirituality, theology, liturgy, etc., so that the gospel would incarnate itself into Indian culture, acquiring in this way a new cultural expression, becoming more catholic (universal) and at the same time purifying and fulfilling another culture. Such an incarnation, however, proved impossible without a living dialogue with Hindus, reading their scriptures, following their philosophico-theological reflection, interpreting their symbols and sharing their way of life and *sadhana* (spiritual pursuit). This tended to be an elite activity. Contact with the people, the poor and a certain impact of the theology

---

27 For Amaladoss, "Culture is the way people live. It is the way people understand themselves, organize themselves and celebrate life. They understand themselves in the context of the world in which they live. Their self-understanding results in a worldview that finds expression in myths and symbols, especially stories of their origin and end, and images of their ongoing life.... Culture is the way in which a community humanizes itself and the world in which it lives." See Amaladoss, "Culture and Dialogue," *International Review of Mission* 74, no. 294 (1985): 170–71.

of liberation made me see inculturation as an integral process of building up a new humanity (the kingdom), in which proclamation, dialogue and liberation had their place and in which I was called to collaborate with all men and women of goodwill.[28]

It is a long quote, but it says it all. First, the meeting of gospel and culture is a two-way process. There are "many good and inspiring things [in Hinduism] that I wished to integrate into my own Christianity." Second, inculturation and universalization (Catholicism) are two sides of the same coin. Third, the study of the Christian Tradition distances the gospel from the most meaningful reality of India. It is not the elite but the poor—those who are marginalized and left behind—who are the subjects of inculturation. Fourth, inculturation is not about expanding Christianity but building a new world in cooperation with other good people and under the mysterious divine action. The coming of the Kingdom, not the growth of Christianity, is the ultimate goal of inculturation. The article is also a testament to Amaladoss's intellectual trajectory: in it, he talks about incarnation, a term he abandoned in his later works.

Another reason why Amaladoss is suspicious of the term *inculturation* is because it creates a sense of a community's culture without a soul. The gospel is supposed to be that soul. To put it differently, he contests the indispensability of the gospel as if local cultures lack what constitutes humanity without the good news. The opposite is true: "Cultures have an autonomy in their own sphere, as recognized by the Second Vatican Council," Amaladoss pointed out.[29] Morality does not depend on Christianity. Morality does not disappear without Christianity. Cultures are not only secularized but also embedded with a plurality of sources, influences, and approaches. A pure Christian community, totally dedicated to the gospel, no longer exists, if it ever did. Religion, however, still plays a crucial role in the people's existence as a force of inspiration and motivation in the background of ultimate and definitive perspectives. "As every culture is animated by one or more religions and ideologies," Amaladoss claims,

---

28   Amaladoss, "Culture and Dialogue," 169–70.

29   Michael Amaladoss, "Inculturation and Ignatian Spirituality," *The Way Supplement* 79, no. 1 (1994): 41.

"the gospel cannot really encounter another culture without encountering these religions and ideologies."[30] Thus, he concludes, "the encounter of gospel and culture becomes also an *interreligious* process" (original emphasis).[31] Amaladoss offers a powerful example of how this interreligious process operates in one of his books, *The Asian Jesus*, which presents Jesus as the Sage, the Way, the Guru, the Satyagrahi, the Avatar, the Servant, the Compassionate, the Dancer, and the Pilgrim.

Religion is not separated from culture. In Amaladoss's view, religion is the deepest element of culture. It provides prophetic function and meaning, in the sense that it delivers the answers to the ultimate questions about the origins and goals of life and the role of others in one's own existence. Religion offers meaning to culture, and culture in return gives form to religion. And yet, the prophetic element of religion is permanently in creative tension with culture, always on the brink of being domesticated, although it "always bounces back in the form of holy people and radical movements for renewal."[32] On one side, religion supports and justifies culture; on the other, it challenges culture to reject or oppose any serious attempts to conform to the course of ordinary, day-to-day living. Religion at its worst is an indistinguishable stream of culture; religion at its best is a countercultural force.

In an exchange with the Argentine Mexican philosopher Enrique Dussel, Amaladoss connected this countercultural character of religion with the early Church: "Christianity began as a counter-culture. Every effort to domesticate it and organize it has always been disastrous."[33] Here Amaladoss reveals the countercultural roots of his theology: Christianity cannot be organized. He also shows the antiestablishment spirit that permeates his view: the Church as an institution ultimately domesticates Christianity. The institution is devoted to domesticating, that is, reproducing the dominant cultural and ideological patterns; it is an obstacle to the full development not only of Christianity per se but even of a better

---

30   Amaladoss, "Inculturation and Ignatian Spirituality," 41.

31   Amaladoss, "Inculturation and Ignatian Spirituality," 41.

32   Amaladoss, "Culture and Dialogue," 171.

33   Michael Amaladoss, "The Future of Mission in the Third Millennium," *Mission Studies* 5, no. 1 (1988): 96.

society. Not surprisingly, Amaladoss had critical words for some aspects of the institutional Church, such as the infallibility of the pope and the strong hierarchical system of power.[34] He also rejected the artificial separation of laity and clergy, the former being confined to the realm of the temporal and the latter being in charge of the life and administration of the Church.[35] He depicted the institutional hierarchical Church as antithetical to the Church as "a community of love and sharing united in prayer, witnessing to God's goodness to us and attracting others to join it."[36] The Dogmatic Constitution on the Church, *Lumen Gentium,* explains that the common priesthood of the faithful and the ministerial or hierarchical priesthood are different but interrelated, but Amaladoss is more interested in questioning the difference than investigating the interrelation.[37] Finally, he does not believe that the ministerial priesthood is at the service of the royal priesthood.

I am unsure whether Amaladoss is familiar with the patristic notion of *Ecclesia ab Abel iusto usque ad ultimum electus,* the notion mentioned in *Lumen Gentium* of a universal Church before Christ and beyond the institutional borders of the Church.[38] This universal Church receives all the just, "from Abel, the just one, to the last of the elect," in God's heavenly community through the salvific universal mediation of Christ. In fact, for Augustine, the body of Christ is made of all the just, including those who lived before the coming of Christ. Therefore, one has the notion of a pre-Christian Church, a Church that precedes Christ and extends beyond the sociological, institutional, and juridical borders of the Catholic Church. In other words, the body of Christ does not identify itself with the Catholic Church. The intention of Yves Congar, the Dominican priest who served

---

34 Amaladoss, *Peoples' Theology,* 13–15.

35 For the reference to the "temporal," see Pope Paul VI, *Lumen Gentium* (Dogmatic Constitution on the Church, Rome, November 21, 1964), no. 31: "By reason of their special vocation it belongs to the laity to seek the kingdom of God by engaging in temporal affairs and directing them according to God's will."

36 Amaladoss, *Peoples' Theology,* 19.

37 Pope Paul VI, *Lumen Gentium,* no. 10. For the quote, see Amaladoss, *Peoples' Theology,* 12.

38 The quote reads, "All the just, from Adam and 'from Abel, the just one, to the last of the elect.'" Pope Paul VI, *Lumen Gentium,* no. 2.

on the preparatory theological commission of the Second Vatican Council and on several committees that drafted conciliar texts, was to reintroduce the notion of *Ecclesia ab Abel* in the theological discourse, and he favored a more theological and spiritual configuration of the Church.[39]

Amaladoss's idea of a community that goes well beyond the institutional borders of the Church resembles that of *Ecclesia ab Abel*, but in some degree, it is more intricate. It can probably be explained through a simple story:

> Hindus all over India do visit the tombs of Muslim Sufi saints, honouring them and exploring their intercession. Such tombs in Ajmer, Delhi and Nagore are well known.... Christians, in general, are more reserved in these matters. But they are known to frequent ritual specialists of other religions for healings and exorcisms. The Muslim shamans are said to be powerful against evil spirits. The parents of a sick child may go to a doctor, to the Church and to a shaman in quest of healing.[40]

What Amaladoss had in mind is a community of people who belong to a network of de-institutionalized religions. In his view, a network of borderless religions allows each individual to freely cross over religious borders without abandoning their own faith. "As a Christian," he said, "I do not see the need of any borders between religions."[41] Religions are naturally inclined to enter into mutual dialogue to enrich each other and make the world better. As a matter of fact, Amaladoss shares Pope John Paul II's vision of a redemptive role of religions—all religions. He often quotes the saint pontiff's address to a group of leaders of other religions in Madras, India:

---

39   Center for the Study of the Second Vatican Council, *Archives conciliaires de Gérard Philips*, 123, CT 5/61:41; Yves Congar, *De Ecclesia, Quomodo exponi exprimique possit nexus inter homines extra Ecclesiam visibilem extantes et Corpus Mysticum* (May 18, 1961), 1.

40   Michael Amaladoss, "Editorial—Imaginary and Inter-Faith Dialogue," *Horizonte* 15, no. 45 (2017): 12.

41   Amaladoss, *Beyond Dialogue*, 195.

> As followers of different religions, we should join together in promoting and defending common ideals in the spheres of religious liberty, human brotherhood, education, culture, social welfare and civic order. Dialogue and collaboration are possible in all these great projects.[42]

This community of followers of borderless religions is the ideal community that Amaladoss has in mind. Unfortunately, within religions there is also a propensity for purity and exclusion. This is true for all three main religions in India. Amaladoss responded to this threat with a reinterpretation of identity and, more specifically, of religious identity: identity is the result of the dialogue with others. Interpersonal interaction, therefore, is the enabler of identity. For this reason, boundaries between individuals are not only wrong; they are dangerous because they contribute to the edification of a static identity that leads to a distorted relationship.[43] Religious identity is characterized by a particular connection with God or the divine. For Amaladoss, the relationship among individuals and their connection with the divine are intertwined: "Each one's identity is finally determined by the free interplay of divine call and human response as it happens in the life of every person."[44] In other words, identity is the product of interpersonal interaction and divine call.

In Amaladoss's writings, the term *inculturation* merges three interrelated activities: "Building up the local church as a particular cultural manifestation of the Word, challenging the culture to be converted in the light of the gospel and the ongoing effort to promote an alternative culture."[45] Thus, the gospel, the community, and its culture are inextricably linked. At a phenomenological level, the encounter between gospel and culture through the community is an ongoing, never-ending process; it is no surprise that Amaladoss believes that the term *inculturation* does not convey the complexity of the phenomenon. To borrow a sentence from Kochurani

---

42   John Paul II, *The Pope Speaks to India* (Bombay: St. Paul, 1986), 86.

43   Amaladoss, *Beyond Dialogue*, 205.

44   Amaladoss, *Beyond Dialogue*, 206.

45   Amaladoss, "Inculturation and Ignatian Spirituality," 39–40. The reference to the Second Vatican Council is Pope Paul VI, *Gaudium et Spes*, no. 59.

INCULTURATION AND DIALOGUE   93

Abraham, for Amaladoss, inculturation "becomes the concrete manner in which a community builds itself as the local church."[46] At the end of the process, the local Church develops her own unique theology, spirituality, and worship. This is Amaladoss's view on inculturation according to Abraham: "the very being of the Church in the new culture."[47]

Inculturation is a process that is not detached from Tradition. Amaladoss explains the link between the two as follows: Tradition is not only embodied in texts but in rituals, symbols, and community structures, too. Tradition is not an entity to study but a reality to live at the level of community. Therefore, Tradition is more precisely *living* tradition, namely, the experience of encountering the Word in the context of the ongoing experience of life of a community. An experience gives rise to reflection, and reflection gives meaning to an experience. In this close relationship between faith and life, everyone contributes to Tradition because everyone can live the gospel and place this experience in the light of their faith. Amaladoss uses this beautiful expression: "[Faith] is not a light that shines from the outside."[48] On the contrary, the experience is an attempt to live the faith in the reality of life.

In several of his writings, Amaladoss has raised the point that Indian theology needs to be about symbols, not concepts. One of the reasons for this recommendation is, in his opinion, that Indians feel more at home with symbols than concepts. Symbols provoke reflection as much as concepts, but a different kind of reflection: one that is interpretative, not logical or deductive. Amaladoss has shown a lifelong interest in symbols. Readers must remember that Amaladoss was originally a sacramental theologian. Symbols were the core of his doctoral dissertation; in the third chapter of that document, which evolved into a published book, he discussed at length the symbolic nature of the liturgy and the powerful link that Augustine and Thomas Aquinas established between the sacrament and the sign.

---

46   Kochurani Abraham, "The Emergence of Local Churches," in *Seeking New Horizons: Festschrift in Honour of Dr. M. Amaladoss, S. J.*, ed. Leonard Fernando (Delhi: Vidyajyoti Education and Welfare Society & ISPCK, 2002), 34.

47   Abraham, "Emergence," 33.

48   Michael Amaladoss, *Becoming Indian: The Process of Inculturation* (Bangalore: Dharmaram, 1992), 71–72.

In his dissertation, Amaladoss also reflected on the recent developments of semiology.[49] Symbols resurfaced in his more recent works, in which he once again confronts the intuitive experience of the Asian way of thinking that is focused more on wisdom rather than mere knowledge. He invites his readers to focus on living experience that finds expression in symbol. "Experience reaches out to Reality that is beyond our rational framework," he claimed. "[Experience] evokes symbols that people need to interpret. But all this happens in the midst of experience, that is life. Life is therefore primary. Praxis is more important than theory. Praxis nourishes theory and sometimes challenges it."[50]

Amaladoss carefully distinguishes between universal and local symbols. Universal symbols are those whose meanings have remained unchanged across the course of history. He identified two universal symbols: washing with water in baptism and eating and drinking together in the Eucharist. It is interesting to think, Amaladoss pointed out, that Jesus chose such universal symbolic actions for two of the important sacraments. Similarly, anointing and imposition of hands are also universal symbols.[51] Amaladoss also observed that different religions have different experiences and images of God communicated through their scriptures and other holy books. When we accept the legitimacy of other religions to facilitate salvific divine-human encounter, we also accept the many images and symbols through which they experience God. This does not mean that these are universal symbols accessible to everyone. They are local symbols, in the sense that they belong to a particular historical and cultural tradition.[52]

DIALOGUE

In a compilation of three essays published in book form in 1985, Amaladoss summarized his personal journey in the field of religious dialogue. He divided his journey into three phases:

---

49   Amaladoss, *Do Sacraments Change?* 29–48.
50   Amaladoss, *Peoples' Theology*, 8.
51   Amaladoss, *Peoples' Theology*, 77.
52   Amaladoss, *Peoples' Theology*, 62.

> Twenty years ago I studied Hindu religion and culture so that I could present Christ to the Hindus in a way more adapted to their mentality. Later I tried to discover the "unknown Christ to Hinduism" so that I might make the Hindus recognize the Christ I preach to them as their own.... Today I dialogue with my Hindu brothers, looking forward to mutual enrichment and collaboration in the building up of a new humanity.[53]

Since then, he has published books and articles on religious dialogue but without modifying the basic conclusion he reached in those essays forty years ago: that other religions are not simply human efforts to reach God but vehicles through which God reaches people outside the boundaries of Christianity. In this task of building a new humanity that Amaladoss considers crucial, other religions are essential participants. In his 2008 book *Beyond Dialogue*, Amaladoss explained that religions are not entities (Amaladoss used the term *objects* to emphasize their supposed passive role) but active forms of mediation of an encounter between God and a community.[54] Each religion is a way chosen by God to enter into relationship with a certain community: "If God has called a person or a group in a particular way, that way is unique for them."[55] Amaladoss did not specify who "God" is in this statement, but the term stands for the Christian God. Thus, Amaladoss turned upside down the popular belief that religions are different paths to reach the divine. The opposite is true: religions are different ways in which the divine reaches humanity. Christians believe that the Spirit of God is present and active in other religions; therefore, Amaladoss concluded, Christians must recognize the presence and action of God in other religions' Scripture.[56] Each Scripture is a vehicle for God of self-revelation to a given community, and that vehicle is properly understood only by the members of that community. The members of one community can approach the Scripture of another community, but not as objects, that is, as artifacts that can be addressed outside the background

---

53 Amaladoss, *Faith, Culture and Inter-Religious Dialogue*, 3.
54 Amaladoss, *Beyond Dialogue*, 72.
55 Amaladoss, *Beyond Dialogue*, 73.
56 Amaladoss, *Beyond Dialogue*, 70.

of reference. They can be "properly and adequately accessed in the context of a dialogical relationship with the community to which they belong," he said. Then he added, "They should not be read and interpreted outside that context."[57]

Amaladoss has struggled for some time to find an image (he calls it a model) that encapsulates his view on the relationship between the religions. In his 1985 book on interreligious dialogue, he uses imagery of different rivers leading to the same ocean and of the different languages that refer to the same reality.[58] He soon dismissed all these images as inadequate to express his vision, which was evolving rapidly. In a shorter, more recent article that is basically a summary of his thought on dialogue, Amaladoss returned to the figure of Swami Abhishiktananda to address the option of intrapersonal dialogue. In the end of life, Amaladoss noted, Abhishiktananda "was experiencing God—the Absolute—in two different ways *and did not have to integrate them*" (emphasis added).[59] It is clear that Amaladoss has increasingly abandoned a form of ingenuous relativism (there is one reality but many ways to see it; there is only one God, but many ways to approach Him) to a more complex understanding of the intertwined reality of religious dialogue.[60]

---

57   Amaladoss, *Beyond Dialogue*, 73. One of Amaladoss's key theological ideas is the concept of "dialogical inculturation," which is the process of integrating the Christian faith into local cultures through respectful dialogue and mutual learning between cultures. Amaladoss believes that this approach is essential for creating a truly authentic and relevant expression of Christianity in the diverse, pluralistic context of South Asia.

58   Amaladoss, *Faith, Culture and Inter-Religious Dialogue*, 8–9.

59   Michael Amaladoss, "Indian Christian Theological Issues in the Context of Interreligious Dialogue," in *Windows on Dialogue*, eds. Ambrogio Bongiovanni, Leonard Fernando, Gaetano Sabetta, and Victor Edwin (Delhi: ISPCK, 2012), 42.

60   In another recent article, Amaladoss investigated the question of truth. He asked, What is a true religion? Is truth a criterion to detect a true religion? He proceeded to offer alternatives, or rather complementary criteria, to truth in the evaluation of a religion. One is the results (Matt 7:15). The other is vision (the vision of the Kingdom) and values (the Kingdom's values). He concluded that religions should be judged by their vision and values and by the saints who live them, not so much by their theological, ritual, and institutional

INCULTURATION AND DIALOGUE   97

His sophisticated framing of religious dialogue may discourage others from following his example. Amaladoss, in fact, has a peculiar interpretation of this word. One way to capture that interpretation is the story of his father's funeral as told by Amaladoss himself:

> My father died about 30 years ago. When the time for the funeral came, I started a small revolution by opting to have the funeral mass at home, not officially permitted, rather than go to a nearby chapel which was rather small. When the mass was over, I was stopped from starting the funeral procession to the cemetery. An old lady appeared from somewhere. Under her direction, my sister-in-law was directed to bring a full measure of rice and was asked to touch the head, the chest, and the feet of my father, starting with a small sign of the cross made over the body, with the measure of rice. Then this rice was taken into the house and was emptied in a corner of the main hall and an oil lamp was placed on the heap of rice. . . . Rice, as food, is the symbol of life. By touching the body of my father his spirit was being absorbed, so to speak, in the rice. . . . During the period of mourning—three days—when relatives and friends from far away came to the house after the funeral, they went straight to the heap of rice with the lamp, expressed their grief and then only sympathized with the people in the house. For them the heap of rice was the spirit of my father. It was taken away once the official period of mourning was over. The ritual was obviously pre-Christian. It was Christianized with a sign of the cross. There was no prayer. But the taking away of the body did not mean, for them, that the ancestor was leaving the house totally. He continued there, at least for ritual purposes, in the symbol of rice. I am sure that the parish priest (and the Church) would have looked on this as a superstitious gesture, without understanding its significance. Probably the Chinese, with their own practice of

---

manifestations. See Amaladoss, "Which Is the True Religion? Searching for Criteria," in *Co-Worker for Your Joy: Festschrift in Honour of George Gispert-Sauch, SJ*, eds. Sebastian Painadath and Leonard Fernando (Delhi: Vidyajyoti Education and Welfare Society and ISPCK, 2006), 45–60.

experiencing the presence of their ancestors through the symbol of tablets, would have understood it.[61]

The story of his father's funeral is emblematic of the point Amaladoss wanted to emphasize: in a religiously pluralistic environment like India, in which people do not split along strict lines of religious affiliation, dialogue is not among religions but individuals.[62] This is particularly true when it comes to spiritual matters. People often hold a vague idea of the theoretical incompatibility between spiritual cosmologies, and yet, they believe in spirits and miracles. People may not pay particular attention to matters of theological coherence, and yet, they refer to a spiritual otherworld that intersects and subverts the rules of this world. In Amaladoss's view, people's belief of the supernatural is more important than their correct understanding of the laws of the supernatural. Amaladoss concluded, "We may not be able to avoid some syncretism."[63] Still, his point is deeper than that.

In fact, it is possible for India and Christianity to proceed together peacefully in the concrete reality of existence, only on the condition of excluding the religious truths from conversation. Competitive religious truths are the premises of conflict; therefore, on religious truths, one must be silent. This is Amaladoss's contribution to the development of a truly Indian Christianity: India and Christianity can meet on the common ground of a peaceful existence at least to a point that precedes the revelation. A peaceful coexistence of India and Christianity is possible up to a certain point, when religious truths become part of the conversation. Of course, Amaladoss articulated his thought in more sophisticated terms: there is the level of existence, he argued, and that of theological speculation. There is the interreligious and intercultural conversation, where a multiplicity of identities can be harmonized, and there is an intraconfessional conversation in which theological speculation is not only allowed but encouraged. One must avoid

---

61   Amaladoss, *Peoples' Theology*, 114–15.

62   *En passant*, I mention that Amaladoss's religious pluralism shares nothing with that of scholars such as John Hicks. For Amaladoss, Hicks is an a priori pluralistic theologian, and for this reason his position should be rejected. See Amaladoss, "Which Is the True Religion?", 48.

63   Amaladoss, *Peoples' Theology*, 114–15.

INCULTURATION AND DIALOGUE   99

confusion between the two levels and the two conversations. This twofold construction allows Father Amal to give coherence to his framework.

Religion operates at two levels: Amaladoss calls the first level "meta-cosmic" and the other one "cosmic." The former is the level of theologians and some rituals; the latter is the level of popular religiosity. He is more interested in the latter and more specifically in the cosmic, indigenous, and tribal forms of religiosity. Why, he asked, should the spiritual cosmology of the indigenous people be replaced with a Christian cosmology when they convert to Christianity? "While we have our own army of angels, saints and devils to do God's bidding and to answer our prayers, we simply reject the local good and evil spirits as pagan."[64] He raised a question of conformity: What would have to change when Indigenous people convert to Christianity? What could be conserved from their past and what must be abandoned? Amaladoss was suggesting a policy of tolerance: he invites recognition of the value of the spiritual beliefs within other religions instead of considering them deviant. It is not a missionary strategy; it is mutual enrichment. "The Indigenous People remind us that God is everywhere. The universe is alive with the divine. . . . The Indigenous people can help us to rediscover this universal 'oneness' in God."[65]

It should be clear at this point that Amaladoss is no longer interpreting the practice of religious dialogue in terms of parallel paths, Christians and non-Christians. Reality is much more complex: the dialogue is related to the diversity that enriches both the world out there and the world within. The experience of living in a pluralistic world implies not only finding harmony in ordinary life within a community but also balancing the different heritages that constitute the basis of each individual's personality. Amaladoss not only recognizes in himself both the Hindu and the Christian heritages but detects a plurality of heritages in each of his Hindu, Muslim, and Christian brothers. There is no purity of race, religion, and culture, just as there is no purity of faith. "The Absolute is within, immanent," Amaladoss observed. "The Absolute is experienced as the depth of one's being."[66]

---

64   Amaladoss, *Peoples' Theology*, 114–15.

65   Amaladoss, *Peoples' Theology*, 119.

66   Michael Amaladoss, "Contextual Theology and Integration," *East Asian Pastoral Review* 40, no. 3 (2003): 271.

The plurality of life, the multiplicity of reality, and the fragments of the cosmos find their integrating principle in this absolute center. In fact, "this integration is not merely personal, but cosmic since, in the Absolute, one rediscovers . . . everything." That is why, in the end, religious dialogue is for Amaladoss not only an existential task but, almost inevitably, a spiritual exercise.[67]

Amaladoss firmly believes that there is salvation outside the Church. Salvation, he argues, has less to do with sin and hell and more with participation in the whole universe in the life of God. God is gathering up all things into unity until God will be "All in all" (1 Cor 15:28). Creatures as well as the entire creation participate in this cosmic harmony. In this communion, people belonging to different religions acknowledge themselves as fellow pilgrims toward the Kingdom. Their enemies are more spiritual than material, namely, Satan and Mammon.[68] Like, say, Abhishiktananda and Panikkar, Amaladoss considers the existence of the non-Christian religions as a stimulus to rethink the role of the Church in the grand cosmo-soteriological plan of God. Like them, Amaladoss highlights the activity of the Holy Spirit outside the visible structure of the Church rather than the singularity of Christ and the Church. But his entry point is different from that of Abhishiktananda and Panikkar. The former famously interpreted the *darshana* of Sri Ramana Maharshi as a testimony that the Spirit is at work everywhere; the latter could not escape the feeling that all priests are the priests of the Kingdom. In the concrete, multifaced reality of India where all religions are somehow entangled, Amaladoss sees the Spirit behind the common, historical, and even supernatural destiny of all people. His intuition is neither "mysteric" (like Abhishiktananda's) nor liturgical (like Panikkar's) but sacramental: he believes not only that all religions are sacramentally related to each other but also that God is really present in all of them. The entirety of humanity actively participates in a greater and mysterious reality to which they point, that is, the Kingdom.

---

67   Amaladoss has found a link between spirituality and creation in the spirituality of creation mentioned in *Laudato Si:* "This is very attractive especially to the Easterners like us." See Amaladoss, "A Spirituality of Creation according to Pope Francis," *VJTR* 79, no. 8 (2015): 575.

68   Amaladoss, "Indian Christian Theological Issues," 37–38.

Amaladoss's interest in dialogue is not universally shared in the microcosm of Indian Christianity. A few notes may help contextualize the work of Amaladoss on religious dialogue. In a short contribution written several years ago, he sadly recalled how his guru, Father Hirudayam, was marginalized around the time of Vatican II for his keen interest in inculturation and in Saiva Siddhanta.[69] Since then, the situation has improved. Father Hirudayam was able to establish himself as a scholar in Saiva Siddhanta and founded his own ashram. Several fellow Jesuits received doctoral degrees in various Indian religions. Research centers and permanent study groups and seminars were initiated in different parts of the country, where the different aspects of dialogue—liturgical, spiritual, textual—were addressed. Academic journals and popular bulletins were published. The interest in religious dialogue has grown in the last decades. But, Amaladoss laments, the religious dialogue remains the dedicated activity of a few people. "On the one hand, some think that religion is not relevant to social ministries. . . . On the other hand, our [Amaladoss addressed his fellow Jesuits] attitude to religions . . . seems to be neutral."[70]

ONE LAST THOUGHT

"What does this alleged shift from the Church to the Kingdom mean for priesthood?" This was the first question I asked Father Amal during our initial meeting in Chennai. The question was framed in a way to connect his ideas to his life but, in retrospect, it was the wrong question to start a conversation. Sure, the relationship between the Church and the Kingdom is at the core of the metaphysical background that sustains and justifies Father Amal's theology. According to Father Amal, all religions have a role in the "way known to God" in the grand plan of salvation.[71] P. R. John published

---

69   Michael Amaladoss, "Dialogue with Cultures and Religions," in *Born Again: Jesuits Back in Tamil Nadu*, eds. Leonard Fernando and Bernard D'Sami (Dindigul: Jesuit Madurai Province, 2002), 263.

70   Amaladoss, "Dialogue with Cultures," 265–66. Yet, "dialogue" has become synonymous with the new way of being Church in Asia. See Peter C. Phan, *Christianity with an Asian Face: Asian American Theology in the Making* (Maryknoll, NY: Orbis, 2003).

71   Pope Paul VI, *Gaudium et Spes*, no. 22.

an extract of his class notes as a senior student at Vidyajyoti College of Theology when Father Amal was his professor. It is a valuable insight into the mind of a mature thinker. At that time, Father Amal was back in India after his long permanence in Rome and before his last relocation to Chennai. The course was called Jesus Christ as the Only Saviour and Mission. Here is the incipit: "Salvation is a cosmic project that is working itself out of history according to the plan of God. The whole of history is therefore salvation history." Then the voice of the old instructor continues: "Salvation is not simply the saving of individual souls. It is social and cosmic."[72] The goal of salvation, therefore, is not merely related to the Church but to the Kingdom, of which the Church is the symbol. What does it mean to be a priest, then? Father Amal is a quiet person with a remarkable ability to remain in silence as long as necessary to formulate an answer. "It means that one is a priest of the Church and the Kingdom," he responded after a while. He might have responded as Panikkar did, that all priests are priests of the Kingdom and to be a Catholic priest is a means or, in Panikkar's own words, "a very narrow entry point" into the Kingdom.[73] He meant that the Catholic priesthood is a secondary reality, subordinated as it is to the priesthood of the Kingdom. This is not Father Amal's position: for him, the priesthood of the Kingdom and that of the Church stand on the same ground. It was a well-crafted answer to an infelicitous question.

The metaphysical is not Father Amal's primary interest—people are. There are theologians who are attracted to a strong mode of thinking, so strong that it ends in silence. These are the contemplative theologians who reach the limit of thought and language and then rest, content to be facing the mystery. Then there are theologians who infuse their faith with intelligence. They are the speculative theologians who enlighten their faith with all the resources that reason has to offer in order to make the divine understandable to all. And finally, there are theologians who are motivated by the divine imperative of charity, *agapé*. Those theologians incessantly work to embed love in the human community, feed the hungry, and clothe the poor. Despite his idiosyncrasy for classifications and definitions, Father

---

72   John, "Towards Indian Christology," 57.

73   Raimon Panikkar, *Entre Dieu et le Cosmos Entretiens avec Gwendoline Jarczyk* (Paris: Albin Michel, 1998), 60.

INCULTURATION AND DIALOGUE 103

Amal would agree with me that he belongs to this third stream of theologians. Of course, he does not literally clothe the poor; his gift is rather to offer a vision of harmony and collaboration among people of different heritages, a horizon of peace, regardless of the finitude of human condition. His message is about hope and faith, but more importantly, love (1 Cor 13:13). And yet, there is a factor of radicality in his message.

I investigated at length the theology of Father Amal and I already mentioned that there is nothing extreme in his thought. When I associate radicality and Father Amal, I do not mean that his thought is radical, but that his message implies a radicality of choice. To make a decision—from Latin, to cut off—is to convert. The message of Father Amal is about conversion. The radicality of this message is hidden in his interpretation of the Kingdom: not the slow progress toward an inevitable destiny led by an invisible deity but a personal decision, taken in total freedom in the midst of the ordinary circumstances of life. There is a personal responsibility, a decision to make. The Kingdom of God is *Entos Hymōn*: "Within You" (Luke 17:21), and Father Amal emphasizes the urgency of this decision. Now, he cries, not tomorrow; the decision should be made now. The time is now. The gospel is not talking about a Kingdom to be established in a distant, mythical future. Oh, no, Father Amal protests. The Kingdom is not a postponed retribution for a current world dominated by injustice and death. The Kingdom is an option for today: "I tell you the truth, today you will be with me in paradise" (Luke 23:43). If people convert, the world can be transformed in this very instant. If they change their path, if they embrace agape, if they have faith in Jesus Christ, the Kingdom can be today. If people embrace the beatitudes (Matt 5:3–12), they are blessed now, not tomorrow. This is the radicality of Amaladoss's message: so simple and so impossible. Is it really impossible?

4

CHRISTOLOGY

THE UNIQUENESS OF JESUS CHRIST

After his return to India from Rome in the nineties, Amaladoss intensified his Christological reflection.[1] His most famous book, *The Asian Jesus*, benefited from that reflection. He has affirmed more than once that all salvation is from God through Jesus Christ. In his article "Jesus Christ as the Only Saviour and Mission," he began with an affirmation of faith: "We Christians affirm that Jesus Christ is the only savior. We believe that every human person who is saved participates in the paschal mystery of Christ in ways unknown to us."[2] This affirmation refers to *Gaudium et Spes*, number 22. The pillar of Amaladoss's Christology deals with the uniqueness and universality of salvation in Jesus Christ. Amaladoss has never denied this. He has, however, sought to explain how this affirmation can be understood in Asia today in light of a growing positive appreciation of other religions.[3] He has rejected the validity of two quick answers as not really addressing the problem: the first is that there are many saviors, and the second is that the one divine salvific mystery is known by many names, including Jesus.

> One quick answer is to say that, in the light of other religions also facilitating the salvific divine-human encounter, the affirmation that Jesus is the only saviour is no longer tenable. There are other

[1]   In this chapter, I depend heavily on Amaladoss's 2013 written response to the Congregation. When no source is provided, readers must assume that the quote refers to that response. A synthesis of the response can be found in the last chapter of Amaladoss, *Experiencing*, 167–83.

[2]   Michael Amaladoss, "Jesus Christ as the Only Saviour and Mission," *The Japan Mission Journal* 55, no. 1 (2001): 219–26.

[3]   Amaladoss, "Jesus Christ," 219.

saviours. . . . A similar answer is to say that God is the only saviour. Salvation is a mysteric process of God's continuing action in the world reaching out to the humans. We encounter this mystery in Jesus. Other people may encounter the same mystery through other names and salvific figures. I think that both these answers simply suppress one pole of the dilemma. So, they do not really address the problem.[4]

In another article he argued:

Most Indian theologians affirm that all salvation, however understood, is from God in and through Jesus Christ. . . . I think that Christian faith supposes such an affirmation. If this is not affirmed then we can stop the discussion right here, because there is nothing to explain or understand. . . . Attempts to explain do not amount to denial.[5]

So, the framework of his search is clear. Amaladoss does not deny the faith affirmation that Jesus is the unique savior but seeks to explain this in the context of a positive appreciation of religious pluralism. He thinks that in Asia, this affirmation of faith must be understood in a twofold context. Amaladoss draws a sharp distinction between "a level in which we make faith affirmations and another level where we speak about what is actually happening at the historical, phenomenological level." At the level of faith, the salvation in Christ reaches out to people in different ways. He often refers to the Indian bishops' response to the *Lineamenta*:

As God's Spirit called the Churches of the East to conversion and mission witness (see Rev 2–3), we too hear this same Spirit bidding us to be truly catholic, open and collaborating with the Word who is actively present in the great religious traditions of Asia today. Confident trust and discernment, not anxiety and over-caution, must regulate our relations with these many brothers and sisters.

---

4   Amaladoss, "Jesus Christ," 219–20.

5   Amaladoss, "Mystery of Christ," 328.

CHRISTOLOGY 107

For together with them we form one community, stemming from the one stock which God created to people the entire earth. We share with them a common destiny and providence. Walking together we are called to travel the same paschal pilgrimage with Christ to the one Father of us all (see Lk 24:13ff, *NA* 1, and *GS* 22).[6]

The bishops went on to say:

In the light of the universal salvific will and design of God, so emphatically affirmed in the New Testament witness, the Indian Christological approach seeks to avoid negative and exclusivistic expressions. Christ is the sacrament, the definitive symbol of God's salvation for all humanity. This is what the salvific uniqueness and universality of Christ means in the Indian context. That, however, does not mean there cannot be other symbols, valid in their own ways, which the Christian sees as related to the definitive symbol, Jesus Christ. The implication of all this is that for hundreds of millions of our fellow human beings, salvation is seen as being channelled to them not in spite of but through and in their various sociocultural and religious traditions. We cannot, then, deny a priori a salvific role for these non-Christian religions.[7]

These two quotes are long but provide useful context. In Amaladoss's opinion, Christians appropriate salvation through a direct and conscious relationship of faith in Jesus Christ, moved as they are by the Spirit. The same Spirit also enables other people to accept or appropriate the salvation-in-Christ, but the Spirit works in them, not through the kerygma and sacraments of the Church or through an explicit confession of faith in Jesus Christ, but through, or facilitated by, other symbolic figures and structures. Following John Paul II, these means may be called "participated mediations."[8]

---

6   Peter C. Phan (ed.), *The Asian Synod: Texts and Commentaries* (Maryknoll, NY: Orbis, 2002), 21.

7   Phan, *Asian Synod*, 22.

8   Pope John Paul II, *Redemptoris Missio* (Letter Encyclical, Rome, December 7, 1990), no. 5.

108   MICHAEL AMALADOSS AND THE QUEST FOR INDIAN THEOLOGY

Amaladoss makes no attempt to equate these symbolic figures with Jesus Christ or to consider them as parallel mediations. Rather, he acknowledges a pluralism of (participated, but real) mediations in the lives and histories of peoples and groups. "Acknowledging this pluralism," he clarifies, "does not in any way mean the denial of the uniqueness of the source or our faith affirmation relating the salvation of all to what God has done in Jesus Christ." As a matter of fact, Amaladoss notes, the talk about the "mysteric" or cosmic Christ by some Asian theologians is precisely meant to affirm this link with Jesus Christ but without any conscious relationship to his humanity. The members of other religions are certainly related to Jesus Christ as a final cause, but Jesus Christ is not part of their religious consciousness and commitment. This is what makes space for dialogue with them at the religious level, and, where possible, proclamation.

At this historical and phenomenological level, the Church is seen and experienced by other people as one among other religions. God does reach out to the believers of other religions without them having any direct, conscious relationship with the visible, institutional Church. "It is at this level," Amaladoss noted, "that we are dialoguing with the believers of other religions. I think that it is legitimate to talk about a pluralism of religions at this level. Such a pluralism does belong to the salvific plan of God." That is why interreligious dialogue is an integral dimension of the mission of God and the mission of the Church. Amaladoss quoted Cardinal Julius Darmaatmadja in response to *Ecclesia in Asia*:

> Yes, it is true that there is no authentic evangelization without announcing Jesus Christ, Saviour of the whole human race. But for Asia, there will be no complete evangelization unless there is dialogue with other religions and cultures. There is no convincing and trustworthy announcement of Jesus as the Saviour, unless along with, or even preceding this announcing, the Church presents the actual loving ministry of Jesus which rescues people from situations of injustice, persecution, misery, and in the place of these brings life, yes, even life in abundance.[9]

---

9   Julius Darmaatmadja, "A New Way of Being Church in Asia," *VJTR* 63, no. 12 (1999): 891.

CHRISTOLOGY   109

In the multireligious situation of Asia, Christians tend to talk, even among themselves, on two registers. There is a practical, pastoral level where Christians speak about pluralism, which is real and based on theological principles. At the ontological, mysterical level, they speak to their faith conviction about the relatedness of all those who are saved to Jesus Christ and to the Church. These are two dimensions of one plan of God, and as a theologian, Amaladoss can and should discuss both. He can distinguish them without separating or confusing them.

These two dimensions should not be posed and compared as if they were made at the same level. At the same time, theological reflection cannot ignore either level. To proclaim the Christian faith and to base this proclamation with transcendental affirmations, is not helpful when Christians talk about Christ to members of other religions at a historical and human level.

> If we take history seriously, our enquiry on the role of Jesus in the history of salvation cannot be answered by a transcendental affirmation. There is no problem in making such affirmations within the Christian milieu. But if we go out on to the public place and engage in historical actions like proclamation and dialogue then we have to give some historical content to our transcendental affirmations. Otherwise, it is better to proclaim our faith and refrain from explaining it.[10]

When Christians say that Jesus Christ is the only savior, they tend to look at the divine in Jesus. But it is difficult to preach the doctrine to members of other religions without downgrading their religious experiences that are unrelated to Jesus. "It represents a high Christology," Amaladoss protested, "that looks on Jesus simply as God."[11] He clarified, "When I encounter the members of the other religions, the church is seen by them as one among the many world religions, whatever may be my own personal awareness of its special character in the plan of God." The members of the other religions are not and need not be aware of this mysterious relationship they

---

10   Michael Amaladoss, "Jésus Christ, le seul sauveur, et la mission," *Spiritus* 41, no. 2 (2000): 148–57, 153.

11   Amaladoss, "Together Toward the Kingdom," 8.

have with Jesus Christ and the Church. Christians cannot ignore this fact in conversation or in their own theological reflection:

> In history, the man Jesus and the Church, which is a community of his disciples, play a special role which does not exclude the other religions. Jesus has gone before us, showing us an example of self-giving love even unto death. Even people who do not know Jesus can participate in his mystery by doing what he did. (cf. Mt 25) This involves a radical secularization of life in which all religions, their doctrines and rituals become relative. What is important is to love God in the other, ready to give one's own life. Such egolessness leads to peace, love and fellowship. . . . Today we cannot think of history without Jesus and the Church. But their role is one of solidarity, symbol and service, not monopoly. The human Jesus has chosen a kenotic (self-emptying) way of service, rather than domination. Asians do not feel comfortable with traditional images like 'Jesus the King' which may have urged missionaries to conquer Asia for Christ. They would prefer to witness to Jesus as the liberator of the poor and the oppressed, Jesus as the Wise Man, as the eschatological Prophet, as a Servant.[12]

Although Amaladoss speaks about the uniqueness and universality of Jesus Christ, he prefers to focus not on who He is but rather what He signifies and does. Jesus is seen as an initiator of a movement of love, opting to be poor and to struggle with the poor or as a countercultural prophet.[13] This way of presenting the saving action of Jesus does not deny the truth that salvation is ultimately rooted in Jesus' paschal mystery. "Our formulation," Amaladoss pointed out, "rather articulates for a larger public an aspect of the saving work of Jesus Christ." On the Chalcedonian formula, for example, Amaladoss wrote in 1996 that "the clear definition of Chalcedon is not

---

12   Amaladoss, "Together Toward the Kingdom," 8–9.

13   The reference to the poor is to Aloysius Pieris, *The Christhood of Jesus and the Discipleship of Mary: An Asian Perspective* (Colombo: Logos, 2000); *Fire and Water* (Maryknoll, NY: Orbis, 1996), 65–78. The reference to the countercultural prophet is to Sebastian Kappen, *Jesus and Cultural Revolution: An Asian Perspective* (Mumbai: Build, 1983).

CHRISTOLOGY 111

quite intelligible in India. Some of those terms cannot even be translated in Indian languages."[14] Yet, it is not simply a matter of translation but one of reinterpretation. For Amaladoss, in fact,

> The council of Chalcedon said that the divinity and the humanity in Jesus should neither be confused nor separated. I think that the tendency in the Western Church has been to affirm the unity of the personhood in Jesus and highlight his divinity, while downplaying the difference of natures and his humanity. In the context of other religions, while it is easy for us to affirm the presence and action of God, the Word and the Spirit in them, it seems difficult to relate them to the historical manifestation of the Word in Jesus, except eschatologically and in mystery.[15]

Here the idea is to reexamine the formulation and make it more suitable to the Indian mindset.[16] In fact, the basic principle behind Amaladoss's Christology is that the Chalcedonian formulations should be relativized. The formulations depend upon context; to put it differently, a distinct Christology is only meaningful when it can be adopted by a local Church in a particular context and in a specific moment in history. And a local Church adopts a distinct Christology only when it is intelligible to the community of reference. Each community is culturally and historically conditioned.[17] The word *adoption*, however, is incorrect: for Amaladoss a local Church develops a distinct Christology that makes possible the formulation of the revelation in an intelligible way and for all people to have access to a definitive communication with God.[18] In

---

14   Michael Amaladoss, "Who Do You Say That I Am?" *VJTR* 60, no. 12 (1996): 782–94, 784.

15   Michael Amaladoss, "Asian Theology: Bilan and Perspectives" (paper presentation, Louvain-la-neuve, May 1, 2001). See Emis Segatti, "The Christological Thought of Michael Amaladoss," *Archivio Teologico Torinese* 7, no. 2 (2001): 345.

16   Amaladoss is not alone in his criticism against the Greek character of the council of Chalcedon. See, for example, the pioneering work of Vilakuvelil Cherian Samuel, *The Council of Chalcedon Re-Examined* (Delhi: ISPCK, 1971).

17   Amaladoss, *Beyond Inculturation*, 99.

18   Xavier Léon-Dufour, *Lecture de l'Evangile selon Saint Jean*, vol. 1 (Paris: Seuil, 1988), 124. The source was mentioned by Amaladoss, who agreed on this point.

summary, a local Church initiates a distinct formulation that is simultaneously revealing of the complex nature of Christ and intelligible to members of the community.

Accordingly, Christology is no longer a matter of adoption of formulations drawn from doctrine but the development of a theological reflection that emerges in the practical reality of life.[19] In Amaladoss's words,

> Every statement is made in a context. The fact that this context may not be explicitly acknowledged does not make the context disappear into thin air. A contextual theological reflection starts from below, from experience, and questions the traditional formulations of faith. . . . Indian theologians dismiss the kind of systematic theology which ignores its own contextual sources as irrelevant.[20]

One of Amaladoss's key theological ideas is dialogical inculturation, which is the process of integrating the Christian faith into local cultures through respectful dialogue and mutual learning between cultures. I addressed this theme in a previous chapter. Amaladoss believes that this approach is essential for creating a truly authentic and relevant expression of Christianity in diverse cultural contexts. Amaladoss's approach can be mistakenly confused for a sort of Indian existentialism; it is rather a "dialogue more with the human and social sciences than with philosophies."[21] He is adamant in his belief that experience is a source of action, the first principle from which reflection begins. Symbols and narrative must be considered to be just as important as concepts. In his view, symbols provoke thought and hermeneutical reflection.[22]

The difference between the adoption of formulations drawn from doctrine (a top-down method) and the development of a theological reflection that emerges in the practical reality of life (a bottom-up method), however, is not only a matter of shifting from one approach to another. Rather, it is a passage from one order of things to another. Questions and

---

19   Amaladoss, *Beyond Inculturation*, 48.
20   Amaladoss, "Mystery of Christ," 328.
21   Amaladoss, "Together Toward the Kingdom," 2.
22   Amaladoss, "Together Toward the Kingdom," 2.

CHRISTOLOGY   113

answers change accordingly. Formulations, in fact, respond to ontological questions: Who is Christ? What is creation? Reflection that emerges from experience instead concentrates on how it is that individuals and communities experience Christ and creation. Rather than, Is Christ present in the Eucharist? the question is, How do we perceive the Eucharist? By reflecting on this abundance of experience, people can then build outward to establish how they know the world. This knowledge, however, is not phenomenological but theological. Amaladoss cautioned against the temptation to consider this approach a kind of epistemology. The questions that are addressed and the answers that are offered are theological. Theology is not a phenomenology of the living experience.[23]

Good theologians are no longer those who quote from their predecessors but who are open to life and contribute to building a peaceful community. Theology is not speculation based on the work of previous theologians: "to be a theologian then is not to have mastered treatises . . . but to be alive to life and experience from day to day . . . and be ready for an ongoing search that does not forget its roots in the past, but is open to the future in constructive and creative ways."[24] Of course, formulations receive their meaning from context. The shift that Amaladoss suggests is more

---

23   With reference to the questions to be addressed, see this passage: "While the phenomenological or comparative study of religions can be a useful exercise to promote a basic understanding of the different religions, the question of uniqueness with regard to a particular religious tradition is not asked at this level. That many people who discuss the question of uniqueness seem to remain at this level, however, does not make the question itself meaningless. Because *the question is not primarily a phenomenological question, but a theological one*" (emphasis added). With regard to the answers, refer to this passage: "When I, as a Christian, say that Hinduism is legitimate, I do not mean to say that Hinduism considers itself as a legitimate religion. On the contrary, I consider Hinduism as legitimate from my own point of view, however I may qualify such legitimacy. That is why my affirmation of uniqueness becomes a problem. *My affirmations* of religious pluralism and of the uniqueness of my own religion *are not phenomenological affirmations, but theological ones, that is, made from within my own faith perspectives*" (emphasis added). Both quotes are from Amaladoss, "Is Christ the Unique Saviour? A Clarification of the Question," in *What Does Jesus Christ Mean?* Eds. Errol D'Lima and Max Gonsalves (Bangalore: Indian Theological Association, 1999), 6–8.

24   Michael Amaladoss, "The Limitation of Theology," *VJTR* 51, no. 11 (1987): 529.

precisely from a doctrinal, ultimately systematic theological context to a sociocultural context. The suggested solution is the integration of Christian belief with today's everyday Indian experience—namely the demythologization of doctrines and specifically those that are related to the nature of Christ. Demythologization consists in the Christians' readings of doctrines and dogmas from the lens of contemporary everyday experience.

JESUS, THE WORD, AND THE SPIRIT

Just as the Word and the Spirit, together with the Father, constitute one God, the one person of the Incarnate Word is constituted by his divine and human natures. Like other (Western and Indian) theologians, Amaladoss holds a distinction between the humanity and divinity of Jesus Christ. He is committed to a distinction, not a separation, between the two natures that constitute this one "person": "We confess two natures in the one Person of Jesus Christ; the Council of Chalcedon said that the two natures should 'neither be separated nor confused,'" he argued. The communication of idioms is legitimate, but it remains a communication of idioms between two natures in the perspective of the unity of the person. Of course, this does not mean that theologians cannot talk about the two natures without confusing or separating them, if and when necessary. "While the 'communication of idioms' supposes that we can attribute to the one person predicates that refer to both the natures," he argued, "it does not forbid us to distinguish between the two natures and speak about them." It is an articulated unity with distinct, not separate or parallel, elements. The affirmation of a distinction is not a denial of unity but an attempt at an articulation of its constitutive elements in the light of experience. But the unity and the relationship are mysterious. "In the context of our experience and our questions the theologians can explore them, open, of course, to correction and improvement."

Amaladoss also suggested a specific reinterpretation of Chalcedon: "I think that the tendency in the Western Church has been to affirm the unity of the personhood in Jesus and highlight his divinity, while downplaying the difference of natures and his humanity." In India, in fact, the context of religious pluralism suggests Amaladoss emphasize both the difference of natures in Christ and His humanity, and that emphasis on the

CHRISTOLOGY   115

humanity of Jesus is critical in the practices of dialogue. That may explain why Amaladoss advocates for the underscoring of the humanity of Jesus without downplaying His divinity. He thinks that it is an act of balance. If the Church has, in the past, highlighted the divinity of Jesus, the reality of Asian Christianity suggests the opposite. "Attempts to articulate the divinity and humanity in Jesus Christ have always been problematic," he noted. "I have tried to keep the balance compared to many other Christological attempts."

One can detect a trajectory in Amaladoss's reflection on the two natures of Jesus Christ. In his early days as a theologian, he distinguished between Jesus and the Christ (following other theologians like Panikkar); he later realized that the term *Christ* means "anointed" and refers directly to Jesus. He started distinguishing between the "Word" (the divine nature) and "Jesus" (the human nature). Although a distinction between the Christ and Jesus may be confusing, a distinction between the Word and Jesus is not. The distinction between the Word and Jesus serves Amaladoss in shedding light on the distinction between the action of the Word and the Incarnated Word. The action of the Word is always related to the incarnate Word, Jesus Christ, though one does not always see and know how this happens:

> By affirming the incarnation and the uniqueness of Christ, I am affirming this relationship, though I accept that I am not explaining it. The idea of Jesus Christ as the "final cause" refers Jesus Christ back, in a way, to the plan of God. To say that Jesus Christ is present in other believers through the Spirit affirms a distinction and relationship between Jesus Christ and the Spirit. I think that to say that the Word is present and active in all humans brings Jesus Christ more closely in relationship to everyone. The Word and Jesus are not parallel mediations. They are two ways of one and the same mediation. They relate to and refer to each other. But they need not be the same. All these are attempts to throw some light on "in a way known to God."

The Word of God was certainly present and active in the world before it became incarnate in Jesus. After it became incarnate, does the unity of the person imply that the distinction between the natures disappears? Or does the unity suppose that all the actions of the Word thereafter are not only related to its human nature in some way but also limited to what the human nature does or can do? Discussing this very question, Dupuis made the following distinctions:

> For clarity's sake it seems therefore useful to distinguish the following: the action of the Word-to-be-incarnate (*Verbum incarnandum*), that is, the Word before the incarnation; the action of the Word incarnate (*Verbum incarnatum*), either in the state of kenosis during his human life or after the resurrection in the glorified state; and the perduring action of the Word as such which continues after the incarnation of the Word and the resurrection of Christ and is not constrained by the limits of his humanity.[25]

What one sees here is distinction in unity, not separation. Amaladoss thinks that there is no problem with the action of the Word-to-be-incarnate and of the Word-incarnate. The question is about the action of the Word, distinct from though related to His humanity, even after the incarnation. In his commentary on John's Gospel, Xavier Léon-Dufour spelled out the different stages of the activity of the Word. He explained that the Logos is working from the beginning of creation (John 1:2–5) as the source of light and life, enabling a personal relationship between God and the humans:

> This enlightening action, insofar as it is welcomed, produces divine sonship. And this is so, even before the Logos takes a human face, that is independently from any explicit reference to Jesus Christ.[26]
>
> The "coming" of the Logos has already been spoken of in 1:10f: he "was in the world" and "he came to his own home." If it is true that the Logos is God communicating himself, this communication has begun not with the incarnation but since creation, and

---

25 Jacques Dupuis, *Christianity and the Religions: From Confrontation to Dialogue*, trans. Robert Barr (Maryknoll, NY: Orbis, 2002), 140.

26 Léon-Dufour, *Lecture de l'Evangile*, 109.

CHRISTOLOGY 117

it has continued through the whole history of revelation. However, the incarnation of the Logos marks a radical change in the mode of communication.[27]

Henceforth, [revelation] happens through the language and the existence of a man among others: this phenomenon of concentration in a man will make it possible for the revelation of God to be formulated directly in an intelligible way, and for all people to have access to a definitive communication with God.[28]

This new stage does not supersede the previous one. The Logos continues to express himself thanks to creation of which he is the author and the witness given to the light: many can receive him and become children of God. Henceforth, however, revelation is also and mostly concentrated in him who will be designated by his name: Jesus Christ (Jn 1:17).[29]

Amaladoss noted that, according to Léon-Dufour, the incarnation is a special manifestation of God through the Word in human nature, but it does not exclude a continuing revelation of God by the Word to people who do not relate to the humanity of the Word, namely Jesus Christ.

For Amaladoss, not only is the Word present and active in all human beings, but the Spirit is too. In the course of his life, Amaladoss has strongly affirmed the presence of the Spirit everywhere, including other religions. He has held that all salvific activity is from God, Father, Son, and Spirit and that this salvific activity is related to the paschal mystery of Jesus Christ. The "how" of this relationship in the case of the other believers is known to God alone.[30] Though all salvation is from the Father, in Jesus Christ, and through the Spirit, in the case of members of other religions, it is not mediated through a direct and conscious relationship with Jesus. On this point, Amaladoss feels in harmony with John Paul II, who spoke on several occasions and in various documents about the action of the Spirit in

---

27   Léon-Dufour, *Lecture de l'Evangile*, 112.

28   Léon-Dufour, *Lecture de l'Evangile*, 124.

29   Léon-Dufour, *Lecture de l'Evangile*, 124.

30   The reference is to Pope Paul VI, *Gaudium et Spes*, no. 22.

118 MICHAEL AMALADOSS AND THE QUEST FOR INDIAN THEOLOGY

Christianity as well, and in other religions.[31] But the relationship of these two groups of people to Jesus Christ—the Christians and the members of other religions—seems to be different. Jesus is present and active in the Christian believers, directly and consciously, in a way that He does not seem to be present and active in the believers of other religions. This is indicated by saying that Christ is present in other religions through the Spirit. It is the same Spirit related to the paschal mystery of Jesus Christ. These two different "ways" of presence of the same mystery are the foundation for differences between the religions at the historical and phenomenological level. Amaladoss clarifies his position:

> I wish to acknowledge and affirm this difference as source of creative and meaningful dialogue between religions. I feel that sometimes some theologians, by affirming that the Spirit present and active in the other religions is the Spirit of Christ, may not sufficiently appreciate this difference between the two ways of the Spirit's presence and their relevance to interreligious dialogue.

He did not affirm an economy of the Spirit more universal than or separate from that of the salvific paschal mystery of Christ. The economy is one. But it may be actualized or realized in practice in different ways. Amaladoss thinks that a relationship with the Spirit is real for all people in a way that a direct and conscious relationship with Jesus is not: "I am trying to affirm this difference because a real difference between religions and the ways in which God, Jesus Christ and the Spirit are active in them is meaningful for dialogue. It is this difference that makes it possible for us to listen to the Spirit speaking to us through the other religions and to learn from the Spirit."

It is because they realize the presence of the Spirit in other religions that theologians like Amaladoss have insisted that Christians can learn from other religions. The Indian bishops have suggested the following in their documents:

---

31   Amaladoss primarily refers to chapter 3 of Pope John Paul II, *Redemptoris Missio.* The activity of the Spirit in the Christians and in the Church is addressed in nos. 21–27 and the activity of the Spirit in the other religions in nos. 28–29.

CHRISTOLOGY   119

It is an accepted principle that we cannot comprehend a mystery; before it, our attitude needs to be one of reverent acceptance and humble openness. God's dialogue with Asian peoples through their religious experiences is a great mystery. We as Church enter into this mystery by dialogue through sharing and listening to the Spirit in others. Dialogue, then, becomes an experience of God's Kingdom.[32]

In Amaladoss's view, what Jesus has revealed to humanity may not be fully grasped by humans because of their human, historical, and cultural conditionings and limitations, although the Church is right in what she grasps and expresses. In his words, "The Spirit may actually be leading us to fuller truth through our dialogue with other religions."

THE RELIGIONS

In Amaladoss's view, his own search on other religions falls within the perimeter assigned by the document *Dominus Iesus*:

In the practice of dialogue between the Christian faith and other religious traditions, as well as in seeking to understand its theoretical basis more deeply, new questions arise that need to be addressed through pursuing new paths of research, advancing proposals, and suggesting ways of acting that call for attentive discernment. (§ 3)

Later in the same document one reads:

With respect to the *way* in which the salvific grace of God—which is always given by means of Christ in the Spirit and has a mysterious relationship to the Church—comes to individual non-Christians, the Second Vatican Council limited itself to the statement that God bestows it "in ways known to himself." (*Ad Gentes*, 7) Theologians are seeking to understand this question more fully. Their work is to be encouraged, since it is certainly

---

32   Phan, *Asian Synod*, 20–21.

useful for understanding better God's salvific plan and the ways in which it is accomplished.[33]

He has no intention of denying anything that pertains to the traditional faith of the Church; at the same time, he remains sensitive to the fact that even traditional faith affirmations need to be interpreted in new contexts. His reflections do not question the overall context of faith; he is trying to make distinctions and clarifications within the doctrines in light of new awareness in new contexts. Traditional doctrine also develops in light of new theological reflection in new contexts. A comment by Francis A. Sullivan, SJ, on *Dominus Iesus* refers to the "way in which the salvific grace of God comes to individual non-Christians" and offers an example of the kind of questions and distinctions that Amaladoss has in mind:

> While the CDF does not offer any solution to this question, it does go beyond speaking of the salvation of non-Christians as having a "mysterious" or even "indispensable" relationship to the Church, by saying: "With the coming of the Saviour Jesus Christ, God has willed that the Church founded by him be the instrument for the salvation of *all* humanity" ($ 22). In the following sentence it even describes this as a "truth of faith." This raises the question whether the CDF means to describe as a "truth of faith" the proposition that the church exercises an instrumental causality in the salvation of everyone who is saved. The texts to which reference is given in support of this statement speak of Christ as the Saviour of all mankind, and of the church as sent to bring his message of salvation to the whole world, but they hardly answer the question whether the church exercises instrumental causality in the salvation of people whom it does not reach with its ministry. Nor does the "universal mediation" of the church in salvation have to be understood in terms of instrumental causality.[34] I believe that the mediation of the

33 Congregation for the Doctrine of the Faith, "Declaration *Dominus Iesus* on the Unicity and Salvific Universality of Jesus Christ and the Church" (Rome, August 6, 2000), no. 21.

34 This is the footnote provided by Sullivan: "Jacques Dupuis, SJ, insists that the mediation of the church in the strict, theological sense, has to be understood as instrumental efficient causality." See Dupuis, *Toward a Christian Theology,*

church in the salvation of those whom it does not reach can be seen in the fact that the church offers the eucharistic sacrifice for the salvation of the whole world.[35] In my opinion it is not likely that the CDF intended to assert as a "truth of faith" that the church exercises instrumental causality in every instance of salvation. I would see that as one of the "questions that are matters of free theological debate" to which the CDF did not intend to propose solutions (§3).[36]

A fine distinction can be drawn between challenging faith affirmations and seeking to explain faith affirmations in the context of a positive appreciation of religious pluralism. This is the approach of contextual theology. "Precisely because I take the issue of religious pluralism seriously in the context of our ongoing experience of and dialogue with the believers of other religions," Amaladoss pointed out, "a priori explanations of the faith which do not take into account our experience of dialogue do not satisfy me. Such, for instance, would be explanations that do not give a place to the other religions in the plan of God for salvation."

A positive appreciation of other religions, however, does not mean they are parallel ways to God or salvation. God's plan of salvation is one. For Amaladoss, the history of salvation has a structure. All religions are integrated into this structure, but their followers may not be aware of it. He explained, "We believe that God through the Word and the Spirit is leading all things to a unity in ways unknown to us." In Asia, there is a growing conviction that other religions do facilitate salvific divine-human encounter. Amaladoss added, "We can also ask whether the one salvific plan of God includes various ways in which God is reaching out to the humans." A positive view of the role of other religions as facilitators of salvific divine-human encounter is common among bishops and theologians in Asia. Both a positive role for other religions in God's plan of salvation and their relationship to the unique mystery of Christ are assured through the Holy

---

350. For this reason, he denies the church's mediation in the salvation of those whom it does not reach with its ministry of word and sacrament.

35 Here Sullivan refers to his own book, *Salvation Outside the Church?* (New York: Paulist, 1992), 158–60.

36 Francis A. Sullivan, "Introduction and Ecclesiological Issues," in *Sic et Non: Encountering Dominus Iesus*, eds. Stephen J. Pope and Charles Hefling (Maryknoll, NY: Orbis, 2002), 50–51.

Spirit that is active in them. The fact that other religions do not consciously and directly relate to Jesus Christ does not in any way deny the uniqueness and universality of the salvific mystery of Jesus Christ. That is why John Paul II said, "The Church's relationship with other religions is dictated by a twofold respect: respect for man in his quest for answers to the deepest questions of his life and respect for the action of the Spirit in man."[37]

Much of Amaladoss's reflection is an attempt to consider this conviction on other religions in understanding the mission of the Church in Asia. He no longer speaks of other religions as salvific or as ways to salvation, and he makes even less effort to present other religions as parallel paths to the way of Jesus Christ. He makes no attempt at all in his most recent writings to assert that all religions are the same or that they are complementary; there is only the suggestion that they have a role in the "way known to God."[38] He argued, "My conclusion from all these reflections is that God's salvific plan for the world and for humankind is one. But this one plan is differently articulated in a pluralism of elements, though they are marked by inter-relatedness." Nothing should lead theologians to introduce any separation or parallelism between these various elements. They remain distinct, though interrelated. It is this pluralism that provides a space for dialogue and collaboration between these different elements. The unity will be fully evident only when all things are united on the last day, and God will be "all in all" (Cor 15:28). According to Amaladoss, salvation is always participation in the paschal mystery, though the ways are known only to God. A mystery is a mystery. The International Theological Commission accepts that this is a point under discussion among theologians. As a matter of fact, theologians have only barely delved into this mystery thus far. In Amaladoss's words: "A search is a search. If someone comes up with more satisfying answers to the questions, I am open to them."

THE CHURCH AND THE KINGDOM

The Second Vatican Council spoke about the "necessity of the Church for salvation." Recognizing the possibility of salvation for those who were not guilty of a sinful refusal to belong to the Church, the Council spoke of them

---

37   Pope John Paul II, *Redemptoris Missio*, no. 29.

38   Pope Paul VI, *Gaudium et Spes*, no. 22.

CHRISTOLOGY   123

as being "related to the church in various ways."[39] The term used is *ordinantur*, or related.[40] Here, Amaladoss quoted Sullivan: "It is obvious that the church has an instrumental role in the salvation of those who belong to it. It is not so clear, nor did Vatican II offer an explanation of, how it is used by God as an instrument for the salvation of those who are not its members."[41] The document *Dominus Iesus* suggests that the way this instrumental role of the Church transpires is unclear: "Theologians are seeking to understand this question more fully. Their work is to be encouraged."[42] Therefore, Amaladoss concluded that how the Church exercises instrumental causality is one of the questions that remains a matter of free theological debate.

It is in this context that Amaladoss explores the relationship between the Church and the Kingdom of God. He does not speak of the Kingdom as a merely sociological and this-worldly reality, but neither is it a purely spiritual, other-worldly reality. Perhaps in an incarnational economy, spiritual and sociological, other-worldly and this-worldly realities should not be opposed but held in the tension of the "already/not yet." Among theologians, Amaladoss claims, there are two views of this relationship. Some still think that the Kingdom is simply the future of the Church, which is its beginnings. Others, in the context of a positive view of other religions in the plan of God, relate the Kingdom to the plan of God and find a place for other religions in the Kingdom. This does not mean, however, that all religions have the same relationship to the Kingdom. The Church claims a special relationship, which is not one of identity with the Kingdom: she argues to be the sacrament of the Kingdom. The Church, although essentially related to the Kingdom of God, is not identical to it, but it is its sacrament. The Second Vatican Council already referred to the Church as "the universal sacrament of salvation," a "sign and instrument, that is, of communion with God and of unity among all men."[43]

---

39   Pope Paul VI, *Lumen Gentium*, nos. 14–16.

40   Pope Paul VI, *Lumen Gentium*, no. 16.

41   Sullivan, "Introduction and Ecclesiological Issues," 50–51.

42   Congregation for the Doctrine of the Faith, "Declaration *Dominus Iesus*," no. 21. But in no. 22, *Dominus Iesus* goes on to say that "God has willed that the Church founded by him be the instrument for the salvation of all humanity."

43   The first quote is from Pope Paul VI, *Lumen Gentium*, no. 48; the second is from *Lumen Gentium*, no. 1.

Amaladoss has never questioned this special relationship of the Church to the Kingdom of God as its sacrament. A sacrament is usually described as sign and instrument. Because these words seem to refer to a material thing, he has tried to humanize the term by talking instead of symbol and servant. The many ways in which God reaches out to all people are part of the one salvific plan of God in which the Church has a special role. Traditionally, this role has been described as the Church being the sacrament of universal salvation. The idea of the sacrament makes space for the presence and role of other religions in the one plan of God. The role of other religions does not exclude the possibility that all humans are ordained to the Church, as the Second Vatican Council stated.[44] Amaladoss shows no hesitation in affirming such a relationship according to the plan of God, pointing out, "I think that many theologians agree that the necessity of the Church for salvation does not demand more than such an 'ordination' or relationship." Amaladoss aligned himself with Pope John Paul II when the latter said,

> One may not separate the Kingdom from the Church. It is true that the Church is not an end unto herself, since she is ordered toward the Kingdom of God of which she is the seed, sign and instrument. Yet, while remaining distinct from Christ and the Kingdom, the Church is indissolubly united to both. The result is a unique and special relationship which, while not excluding the action of Christ and the Spirit outside the Church's visible boundaries, confers upon her a specific and necessary role.[45]

Amaladoss noted that although Pope John Paul II affirmed an "indissoluble relationship" between the Church and the Kingdom, he also pointed to a distinction so that the Kingdom is also present, even if inchoatively, outside the Church's confines, and the Church's missionary activity also includes the promotion of gospel values among people outside her confines. I refer to a previous remark: for Amaladoss, there is a level where Christians make faith affirmations, and there is another level where they

---

44 Pope Paul VI, *Lumen Gentium*, no. 16.
45 Pope John Paul II, *Redemptoris Missio*, no. 18.

CHRISTOLOGY 125

speak about what is actually happening at the historical, phenomeno-logical level. These two dimensions are relevant when one addresses the relationship of the Church to the Kingdom. Amaladoss does not pro-pose a "regnocentric" (i.e., kingdom-centric) theory of mission. On the contrary, he has repeatedly asserted that the goal of mission is twofold, namely the building of the Kingdom and of the Church as its symbol and servant:

> Just as we neither separate nor confuse Jesus and God, we need neither separate nor confuse the Church and the Kingdom. The goal of mission then can be redefined as helping to build the King-dom and the Church as its symbol and servant.[46]

In his view, it is precisely because there is a double goal with two elements, distinct though not separate, one from the other, that it is possible to think that the other religions can collaborate with the Church in building the Kingdom of God.[47] Addressing other religious leaders in Chennai, Pope John Paul II said,

> By dialogue we let God be present in our midst; for as we open ourselves in dialogue to one another, we also open ourselves to God. . . . As followers of different religions, we should join together in promoting and defending common ideals in the spheres of reli-gious liberty, human brotherhood, education, culture, social wel-fare and civic order.[48]

---

46 Michael Amaladoss, "The Trinity on Mission," in *"Mission is a Must": Inter-cultural Theology and the Mission of the Church*, eds. Frans Wijsen and Peter Nissen (Amsterdam: Rodopi, 2002), 104.

47 Amaladoss sets the relationship between the Church and the religions in the following terms: "The Church then cannot set itself as a criterion to judge all the other religions. Jesus is the Truth incarnate. The Church is called and sent by Jesus. But it does not possess Jesus. It is a pilgrim. It is slowly deepening its own experience of God. It is also affected by the human limitations and frailties of its members." See Amaladoss, "Together Toward the Kingdom," 7.

48 Pope John Paul II, "Address on the Occasion of the Meeting with the Expo-nents of Non-Christian Religions," Madras, February 5, 1986.

126   MICHAEL AMALADOSS AND THE QUEST FOR INDIAN THEOLOGY

Here the pontiff was obviously speaking about collaboration between religions in the presence of God. He referred to a similar project in *Redemptoris Missio* when he spoke about the Church serving "the Kingdom by spreading throughout the world the 'Gospel values.'"[49] Amaladoss noted that it is in the same perspective that Pope John Paul II frequently called the leaders of other religions to come together to pray for peace in the world, because he believed that "every authentic prayer is prompted by the Holy Spirit, who is mysteriously present in every human heart."[50]

DE-DOGMATIZATION

In this chapter, I have referred several times to the term *demythologization*, although only once explicitly. It is time to return to it and explain why it plays a certain role in Amaladoss's Christology. As far as I know, Amaladoss does not mention the term in his writings. It is open to debate if he knows the work of German Protestant theologian Rudolf Karl Bultmann (1884-1976), but there is some resemblance between Bultmann's explicit and Amaladoss's implicit project of demythologization. The questions they raise are equivalent. Bultmann asked, How can individuals living in a modern scientific society accept the mythical world picture of the gospel as true? Amaladoss asked, How can the members of other religions who live in a pluralistically religious society accept the doctrine of faith of Christianity as true?[51] The answer each author offered is also similar. Bultmann argued that the modern Christian cannot be expected to take this mythical world seriously, and so "there is nothing to do but to demythologize it."[52] Amaladoss claimed that the members of the other religions cannot be expected to take seriously the doctrinal truth of Christianity, and, therefore, he suggested the removal of doctrine from conversation. Bultmann

---

49   Pope John Paul II, *Redemptoris Missio,* no. 20.

50   Pope John Paul II, *Redemptoris Missio*, no. 29.

51   See, for example, this sentence: "Ninety-seven percent of Asians today do not actually have any conscious relation to Jesus Christ. Some of them may even consciously distance themselves from him." See Amaladoss, "Mystery of Christ," 319.

52   Rudolf Karl Bultmann, *Neues Testament und Mythologie: Das Problem der Entmythologiesierung der neutestamentlichen Verkündigung* (München: Kaiser, 1985), 9. The translation is my own.

CHRISTOLOGY   127

was concerned with the mythology of the Christian kerygma, the apostolic proclamation of salvation through Jesus Christ; Amaladoss was instead concerned with the current role of doctrines and dogmas. Neither author disputed the value of mythology nor the exactingness of doctrines, and both come to the same conclusion: accommodation. For Bultmann, the removal of mythology from the Christian kerygma makes it comprehensible to modern Christians; for Amaladoss, the removal of dogmas from the conversation makes possible conversation with the members of the other religions.

The question of demythologization (*Entmythologisierung*) is raised in Bultmann's work as a result of a supposed impossibility. It is impossible, for the person who lives in a modern world dominated by science and technology, to believe in the "mythical vision of the world" (*mythische Weltanschaaung*) that is present, according to the German theologian, in the texts of the gospel. Bultmann summarized the problem in the following terms:

> Can the Christian proclamation today expect men and women to acknowledge the mythical world picture as true? To do so would be both pointless and impossible. [. . .] It would be impossible because no one can appropriate a world picture by sheer resolve, since it is already given with one's historical situation.[53]

The impossibility, in other words, is an epistemological impossibility, an incommensurability between the world picture of the early Christians and that of the modern Christians. For Bultmann, it is impossible to use electric power and cars or clinical tools and modern medicines in case of illness and at the same time believe in a world inhabited by spirits and miracles. And even if some individuals personally believe in the mythical world of the gospel, then they must remain silent on it, because they risk making the Christian proclamation incomprehensible to their contemporaries.[54] To put it differently, the kerygma exists, but the historical events of which the gospel speaks are no longer current. And by saying they are no longer

---

53   Bultmann, *Neues Testament und Mythologie*, 14.
54   Bultmann, *Neues Testament und Mythologie*, 16.

current, Bultmann acknowledged that science has profoundly modified the mentality of today's men and women. Those people do not have the option to believe in the resurrection and the ascension because neither the former nor the latter find credence in the modern consciences reframed by science and technology.

Amaladoss's line of thought mirrors that of Bultmann. A doctrinal interpretation of Christianity must be superseded by an experiential interpretation that opens the dialogue between Christians and the members of other religions. The question of accommodation comes to Amaladoss as a result of "the newer dimensions of evangelization [that] are not yet fully understood. They are also more relevant and urgent for us at the present historical context." The question is raised because of a totally new historical and social circumstance. Of course, for Christians, other religions are not mere human and historical facts. "Since we recognize the presence and action of the Spirit of God in them (*Redemptoris Missio*, 28)," Amaladoss argues, "they are also theological facts." They are elements in the salvific plan of God for the world. And this is, so to speak, the theological level. Then there is the historical and social level. At this level, Amaladoss notes, the Church engages in dialogue with the members of other religions: "When I encounter the members of the other religions, the Church is seen by them as one among the many world religions, whatever may be my own personal awareness of its special character in the plan of God." Those members of other religions are not interested in Christians' faith affirmations. For Amaladoss, faith affirmations are not only incomprehensible to the members of other religions, but most importantly, they are inconvenient because they hinder dialogue among religions. Thus, the problem is not so much epistemological as it is existential.

By avoiding faith affirmations, however, Amaladoss avoids the question of truth. In his opinion, theology keeps getting stuck on one simple question: Who owns the truth? In an audacious move, he has argued that, on the one hand, although the question is legitimate and interesting, it is also unanswerable in a pluralistic environment; on the other hand, it is of minor importance compared to the difficulties it has caused. Instead, theologians should bracket the question of truth and concentrate on how it is that individuals of different religions experience it. Rather than, Is my religion true? people should ask, How we can live together peacefully? By

CHRISTOLOGY 129

addressing the world of experience, theologians can pursue a much more valuable job than just repeating dogmatic formulas.

Both Bultmann and Amaladoss sense a limit within Christianity, and both seek a solution within Christianity, that is, a change of the parameters. For Bultmann, the task of theology is to make the Scripture less mysterious and mythical so that Scripture takes a more human face; for Amaladoss, the task of theology is to make the religious conversation less doctrinal and dogmatic so the religious conversation assumes a more colloquial style. Of course, the two projects differ to some degree. Bultmann's proposed project is a demythologization of Scripture, but Amaladoss's intent is more precisely a de-dogmatization of theology, so that theology becomes an open and eventually neutral space of dialogue, comparison, and mutual enrichment. For Bultmann, the assumption of the incompatibility between the evangelical message and the scientific mindset translates into a need to bring the former closer to the latter. He determined that the relationship between the two elements is unbalanced on this side: if modern reason is incapable of appreciating the sacred text, it is because the latter is expressed through an allegorical, mythological language that fails to reconcile with scientific reasoning. It will, therefore, be on the mythical nature of the interpretative content, not on the interpreter's scientific *forma mentis*, that the tools of demythologization will be applied. In brief, Bultmann suggests converting the *mythos* into *logos*. Similarly, in Amaladoss, the incompatibility between the Christian doctrines and non-Christian religious mindset translates into the need to bring the former closer to the latter. The de-dogmatist intervention takes place on the side of doctrine rather than on the side of the hermeneutical subject: it is the former that is called to meet the needs of understanding of the latter. If Hindu and Buddhist and Muslim individuals are not available to appreciate the truth of Christianity, it will be on the Christian truth, and not on the non-Christian mindset, that the tools of de-dogmatization must be applied. In short, Amaladoss's advice is to convert the logos into culture.

In Bultmann, the kerygma is totally dehistoricized; in Amaladoss, instead, the Christian faith is rather de-dogmatized. If the content of Christian faith is entirely expressed by means of cultural artifacts, the transcendental truth of Christianity in the public space amounts to nothing. Conversation with members of other religions can be pursued regardless of their professions of faith. Stated logically, if A is in every way disconnected from B, then A is irrelevant to B. The doctrines and the dogmas survive, but they are relevant only within the borders of a given community. They are, so to speak, privatized, although not at the level of the individual but of the confessional group. What matters, then, is not so much the truthiness of the Christian revelation but the personal inclination, the good intent, and the collaborative spirit. The dialogue, therefore, appears to be a process wholly immanent, not only because it is based on a gap between the dogma and the other religions, but more radically because it tries to bridge that gap in a way that conforms to cultural models of interaction, namely by silencing the dogma itself.

Throughout its history, Christianity has built a monumental two-story (*duplex ordo*) intellectual edifice in which being and becoming coexist.[55] Entities—principles, laws, God—are immutable. Becoming is the flow of history, the coming into the world and leaving this world. Amaladoss recognizes both levels but prioritizes the latter and minimizes the role of the former. His project of weakening dogmas is complementary to his adamant defense of the order of existence. What comes next, then? Can Christianity coexist with a minimal, untroubling order of necessity and a predominant order of contingency? What is the supposed synthesis?

---

55   More precisely, the reference is to a "duplex ordo cognitionis," that is, "two-fold order of knowledge [that is] distinct both in principle and also in object." Pope Pius IX, *Dei Filium* (Dogmatic Constitution of the First Vatican Council, Rome, April 24, 1870).

5

A TRUE INDIAN THEOLOGY

INDIAN TRADITION

In his *Life in Freedom*, Amaladoss focused on the Asian stream of liberation theology. Although he does not identify with it, he has devoted a great deal of work to detecting not only the voices of Christian theologians in South Korea, the Philippines, and India but also those of Christian and non-Christian men and women who struggle to reach human liberation in its multifaced nature. In the book, Amaladoss wrote this beautiful passage:

> When one is open to other believers and is in conversation with them, one is not only sharing one's own perspectives with the other but also being influenced and challenged by the other. Such a challenge may lead me to rethink my own perspectives, to see new aspects of my own tradition that I had not seen before, to reinterpret my tradition, even abandoning perspectives that were taken for granted before, and finally develop my own tradition in new directions by creatively integrating elements from other traditions. Such a process liberates me from the social, cultural and historical conditionings of my own religion—the liberation of faith and theology from the constraints of my own religious institutions."[1]

It is a dense passage, but the core message is clear: Amaladoss is suggesting a creative exercise in which dialogue with members of other religious traditions serves as a hermeneutical key to interrogating the sources of Christian faith. In turn, this reinterrogation of the sources of Christian

---

[1]   Amaladoss, *Life in Freedom*, 134.

132 MICHAEL AMALADOSS AND THE QUEST FOR INDIAN THEOLOGY

faith deepens the understanding of Tradition and avoids any temptation for ossification. Accordingly, the living Tradition is open to be enriched by other cultures and religions and ultimately supports a liberation from the past and the emergence of one's own tradition in new directions.

As I noted, the quoted material is dense, and I can only discuss a few elements of it, one of which is "my own tradition." What tradition does Amaladoss have in mind? Is it the universal Tradition of the Church or a more local reincarnation of it? A second element is novelty, the new. What does "new" mean in Amaladoss's passage? And what is the relationship between this new and its past—new in continuity with the preexisting or new as a discontinuity? The latter seems more likely because he argued that "the more I creatively integrate elements from other traditions into my own tradition, the more I liberate myself from the legacies of the past." The new is instrumental in liberating Amaladoss from the captivity of the past.

When Amaladoss mentioned his own tradition, which tradition did he have in mind? In the previously mentioned chapter he wrote for the Festschrift honoring one hundred years of life of Father Josef Neuner, SJ, Amaladoss addressed the question of mediation. He argued that "the efforts of Indian (Asian) theologians to focus directly on God's self-revelation in the Bible and to respond to it in terms of the Indian context and culture, independently of the mediation of Greek culture and philosophy."[2] Then he further clarified: "We do not wish to ignore two thousand years of doctrinal and theological development. But a pole of dialogue is different from a norm."[3] Those passages contain much more than I want to disentangle here, but the sense is obvious enough: Amaladoss believes that it is possible to access revelation as it is contained in the Bible without the mediation of Greek culture and philosophy. At this point, the meaning of the initial quote is clear: Amaladoss is arguing that the encounter with believers of other religions led him to rethink his own tradition (the universal Tradition, with a capital *T*) and develop his own Indian tradition (with a lowercase *t*). For Amaladoss, Indian theology is a theology with its own (existing or in formation) tradition. There are at least two questions to be

---

2   Amaladoss, *Life in Freedom*, 134.

3   Amaladoss, *Life in Freedom*, 134.

A TRUE INDIAN THEOLOGY 133

clarified in Amaladoss's statements. One is concerned with what is a tradition that accesses God's self-revelation in the Bible from the perspective of the Indian context and culture. The other refers to the reasons why the Greek mediation is considered normative by the Church's official teaching and why Amaladoss instead proposes to bypass it.

The first question is a worthwhile starting point. In the first half of the twentieth century, Monchanin saw Christian Tradition as composed of two parts: an "infrangible core of the Revelation itself," the dogma at its pristine state, and several "constellations" formed around this nucleus—the subsequent development that began in the times of the apostolic fathers and carried on through the course of the European history of Christianity.[4] Thus, Indian theology is, in effect, the development of another constellation, framed in an Indian context independent of the Greek mediation. If I am correct, the phrase "pole of dialogue" plays the same role in Amaladoss's remark that constellation plays in Monchanin's.

When Monchanin introduced the notion of constellation, he offered some examples of what he meant by that term: "Origenist, Augustinian, Scotist, Thomist . . . or Newmanian."[5] The list is generous, as it seems that Monchanin did not limit himself to mentioning the giants, i.e., Augustine and Thomas Aquinas and their majestic Neoplatonic and Aristotelian synthesis, but included those syntheses that arose as a legacy of the work and thought of thinkers such as Origen, Duns Scotus, Newman, and their followers. What the list makes evident is that a constellation is a specific theological and philosophical system or school raised in a specific historical context in response to a distinct set of questions related to a diverse, rich, and profound intellectual heritage. A constellation comes out of a reinterrogation of the sources of Christianity, and it is a new synthesis that offers a new interpretation of the mystery without contradicting a dogma in its pure condition. That new synthesis resonates well beyond the historical limits of the period in which it was conceived, and it gradually becomes

---

4   The original quote reads, "autour du noyau infrangible de la Révélationelle-même, . . . ensuite équilibrée en des figures intelligibles, pareilles à des constellations." See Monchanin, *Théologie et Spiritualité Missionnaires*, 86.

5   The quote reads, "origénisme, augustianisme, scotisme, thomisme, newmanisme." See Monchanin, *Théologie et Spiritualité Missionnaires*, 86.

assimilated within the Tradition of the Great Church. In other words, the system becomes a doctrine. Another way to express the same idea is this: Christian doctrine shows a remarkable sense of unity, which is the result of not only the fact that systems of thought that are so different—among them Origenism, Augustinianism, and Scotism—nevertheless share the same core, and that this process of assimilation demands a geological patience. If Monchanin's idea of constellation is taken at face value, an Indian constellation is a system of thought, not a national theology (a theology in Indian forms made by Indians for Indians), offering a new synthesis among Christianity and the vast and deep religious treasures of India. This synthesis, although eventually born in India, is not limited to India in its value and application, but has, so to speak, a compass that includes the entire universal Church. If the past is any indication, an Indian constellation will take the name of the genius who first conceived the synthesis. I will return to the subject of Indian tradition in the post scriptum.

DEHELLENIZATION

The matter of the status of Greek influence on the development of Christian thought is equally crucial. For Pope Benedict XVI and the Church's official teaching, the Greek matrix is not another inculturation but "an initial inculturation which ought not to be binding on other cultures."[6] The hellenization of Christianity is an indispensable and nonnegotiable foundational ingredient of the Christian synthesis emerging from the encounter of the Scripture with Hellenism achieved in the early Church. For this reason, Greek culture is not really a mediation and cannot be compared nor replaced by another, as it rather participates at the core of Christianity. Instead, for Amaladoss, the hellenization of Christianity is one among the many inculturations; it is, therefore, a mediation to relativize.

Amaladoss is an original and profound thinker who has spent his adult life mediating between Indian nationalism and Catholic universalism. Clearly, his purpose is to develop an approach to the problem of integrating Christian belief with the everyday experience of contemporary

---

6   Pope Benedict XVI, "The Regensburg Address" (University of Regensburg, Regensburg, Germany, September 12, 2006).

Indian people. He aims for an integration of Christian faith with the post-colonial stage of Indian Christianity. What is at stake, in his opinion, is the unity and integrity of Indian Christianity and, more specifically, Indian Christian consciousness. The crux of the matter is whether one can be, simultaneously, a Christian while complying with the requirements the everyday reality of India requests. So much for the problem. Dehellenization stands as a possible solution: for Amaladoss, Indian Christianity must transcend the Hellenic past of the Church and be integrated into both the context and conscious of its postcolonial condition. To put it differently, dehellenization is what Indian Christianity needs for the sake of its future, even if this involves calling into question the dogmas of Chalcedon.

The dehellenization of dogma is not a new idea. The Canadian philosopher Leslie Dewart proposed as much in his 1966 book, *The Future of Belief: Theism in a World Come of Age*, as a measure to heal the increasing alienation of Catholic doctrine from the modern worldview.[7] Dewart believed that alienation was the result of the inability of Catholic theology to recognize "that its traditional form has necessarily and logically been childish and infantile to the very degree that it corresponded to an earlier, relatively childish, infantile stage of human evolution."[8] In other words, Catholic theology is still too dependent on antiquated and essentially premodern philosophical modes of thought. Mutatis mutandis, dehellenization is necessary to bridge the persistent alienation of the Catholic doctrine from the Indian world. Amaladoss has argued that this alienation is the result of a foreignism that has its roots in dogmas that have been framed with Greek modes of thought, which brought him to call into question the dogmas of Chalcedon, or at least their articulation.

By his own admission, Amaladoss is not a systematic theologian. Therefore, one must distinguish his ideas from his work. As I showed in the previous chapter, Amaladoss may have doubts about the persistent efficacy of the articulation of the dogmas; in his work, however, the option of the dehellenization of dogmas and doctrines is seldom raised. A question more frequently raised in his work is instead whether Christianity should

---

7   Leslie Dewart, *The Future of Belief: Theism in a World Come of Age* (New York: Herder and Herder, 1966).

8   Dewart, *Future of Belief*, 51.

be divorced from its roots in ancient Greek philosophy. Amaladoss's target, the *Titanic* he aims to sink, is Tradition, or in his own words, "the bypassing of Patristics."[9] The relationship between Christianity and Greek thought obscures the original and primitive nature of Christianity and consequently hinders Indian theologians' direct, unmediated access to the sources of revelation. Amaladoss thinks that patristics should be bypassed because it is an obstacle to a genuine attempt to access the primordial form of faith and therefore to the development of a true Indian Christianity.

The delicate problem of hellenization, and by consequence the eventual dehellenization of Christianity, has been the object of many studies, and a renewal of interest in the theme has emerged during recent decades. At first, there was a tendency to denounce hellenization as a corruption of Christianity. Then, and especially in more recent years, scholars became meticulously devoted to investigating the different dimensions—historical, philological, biblical, and patristic—of this extremely complex issue and reached a more nuanced conclusion. The hellenization of Christianity is a category, a theory, and a historical process. First, it is a central modern category to construct, codify, and grasp a moment in the history of early Christianity. Second, it refers more specifically to a theory, that is, the mutual influence of Judaism and Hellenism in the first centuries of the history of Christianity. Finally, hellenization refers to historical patterns of transformation and the integration of Judaism and Hellenism. Hellenization is a problematic category, and the problem lies in the inescapable question of *essentialization*—that is, excessive generalization. It implies the transformation of one culture or religion by another. Christianity, and eventually Judaism, had been hellenized through a set of clearly identified

---

9   Amaladoss has studied Latin: his first book, *Do Sacraments Change?* reflects his doctoral studies in Paris and shows Amaladoss's familiarity with Latin. I am not sure he reads Classic Greek. When he addresses the work of the Latin and Greek Fathers, he preferably refers to translations and manuals. Often the selection is outstanding, like in the case of the notes based on Cyprian Vagaggini, *Doing Theology* (Bangalore: IJA Publications, 2003). Occasionally, the selection is questionable, like in the case of the paragraphs on patristics that he based on an undergraduate textbook: Justo L. Gonzales, *Christian Thought Revisited: Three Types of Theology* (Nashville: Abington, 1989). The references to Vagaggini and Gonzales are included in Amaladoss, *Quest for God*, 19–20, 29, and 46–49.

changes. More precisely, hellenization implies, to borrow a line from Friedrich Nietzsche, that "a foreign civilization may be transplanted" into another.[10] Moreover, hellenization—or perhaps better, Hellenism—is a term often adopted to express specific ramifications of the phenomenon, including Christianity and Platonism, faith and reason, and philosophy and theology.[11] A third problem is that the terms may have different meanings for different people. Glen Bowersock and Georg Essen distinguished between hellenization as inculturation and hellenization as domination. Only the first is relevant; the second is a modern category that is anachronistically applied to the Christian past.[12] Inculturation stands for the slow process through which a religious movement beginning in small villages of Galilea was incorporated into the Greco-Roman world. One must remember that before becoming part of the Roman Empire, for the three centuries of the Maccabean period Israel had been a colony of the totally Greek Seleucid Empire. The Hellenistic elites of those days dominated, that is, exercised a form of hegemony over the movement. A fourth problem is the supersessionist form that hellenization took in the Protestant theological milieu of the nineteenth century (think of Adolf von Harnack), so if scholars could rewind the thread of history and proceed backward, dehellenization would be the process that returns them to the original Christianity.[13]

These initial considerations help readers see that, in effect, two main theses confront anyone concerned with hellenization. The first thesis suggests that hellenization is at the roots of Christianity because the very first Jewish communities were already hellenized, as was the rest of Israel. Christianity never became hellenized because it was born already

---

10 Friedrich Nietzsche, *Richard Wagner in Bayreuth*, trans. Anthony M. Ludovici (Glasgow: Good Press, 2021), 34.

11 Christoph Markschies, "Does It Make Sense to Speak About a 'Hellenization of Christianity' in Antiquity?" *Church History and Religious Culture* 92, no. 1 (2012): 34. http://doi.org/10.1163/187124112X621581.

12 Glen Bowersock, *Hellenism in Late Antiquity* (Ann Arbor: University of Michigan Press, 1990); Georg Essen, "Hellenisierung des Christentums? Zur Problematik und Überwindung einer polarisierenden Deutungsfigur," *Theologie und Philosophie* 87, no. 1 (2012): 1–17.

13 Adolf von Harnack, *Das Wesen des Christentums*, ed. T. Rendtorff (Gütersloh: Kaiser/Gütersloher Verlagshaus, 1999).

hellenized. The second thesis argues that hellenization is a process that happens upon an original, genuine, self-sufficient form of Christianity in the second and third centuries. The conciliation of Scripture and Greek thought, that is, Christianity, is the result of the fusion of the two traditions. In both cases, however, hellenization played a fundamental role in defining the theology of the Trinity as well as the Christology of the councils of the fourth and fifth centuries and, as such, is normative. According to David Tracy, "The Hellenistic tradition provided the necessary conditions of possibility for a clearer affirmation of the divinity of Jesus Christ and the universality of the eschatological self-revelation of God in the face of Jesus."[14] In the words of Pope Benedict XVI, a "critically purified Greek heritage forms an integral part of Christian faith."[15]

In brief, according to some scholars (and this is the first option), hellenization is a process of internationalization of the Greek forms of life and thought that initiated with Alexander the Great and his conquest of Israel in the third century BC and continued for centuries, well beyond the end of the Seleucid Empire in 63 BC and the entry of the Roman legions in Jerusalem. It was a long, slow, and successful experiment of inculturation of the Greek culture within the Jewish mind so the later encounter between the Scripture and Greek philosophy was almost inevitable. To put it another way, hellenization is the intellectual and cultural tapestry on which Christianity was born and grew. Others believe instead (and this is the second option) that hellenization was a transformation of a basically Jewish community that, despite hellenization in progress, remained faithful to its religion, worship, and Scripture and was therefore almost isolated from such hellenization. This primitive community, made up of Galilean fishermen, grew up; generation after generation, their simple faith became the religion of the members of the highest class who had the means and the will to

---

14 David W. Tracy, review of *Jesus-God and Man*, by Wolfhart Pannenberg, Lewis L. Winkins, and Duane A. Priebe, and *Revelation as History*, by Wolfhart Pannenberg and David Granskou, *Catholic Biblical Quarterly* 31, no. 2 (1969): 287.

15 Pope Benedict XVI, "Regensburg Address." For a brief but exhaustive comment on Ratzinger's view of dehellenization, see Tracey Rowland, *Ratzinger's Faith: The Theology of Pope Benedict XVI* (Oxford: Oxford University Press, 2008), 105–22. I intentionally focus on scholarly literature rather than formal or informal papal interventions because I am interested in showing the scholarly rather than the doctrinal side of the matter.

A TRUE INDIAN THEOLOGY   139

articulate theological systems. And it was at that moment that hellenization occurred. This hellenization had two faces: first, the assimilation of Greek philosophy within Christian theological reflection and second, the transformation of the existing forms of Greek philosophy, particularly those celebrated in Alexandria, because of its clash with Christian theology. In both options, the normative dogmatics of the Councils and the theology of the fathers of the Church are neither a reinvention of Judaism nor a supersession of it but the consolidation of a new civilization, Christianity. Christianity absorbed much from the Hellenic culture, but with certain limits; only in this sense can one talk about the hellenization of Christianity.

In his critical comments about the grip that the Greek thought still holds on Tradition, Amaladoss did not elaborate on which interpretation of hellenization he shares. It is safe to say, however, that he believes that Greek inculturation is not normative; it is one of the many—actually the first of all the possible inculturations. If hellenization is the primordial inculturation, then dehellenization is a form of deculturation; once Greek mediation is bypassed, Indian theologians would access original Christianity.

TRADITION AND MODERNITY

Amaladoss is a major figure in contemporary Indian theology and is considered one of the pioneers of an indigenous theology on the subcontinent. In some ways, Amaladoss is for Indian theology what the psychologist Ashis Nandy is for social sciences in India. It is as difficult to study India from a theological viewpoint and not come across Amaladoss's work as it might be to avoid Nandy in the humanities and social sciences. If Nandy's work is the search for a way of speaking to Indian politics from a South Asian perspective, Amaladoss's work is the search for a way of speaking to Indian Christians from a South Asian perspective. Nandy is a critical traditionalist, and Amaladoss is a critical modernist. Like Nandy, Amaladoss is a scholar who maintains his autonomy from schools of thought and academic circles.[16] Like Nandy, Amaladoss is unconventional and fond of Carnatic song; unlike Nandy, he is neither dissenting nor confrontational.

---

16   I found this connection between Ashis Nandy and Amaladoss revealing. Unfortunately, I cannot locate the source that proposed it.

Amaladoss is a critical modernist because the India he writes about is not necessarily the India one can read about in current newspapers. This is not to say that he does not maintain currency and engagement with all things Indian; it is that the filters he adopts to decode the information he collects belong to a different era. This temporal shift poses no negative consequences to his existing work or to his legacy, which was cemented decades ago. It is rather a sign that Amaladoss is the product of a certain India, and it is to this India—an India in which no one is haunted from morning until night by the calls for modernity and all have time to occupy themselves with religion—that he constantly returns. It is an India that the Western readership easily falls in love with, where solidarity is a constant, and tight-knit neighborhoods and family connections are valued beyond wealth. Sure, the hospital can be far away, schools can be underrated, and transportation services like buses or taxis are occasionally tardy, but friendship is honored, the change of seasons is celebrated, and elders are protected and respected. In Amaladoss's India, festivals, family parties, and social interactions keep the community engaged and united. Although there is no trace of recognizable forms of escapism, in Amaladoss's writings, India is a reminder of the simplicity and truth of yesterday compared to the complexity and moral ambiguity of today. He spent most of his adult life in places as far removed from his home village as is culturally and geographically possible, and yet he conveys the feeling that there is no other place he would rather be. It is precisely this trait that makes his account of India as endearing and enduring as it is. That said, no one would care one iota about Amaladoss's nostalgia for the village life if his books were poorly written or his theology failed to intersect with the zeitgeist of an age.

Beginning in the fifties, India as a country initiated its postindependence transformation from a largely agrarian, relatively poor country into one of the economically and socially advanced countries of Asia. The most striking effect of the ongoing transformation has been the mass migration it encouraged, as Indians moved in vast numbers from rural to urban India. Without considering the details of rural, understood as a physical, social, and cultural concept that is the counterpart of urban, one may say that most of the Indian theology of the last decades can be seen as a theological response to the societal hardships and economic injustices of the new urban society taking form during the Nehruvian age. Amaladoss's interest, however, is slightly different. Of course, he wrote about the social consequences of the passage from a rural to an urban society, but the specific focus of Amaladoss's theology is rather the identity struggle of a community that resembles in his writings a premodern or pseudomodern condition in which family ties and mutual assistance prevent the full effect of modernity.[17] The struggle can be summarized in the following terms: is India still India in a globalizing world in which modernity becomes the common denominator of societies in both the West and the East? Amaladoss claimed, "We need to distinguish between modernity and Western culture and between the instrumental and categorical aspects of cultures. Asians are ready and open to the use of science and technology. But they remain attached to their way of looking at the world, relating to the others and living as a community."[18] India and Asia can become modern, but their modernity is not the same modernity as in the West.[19]

Amaladoss is not against modernity. Interestingly, he never considers in his writing a Gandhian option, an alternative option to modernity. He would concede in private conversation a certain consonance with Gandhi's view of a society built on villages and communities, a view that was not altogether indifferent to the flow of Indian civilization: its ethics, epic, and history. As a theologian, driven by the conscious urge to understand the religious traditions and spiritual depths of the Indian civilization as well as to embrace some kind of social progress, however, Amaladoss naturally turns his attention to modernity. In his mind, modernity is a necessity in the sense that the modern project is the inevitable result of a certain philosophy of history focusing on the advancement of humanity. His problem is rather to situate the Indian modernity in a realm other than the Western

---

17 See, for example, the description of a community as "families [who] live together in a village or other similar unity," in Amaladoss, *Peoples' Theology*, 1. A full description of the negative consequences of modernity to communities and families can be found in Michael Amaladoss, *Walking Together: The Practice of Inter-Religious Dialogue* (Anand: Gujarat Sahitya Prakash, 1992), 164–66.

18 Amaladoss, *Peoples' Theology*, 6.

19 See, for example, his work on Indian secularism: Michael Amaladoss, *Living in a Secular Society* (Chennai: IDCR, 2010). An interesting article on the same subject is Michael Amaladoss, "Secularization and India: Modernization and Religion in an Eastern Country," *Exchange* 21, no. 1 (1992): 34–48.

modernity. With its long and curved history, its religiocultural matrix, its darkness and brightness, and its contradictions and possibilities, India deserves a modernity that is different from Western modernity. It means to look at a project of modernity that does not necessarily alter the identity and aspirations of India.[20]

Although Amaladoss may be skeptical of some concrete effects of modernity, he accepts and masters the intellectual core of modernity. He is a critical modernist because he embraces a certain idea of history and a distinct relationship with the past. He believes in historical linearity or progress. That progressive history becomes a criterion for defining the characteristics of existing subjects (in favor of progress or against it) and for measuring the historical role of individual events. These events are ordered in a coherent, progressive design and in a narrative that moves toward its happy ending. Amaladoss is a modernist because he believes in a historical periodization that breaks history into periods: the past is separated from the present. The periodization implies a renewal that does not proceed with a return to the sources but opens to the new. In fact, the difference between the renewal movements and Amaladoss is that the former propose a return to primitive Christianity, but the latter is characterized by the novelty. This break with the past, this *renovatio* that does not transcend the past but moves away from it, is the very definition of modernity. Modernity is liberation from the ancient without going back to the sources. The spirit of modernity, at least in Amaladoss's interpretation, maintains the Christian transcendence of the human being but excludes the supernatural. Consequentially, the human transcendence is transferred to the intramundane level.

---

20   On this point, Amaladoss shares the same path of Asian historians, sociologists, and political theorists like Gaonkar, Kaviraj, Chatterjee, and Dirlik. See Dilip P. Gaonkar, ed., *Alternative Modernities* (Durham, NC: Duke University Press, 2001); Sudipta Kaviraj, "An Outline of a Revisionist Theory of Modernity," *Archives of European Sociology* 46, no. 3 (2005): 497–526; Partha Chatterjee, *Lineages of Political Society: Studies in Postcolonial Democracy* (New York: Columbia University Press, 2011); Arif Dirlik, *Global Modernity: Modernity in the Age of Global Capitalism* (Boulder: Paradigm, 2006); and Arif Dirlik, "Revisioning Modernity: Modernity in Eurasian Perspectives," *Inter-Asia Cultural Studies* 12, no. 3 (June 2011): 284–305.

Indian modernity is the sign of a new era in India's history, a new context that has generated an entirely new style of theology. Indian theologians moved away from the sober examination of texts and the working of the spirit, shifting inward to a more concrete social realism. To borrow a sentence from Amaladoss, "Contemporary theologies of religions in the West tend to look at other religions in the abstract. For us Asians, they are realities of our daily experience. We are in contact with people in whom we can see their fruits."[21] The examination of the changing life of the village inhabitants and the modernization of old customs and traditions advanced together with growing urbanization and the submersion of the individual into the machinery of the industrial labor force. This is certainly one reason to consider Amaladoss's interest in modernity. The other, however, is even more decisive. Once Amaladoss separates Indian Christianity from Tradition, he inevitably deprives Indian Christianity of a fundamental hermeneutical key for the interpretation of history. History is crucial in Christianity because God entered human history through incarnation. If Tradition is no longer suitable as a hermeneutical key to interpret history, then it is inevitable that another key should be adopted; for the necessity of an ultimate organizing logic of history, modernity becomes that key. And modernity comes with an interpretation of history as progress, a break with the past, and a new beginning.

Of course, liberal and Marxist philosophies of history share the same modernist concept of new beginnings, but with one difference: only Marxism embraces the primacy of practice over speculation. The idea, for those like Amaladoss who reject Marxism as an ideology, is to separate historical materialism from dialectical materialism, that is, the philosophy of history from the doctrine of the revolution. In this way, Marxism, liberated from its ideological envelope, is nothing more than a philosophy of history built around the primacy of praxis. I cannot say whether Amaladoss intentionally separated historical materialism from dialectical materialism, but this is de facto the result of the adoption of a modernist philosophy of history driven by praxis. Besides, this conception of history as action opposes any metaphysics, including Greek metaphysics. At this point it should be clear how the acquisition of an anti-Tradition posture implies not only the

---

21   Amaladoss, "Mystery of Christ," 320.

assumption of a modernist (although critical) position but also an anti-metaphysical philosophy of history. In other words, in Amaladoss, the rejection of Tradition, the call for dehellenization, and the preeminence of practice are distinct ramifications from the same core principle: a particular although critical acceptance of modernity.

But what is this new beginning? The new is only new inside the semantic domain that constitutes it as such; in other words, the new is only new in comparison with something older that is part of the same semantic domain to which the *novus* belongs. But, then, does not a process similar to the idea of progress establish itself with all the connections to the Western idea of modernity? In fact, this way to proceed is the cumulative way and therefore implies a linear process that exhausts itself in the Western idea of progress. In brief, this is new but only in the system that has constituted the new as such; therefore, the new is encouraged to seek reconfirmations and validations within the theoretical domain that was constituted before it. The new is not the absolute new, the new that comes by venturing into unexplored regions, but the new that seeks confirmation of its way forward. Therefore, the new is not novelty but a place of certainty and reflection where categorical thought applies prospective and Western analyses. But this is exactly the trap Amaladoss and others want to avoid: they want to change the metatheory, the semantic domain that determines what is old and what is new. In their perspective, the new implies the possibility to be new irrespective of something that preexists or of something that is part of the semantic family to which the *novus* belongs.

The idea of a restart proposed by Amaladoss (and others) is not original; it has its own story.[22] To state that it is possible to innovate even irrespective of something that is part of the semantic family to which the *novus*

---

22   Already in 1969, Pope Paul VI had highlighted the risks of a new, unrooted Church: "One cannot invent a new Church according to one's judgment, or one's personal taste. Today it is not uncommon for people . . . who believe they are capable of denouncing the entire historical past of the Church, the Post-Tridentine one in particular, as inauthentic, outdated and now invalid for our time; and so, with some now conventional, but extremely superficial and inaccurate term, they certainly declare an era closed (Constantinian, preconciliar, juridical, authoritarian), and another era begun (free, adult, prophetic) to be inaugurated immediately, according to criteria and schemes invented by these

A TRUE INDIAN THEOLOGY   145

belongs is the same as proceeding without the inclusion of the old in the new, as passing to an Other that is not implicit, contained, or predictable in the old. In this case, the new implies a jump, a dislocation with respect to seriality, and it makes itself visible as discontinuity, assuming the characteristics of alterity: an Other compared with that which is known and is implicit. And this is what Amaladoss has in mind: where Thomas Kuhn's *The Structure of Scientific Revolutions* taught readers to recognize the process that modifies a structure of science in another, Amaladoss invites us to foresee the passage from one semantic domain to another.[23] Of course, this new that is other than the old comes with ramifications and questions. I offer one as an appetizer: Steven Toulim maintained that "no formalism can interpret itself; no system can validate itself; no theory can exemplify itself; no representation can map itself; no language can predetermine its own meanings."[24] He suggested that no language—and therefore no theology—can call itself new. I rest here.

TRADITION AND MAGISTERIUM

Sacred tradition, or Tradition, in Catholicism begins with the transmission from Christ to his disciples of a deposit of truth to be spread over the centuries to the ends of the earth. Tradition, therefore, is the teaching of Jesus to the apostles, handed down by them from generation to generation (*tradition apostolica* or *depositum apostolicum*). Tradition is not only the deposit of faith (*depositum fidei et morum*) that is officially transmitted by the Church. It is not only the formal transmission of revelation; Tradition is also the deposit of faith that is believed and safeguarded by the whole Church. Tradition is both the *Ecclesia docens*, the teaching Church, and the *Ecclesia docta*, the learning Church. The former teaches the revelation,

---

new and often improvised masters." Pope Paul VI, "Udienza Generale" (Rome, September 24, 1969). The original text is in Italian; the translation is my own.

23   See Amaladoss, *Making All Things New*, 271, where he states, "The Second Vatican Council inaugurated a paradigm shift in the theology of Mission." Thomas S. Kuhn, *The Structure of Scientific Revolutions*, 3rd ed. (Chicago: The University of Chicago Press, 1996).

24   Steven Toulmin, *Return to Reason* (Cambridge, MA: Harvard University Press, 2001), 80.

but the latter receives and conserves it (1 Tim 6:20). Both are indispensable because only the totality of the *Ecclesia docens* and the *Ecclesia docta* guarantees the *sensus fidei*. Thus, the primary organ of Tradition is the Church as a whole, in which the teaching—when the Church is teaching—and the *sensus fidei*—when the Church is learning—are the subjects of Tradition.

The Magisterium is not Tradition; the Magisterium can neither create nor change Tradition, only discern and express it.[25] One should distinguish between the Church, the subject of Tradition, Tradition, the *depositum fidei* and *morum*, and the Magisterium, which is a function within the *Ecclesia docens*. The Church is the totality of the *Ecclesia docens* and the *Ecclesia docta*, the ecclesiastical authorities and the body of the faithful. It is in the Church in her totality that the Holy Spirit testifies the truth (John 15:26). The Church knows no news, no novelty, no new revelation, only the deepening, the further clarification, and the making explicit of the original revelation. Thus, Tradition concerns truths but also the ways in which these truths are transmitted and the symbols and rites with which they are expressed. The Magisterium is not a proper *locus theologicus*; it is a means for the *Ecclesia docens* to exercise the power of teaching. Thomas Aquinas analyzed in depth the two episcopate powers called orders and jurisdiction. The power of orders (*potestas ordinis*) validates sacramental acts and uses symbolic language. The power of jurisdiction (*potestas iurisdictionis*) refers to the power of governance.[26] The Magisterium belongs to the power of jurisdiction and, more specifically, to the power of teaching the truth.

I offer these details because I want to answer a simple question: if Tradition is not normative, what is normative for Amaladoss? Is there anything that he believes to be normative for his own theology? In other words, on which authority does he build his own theological edifice? In the previous chapter, I showed that Amaladoss upholds a complex position with regard to the Magisterium and, therefore, the doctrine. On one hand,

---

25   The identification of Tradition with the Magisterium is an unfortunate result of Pius XII's encyclical *Humani Generis*, where it is stated, "This deposit of faith our Divine Redeemer has given for authentic interpretation not to each of the faithful, not even to theologians, but only to the Teaching Authority of the Church." Pope Pius XII, *Humani Generis* (Letter Encyclical, Rome, August 12, 1950), no. 21.

26   Thomas Aquinas, *Summa Theologiae* (Steubenville, OH: Emmaus Academic, 2018), II-IIae, q. 39, a. 3, resp.; III, q. 6, a.2.

he tenaciously defends his right as a theologian to make distinctions and clarifications in the context of the traditional faith of the Church. On the other hand, he rightly proclaims his orthodoxy. That said, my answer is that Amaladoss considers the Magisterium normative. However, which Magisterium he considers normative is also a crucial question. The Dogmatic Constitution on Divine Revelation *Dei Verbum*, in effect, distinguishes three distinct functions within the Church: the *munus sanctificandi* (that mirrors the original *potestas ministerii*), the *munus regendi* (that reflects the original *potestas iurisdictionis*), and finally the *munus docendi* (referring to a potential *potestas magisterii*). It seems that the Divine Constitution identifies not two but three powers, although it establishes a sort of hierarchical relationship among them.[27] The elevation of the Magisterium among the autonomous powers, instead of being a simple faculty of the power of jurisdiction, is probably a concession to the nineteenth-century liberal theology of Protestantism that proclaimed the primacy of the word belonging to all the baptized.[28]

As previously mentioned, the Church transmits Tradition from one generation to another. But who interprets Tradition? In the premodern era, the question was nonsense because Tradition itself was *regula fidei*, namely, a principle of interpretation. A few years ago, Pope Benedict XVI reasserted the same principle by saying that sacred Scripture and Tradition constitute "the supreme rule of faith."[29] It is only in the last centuries, with the rise of modern subjectivity, that Tradition from criteria has been

27 According to the Pope Paul VI, *Dei Verbum*, in fact, "the task of authentically interpreting the word of God, whether written or handed on, (8) has been entrusted exclusively to the living teaching office of the Church, (9) whose authority is exercised in the name of Jesus Christ. *This teaching office is not above the word of God, but serves it, teaching only what has been handed on, listening to it devoutly, guarding it scrupulously and explaining it faithfully in accord with a divine commission and with the help of the Holy Spirit, it draws from this one deposit of faith everything which it presents for belief as divinely revealed* [emphasis added]." See Pope Paul VI, *Dei Verbum* (Dogmatic Constitution on Divine Revelation, Rome, November 18, 1965), no. 10.

28 Yves Congar, "Pour une histoire sémantique du terme 'magisterium,'" *Revue des sciences philosophiques et théologiques* 60 (1976): 94–95.

29 Pope Benedict XVI, *Verbum Domini* (Post-Synodal Apostolic Exhortation, Rome, September 30, 2010), no. 18.

reframed as an object of interpretation. So, who is the subject? The whole Church—the people of God as a whole—is the subject of Tradition; it fulfills its *munus* through both the Magisterium (when the Church teaches) and the *sensus fidei* (when she believes). It means that the Holy Spirit assists not only the *Ecclesia docens* but the *Ecclesia docta*, too. And just as there is an infallibility of the *Ecclesia docens*'s teaching, so there is an infallibility of the *Ecclesia docta*, based on the *sensus fidei*. According to St. Paul, the faithful own the *sensus fidei*: "No autem sensum Christ habemus" (1 Cor 2:16). The sense of faith that the believers receive from Christ is the supernatural ability to grasp the revealed truth in their life, thanks to the action of the Holy Spirit. This explains why the humble and simple can be more enlightened in the faith than pastors and theologians. This illumination comes from grace and is nurtured by the gifts of the Holy Spirit.

It is clear at this point that the *sensus fidei* is a criterion not to interpret Tradition but an organ to conserve and protect Tradition. The *sensus fidei*, or in the vulgate of Vatican II, the *consensus fidelium* or *communis fidelium sensu*, is one of the organs of Tradition.[30] The relationship between the Magisterium and *sensus fidei* covers a wide arc of options: it can manifest itself in the simple submission and obedience of the latter to the former. It can also express itself in the orientation and even in the resistance of the *sensu fidei* to the Magisterium when Tradition is at risk. The paramount example is the resistance of St. Paul to St. Peter during the Council of Jerusalem. Now, it would be natural to assume that Amaladoss detects the possibility of resisting the Magisterium in the name of the *sensu fidei*. This, however, is not his line of thought. I believe that he instead establishes a hierarchy of the living Magisterium over the universal Magisterium. The living Magisterium, mentioned in the *Dei Verbum* as the "living teaching office of the Church," is the Magisterium of this present time; the (ordinary and) universal Magisterium, instead, is a teaching on which all bishops (including the Pope) universally agree and is considered infallible. The universal Magisterium is not universal only in space but also in time; this means that it covers all the Church's ages.[31]

---

30 Pope Paul VI, *Dei Verbum*, 12.

31 Tarcisio Bertone, "A proposito della ricezione dei Documenti del Magistero e del dissenso pubblico," *L'Osservatore Romano* (Vatican City), December 20, 1996.

When Amaladoss writes statements such as, "We must learn to trust the believers with their *sensus fidelium* and the creative Spirit that animates them," which believers does he refer to? When he argues that "[we must be] open to the future in hope rather than keep looking to the past in the name of tradition," to whom does he refer?[32] I think the answer is this: in Amaladoss's thought, the living Magisterium, the present Magisterium of the bishops in Asia, becomes the objective Magisterium and the criteria of interpretation of Tradition, in case one bothers to care about it. Here the living Magisterium is considered a *locus theologicus*, autonomous and independent. On the contrary, the universal Magisterium becomes the Magisterium that must be resisted. Amaladoss does not ignore the universal Magisterium, but he unquestionably resists it. His resistance is expressed in two precise modes: sometimes he picks up some statements of the universal Magisterium, including those of the Second Vatican Council, and uses them against other statements of the universal Magisterium to make his point. At other times, he simply refers to the living Magisterium of the Asian bishops as the ultimate source of authority.

It is almost impossible to find in Amaladoss's books and articles traces of disrespect or condescendence toward the universal Magisterium. Neither does he advocate a parallel magisterium of theologians, "in opposition to and in competition with the authentic Magisterium."[33] However, he is unafraid to criticize the universal Magisterium. He does not follow Küng, to mention one name, on his criticism that the universal Magisterium is arbitrary; rather, he claims it is intrinsically Western (or more precisely, it is an expression of a Western ideology) and therefore irrelevant to India (and Asia). The essential dispositive of Amaladoss's theology is the replacement of Tradition with the living Magisterium of the Asian bishops. Once the Magisterium of reference is no longer the organ of the universal Church but only that of the Asian Church, the latter is the *regula fidei* because it interprets Tradition rather than teaches it. As a matter of fact, the living Magisterium of the bishops and the parallel Magisterium of the theologians constitute a mechanism through which one can produce a

---

32   Amaladoss, *Beyond Inculturation*, xv.

33   Congregation for the Doctrine of the Faith, "Instruction *Donum Veritatis* on the Ecclesial Vocation of the Theologian," (Rome, May 24, 1990), notes 27 and 34.

new Tradition. When there is a disagreement between Tradition and living Magisterium, or a misalignment between universal Magisterium and living Magisterium, Amaladoss always takes the side of the latter. He considers normative the living Magisterium of the Asian bishops.

Of course, questions arise out of this interpretation. Can the living Magisterium of the Asian bishops, a teaching organ that is expressing itself in the present times, be considered a sound basis for a theology that refuses Tradition and resists the universal Magisterium? Is the transformation of an ecclesial body into a *locus theologicus* justified? To be part of Tradition, a truth must be taught by the Church not once but in a constant manner; Cardinal Bertone clarified this by noting that the Magisterium can teach a doctrine (truth) on the condition that that doctrine is "constantly handed down and maintained by tradition and handed down by the ordinary and universal magisterium."[34] Ratzinger explained that the universal character of the universal Magisterium must be understood both in a synchronic sense, by all the faithful in all parts of the world, and in a diachronic sense, that is, effective in all the ages of the Church.[35] Do the resolutions of the FABC fall into the same category? I leave these questions unanswered.

VATICAN II

I conclude this chapter with a final note on the Second Vatican Council, which has played and still plays an important role in Amaladoss's theology. A celebrated passage of the *Nostra Aetate* underscores the value of other religious traditions; the Church "rejects nothing of what is true and holy" in these religions; she has high regard for anything that may "reflect a ray of that truth which enlightens all men."[36] Another fundamental document of the Council, *Gaudium et Spes* states that the Holy Spirit also operates outside of the Church.[37] A crucial outcome of the Council has determined a change in the mode of theologizing in India. In the *Dei verbum*, one of the

---

34   Bertone, "Proposito."

35   Congregation for the Doctrine of the Faith, "Instruction *Donum Veritatis*," note 17.

36   Pope Paul VI, *Nostra Aetate* (Declaration on the Relation of the Church to Non-Christian Religions, Rome, October 28, 1965), no. 2.

37   Pope Paul VI, *Gaudium et Spes*, no. 22.

principal documents generated during the Council, the counciliar Fathers offered a long-awaited revision of the concept of Tradition. Tradition (in terms of sacred tradition) can be explained in terms of a living Tradition, that is, it happens in the ongoing life of the Church Tradition; in the words of the Asian bishops, it is "growth in the understanding of realities and the words handed on [which] takes place 'through the contemplation and study made by believers, who treasure these things in their hearts (Luke 2:19, 51), through the intimate understanding of spiritual things they experience, and through the preaching of those who have received through Episcopal succession the sure gift of truth' (DV 8)."[38] In other words, the living reality is an addition to the doctrinal teachings of the councils, symbols of faith, creeds, and liturgical traditions of the Church (*lex orandi, lex credendi*). These are the conciliar pillars of Indian theology and its vision of an Indian Christianity.[39]

One main effort of Indian theologians in the last four decades has been driven by the purpose of contributing to the construction of a Catholic Church with a distinct Asian—that is, non-Western—flavor. In turn, these theological contributions heavily rely on the outcomes of the Second Vatican Council and more specifically on a distinct hermeneutical key by which to assess these outcomes: "the spirit of Vatican II." Through this lens, the definitive significance of the Council primarily rests not on the magisterial documents it produced, but—and this differs from the other ecumenical councils—on the impulses for change and reform that the event inspired, even if they appear to overcome established Church teaching. To put it differently, the spirit of Council stands for the belief that the Holy Spirit protects the texts of the Council from errors that would contradict the Church's essential doctrines. Consequently, the doctrines are interpreted in light of the conciliar texts rather than the other way around.

One decade ago, the late Giovanni Franzoni clarified the crux of the matter: "Wanting to synthesize, this is how I would describe the knot of contrast that has been hanging over the Catholic Church for decades:

---

38   See *FAPA: Federation of Asian Bishops' Conference Documents From 1997 to 2001*, vol. 3, ed. Franz-Josef Eilers (Quezon City: Claretian, 2002), 362–63. Here the text cites Pope Paul VI, *Dei Verbum*.

39   Amaladoss, *Experiencing*, 169–70.

Wojtyla and Ratzinger see Vatican II in the light of the Council of Trent and Vatican I. For us, on the contrary, these two councils should be seen and downplayed in the light of Vatican II. Therefore, given these divergent points of view, the contrasts cannot be eliminated."[40] A monumental confrontation within postconciliar Catholicism was raised between those who believe in progress and those who believe in Tradition. For the former, the long postconciliar period before the elevation of Cardinal Bergoglio to the Holy See consists of a constant and self-evident attempt to betray the spirit of the Council, expressed by its theological documents. The spirit of renovation emerging from the Council was rapidly challenged, then minimized, and finally imprisoned in a sort of counterreform. It is the thesis of a betrayed Council, the betrayed revolution that was supposed to be and never was. For the latter, the long postconciliar period between Paul VI and Francis is an unacceptable attempt to betray the theological documents of the Council by interpreting them outside the lineage of Tradition. Vatican II was not a break from the past but an attempt to renew the language through which the Church presents its ancient message and to authorize sets of internal reforms to adapt its activity to modern conditions. Those who insist there was a break between a preconciliar and a postconciliar Church, the narrative goes, ignore the far greater continuity between the Council and earlier Tradition. The blame for the disappointment of hopes for renewal belongs to those who have gone far beyond both the letter and the spirit of Vatican II. These are, in brief, the two alternative positions.

Amaladoss frequently mentions the Council in his writings.[41] However, his interest seems to be oriented toward the reception of the Council rather than the Council itself.[42] Therefore, I can only offer my synthetic

---

40   The late Giovanni Franzoni was a former Benedictine abbot of the basilica of St. Paul Outside-the-Walls (second only to St. Peter's among the great basilicas of Rome), a Catholic theologian, and conciliar Father. The quote is from Giovanni Franzoni, "Concilio Tradito. Concilio Perduto?" (address, 31st Congress of the Asociación de Teólogos y Teólogas Juan XXIII, Madrid, September 18, 2011).

41   See, for example, Amaladoss, *Quest for God*, 55–56 and *Beyond Inculturation*, 5–6.

42   See Amaladoss, "The Liturgy: Twenty Years after Vatican II," *VJTR* 47 no. 5 (1983): 231–39; "Inculturation and Dialogue," *Vatican II 20 Years Later* (Rome: Centre of Ignatian Spirituality, 1986), 151–76; "L'église en Inde: vingt ans après Vatican II," in Paul Ladrière et René Luneau (eds.), *Le retour des certitudes*

interpretation of his view of Vatican II. For Amaladoss, as for all progressives, the light that guides the process of the Indianization of the Church, and its break with Tradition, is the Second Vatican Council. The Council has never been qualified as dogmatic in character, but rather as pastoral. The Council was proclaimed not to condemn errors or formulate new doctrines but to update the interpretation of Tradition. As Pope John XXIII said on his deathbed, "It is not the Gospel that changes; it is we who begin to understand it better."[43] Together with many others, Amaladoss believes that the primacy of pastoral can be interpreted as the primacy of praxis over doctrine. Thus, the Council can be seen as a change not in the doctrine but in the nature of the doctrine, including its aims, boundaries, and methods. From this perspective, the Council is the turning point in the marginalization of centuries of metaphysics in favor of anthropology and social theory. Once the primacy of practice has been accepted, the primacy of action (experience, ethos, immanence) over contemplation (authority, doctrine, transcendence) is established. More importantly, a new hierarchy between tradition and progress, past and present, can be affirmed.

The Second Vatican Council is the supreme (but not infallible) ordinary Magisterium, not because the ordinary Magisterium cannot be infallible, but because it is infallible only when it receives confirmation from Tradition. Although John Paul II and Benedict XVI have argued that the documents of the Council require an alignment with Tradition, others have instead considered those documents as a departure from Tradition.

(Paris: Centurion, 1987), 13–33; "Mission from Vatican II into the Coming Decade," *VJTR* 54, no. 6 (1990): 269–80; "Dialogue between Religions in Asia Today: 40 Years of Vatican II and the Churches of Asia and the Pacific—Looking Back and Moving Forward," *East Asian Pastoral Review* 42, no. 1–2 (2005): 45–60; "Interreligious Dialogue 50 Years after Vatican II: Challenges and Opportunities," *VJTR* 79, no. 2 (2015): 85–99; "The Church Open to the World from Vatican Council II to Pope Francis with Special Reference to Asia," in *Towards Renewing Church and World: Revisiting Vatican Council II through the Eyes of Pope Francis*, eds. Francis Gonsalves et al. (Delhi: ISPCK, 2020), 59–69.

43   The original in Italian reads, "Non e il Vangelo che cambia, siamo noi che cominciamo a comprenderlo meglio." The translation is my own. See Mario Benigni and Goffredo Zanchi, *Giovanni XXIII: Biografia ufficiale* (Milan: San Paolo, 2000), 428.

In this case, the alignment between those documents and Tradition is considered a plus as if the Council is the *regula fide*, the criteria of interpretation on Tradition. This departure, however, makes the Magisterium of those documents supreme but not infallible. In fact, Tradition and Scripture, namely the deposit of faith, are always divinely supported; the Magisterium is only divinely supported when it expresses itself in extraordinary form (for example, the infallibility of the pontiff) or in ordinary form when it is in continuity with Tradition. Or one must conclude that Vatican II was a kind of supercouncil whose authority is superior to the authority of the previous councils. I put the issue to rest.

CONCLUSION

AMALADOSS AND INDIA

Michael Amaladoss is a dominant figure within Indian Christian theology. He is an Indian Jesuit priest, theologian, and author who has made significant contributions to the development of contextual theology in Asia. His theology is deeply rooted in the social, cultural, and religious realities of Asia, and he emphasizes the importance of inculturation and interfaith dialogue in the Church's life. He has also produced advancements in the field of Christology, and I dedicated part of this book to his epistemological contribution. Another part is focused on the epistemic contribution, namely, Amaladoss's project of a true Indian theology, a theology that is built in alignment with the Magisterium, in relativization of Tradition, and in total autonomy from Western theology. I return to the latter in the post scriptum. Here, I seek to provide a brief summary of the study, including some comments on Amaladoss's theological framework and an evaluation of his legacy.

There are authors—one thinks of de Lubac—who understand all their own completed works as an approximation to an ever-elusive center. Amaladoss is the opposite: from his center—Indianness—his works burst out in all directions. Indianness is, in first approximation, the relationship between Christianity and India, so Amaladoss cannot write theology without its essential Indian substrate; still, no idea of India is practical without its connection to Christianity. In the last half century, a shift has occurred in Indian Catholicism: the major ecclesial and theological efforts have moved from converting India to making Christianity more Indian. A new generation of priests and theologians has found a natural starting place for

156   MICHAEL AMALADOSS AND THE QUEST FOR INDIAN THEOLOGY

their pastoral and intellectual work in the reality in which they lived, not in abstract principles and goals. A respect for the fine and rich plurality of Indian spiritual and religious traditions added additional motivation to the change of perspective, and this respect was legitimized and justified at a conciliar level. The task of making India Christian was replaced with other tasks: how to peacefully cohabit with the members of other religions; how to solve the millenarian plagues that affect Indian society, including caste, poverty, and corruption; and how to consequently reconceptualize theology. *Mission*, understood as conversion, initially became an obsolete word, tainted as it was with colonial reminiscences; later, the word was banned as a source of division with Hindu radicals and, unfortunately, of persecution. If there was a time in recent history in which questioning whether India can be Christian were not only a provocation but an absurdity, this is it.

The first generations of theologians emerging after independence saw their role as contributors in building the Indian version of Christianity. Sometimes consequentially, sometimes instrumentally, they built the two polarities, Western theology and Indian theology, to affirm a distinction that was also an affirmation of autonomy. India, one of the mothers of human civilization, was finally independent from foreign subjugation and free to follow its own path. Indian Christians had their own questions to answer, for example, how to be an Indian and a Christian in harmony, and much work to do, particularly integrating (i.e., inculturating) the Church in the local setting. Theologians developed new methods of theologizing that leveraged local material instead of applying, to paraphrase a sentence of Rayan, "a ready-made theology imposed by Western tradition on India."[1] The period of the rise and dominance of this phase of Indian theology mostly corresponds to that of the grip of the Indian National Congress's values of social justice, freedom, and state's neutrality in religious affairs over Indian society. These values form the background of most of Amaladoss's theology.

Amaladoss's entire oeuvre represents an attempt to generate a new Christianity that is totally and inherently Indian. The attempt consists not

---

[1]   The original quote of Rayan reads, "a ready-made Church imposed on India." Quoted in Georg Evans, "My Experiences with Asian Theologies," in *Seeking New Horizons, Festschrift in Honor of Dr. M. Amaladoss, S. J.* (Delhi: Vidyajyoti and Welfare Society, ISPCK, 2002), 112.

CONCLUSION   157

of an assimilation by Indian theologians of the basic character of the Christian theology, but rather the opposite; it is an operation of anti-assimilation. The origins of this idea can be traced to Amaladoss's early life. He claims that the meeting with Father Hirudayam played a decisive role in his Indian turn. This meeting continued to animate his thinking as his fame and influence within Asian Christianity increased over the following decades. He not only sought to theologize Father Hirudayam's nationalistic sensibility, he also elaborated the distinction between an inauthentic existence—in which Christians have a conflicting relationship with their own Indian life—and authentic being, in which one reaches the full range of being Christian as well as Indian. For Amaladoss, a Western cultural framework has imposed and still imposes inauthenticity on most Indian Christians by subordinating them to its abstract rites, rules, and doctrines. Authenticity, by contrast, is the capacity to liberate latent potential within Indian Christianity.

Amaladoss's work has been dominated by an attempt to reflect theologically the tensions between the past and the present, tradition and modernity, West and East. As an unsystematic theologian, not indifferent to singular events but always concerned with inscribing them into a broader social context, Amaladoss has focused on a variety of topics such as intercultural and interreligious dialogue, inculturation, the caste system, spirituality, and liberation. In this sense, he could be defined as a typical representative of the Indian homeless theology, a theology without school affiliations: critical, progressive, nationalist, and clearly influenced by socialist ideas but far from Marxist orthodox or dogmatic. The core of Amaladoss's thought is the category of postcolonialism, or even anti-colonialism, that he declines in terms that are different than the subaltern school. In Amaladoss, postcolonialism is a vision of the history of the Indian Church rooted in the idea that colonialism, and not nationalism, carries the responsibility for the main problems of the era.[2] Accordingly, these problems are always seen as coming from the outside. When the last of the colonial heritage is expelled from the country, Indians will be liberated. To put it differently, postcolonialism is the unique category that promotes the passage from a domain of necessity and alienation to a domain of liberation.

---

2   In Amaladoss's words, "The problem comes not from Hindu nationalists but from Europe and Christian conservatives."

In Amaladoss's words, "Since anyone who claims to do contextual theology is . . . dismissed as unworthy of attention, I feel obliged . . . to show that I am . . . part of a history."[3] To his detractors, he argues that history is a complex reality, not a series of abstractions. In his work, Amaladoss reflects on one of the great questions on history: What is the relationship between people and history? Amaladoss makes an unusual assertion in response: people make history as well as history makes people. People can be either masters or victims of history. In the end, it depends on them. He believes that people need to fight what can be seen as a deterministic character of history and build their own history. People need to transform history from an inertial process to an active moment of creativity. More precisely, Indian people need to unleash from a West-centric history and manufacture their own destinies. This implies a certain way of theologizing: reflection confines itself to the mere study of things as they are, but the perception that things can be changed by praxis suggests seeing things as they could be. To put it differently, there is no doubt that Amaladoss's Indian origins pushed him to think historically within national patterns and ecclesial borders. But thinking locally needs a methodology and, to a certain extent, it implies a philosophy of history. It is a certain philosophy of history as praxis that has shaped, more than anything else, Amaladoss's style of thinking; without endorsing any Marxist orthodoxy, he looks at theology through the connections between theological work and social structures, religious and cultural conflicts, and forms of domination and liberation.

In Amaladoss there is a predominance of the social body and, therefore, an excess of historicity over philosophy and in turn of social life over thought. Certainly, Amaladoss's thinking echoes a season of quasi-omnipotence of history, a season in which history was deemed the main transforming power and a season that seems to have passed by now. The young Indians who populate cubicles and workspaces in Bangalore and who travel all around the nation believe that technology, not history, changes the world.[4] Young people no longer believe that history as a historical process is a force for change. Previous generations, including Amaladoss's, share this idea that the modern form of history (or simply

---

3   Amaladoss, *Quest for God*, 15.
4   Ross Bassett, *The Technological Indian* (Cambridge, MA: Harvard University Press, 2016).

modern history), which deems history an intellectual category, has an inherent character that makes it different from the previous forms of history. What distinguished modern history is precisely that it is a process, a progression—a movement toward the future. Accordingly, humanity will be redeemed in history and through history, in the sense that history is an unstoppable advancement toward liberation from the limits that still imprison human beings. This nexus between history as a concrete process and history as an intellectual category, that is, the link between political history and philosophy of history, is uniquely characteristic of modern history.

Young Indians have lost this idea of the nexus between political history and philosophy and therefore of history as progress; they have replaced it with the notion that technology changes the world. Accordingly, they have lost interest in the intellectual battles around history as an intellectual category: what it is, how it can be interpreted, and who owns it have degraded in importance. That does not mean that intellectual battles are over. In India, a furious battle is ongoing between intellectuals close to the right-wing government and scholars who entered academia during the long Nehruvian age. The former rewrite history to make India a Hindu nation; the latter defend a history of India as a pluralistic nation. These battles on the political use of the past, however, do not excite the younger generations and are thus rearguard actions among old generations to settle the scores of the past. History is no longer the primary vehicle of utopias of infinite progress and dreams of heaven on earth; history is neither a central prism through which one can interpret this present time. History as a product of the grand narratives of science, reason, and progress that dominated the intellectual circles in the nineteenth and twentieth centuries did not survive the collapse of those narratives.

AMALADOSS AND THE WEST

In this era of globalization, it seems that Indian theology stands as a sort of countermobilization: Indian theologians celebrate their own historical and national peculiarities and claim a certain irreducible originality and autonomy. By his own admission, Amaladoss is a resistant, pushing back on the different forms of imposition taken by Western powers, secular as well as ecclesiastical. In his words, "westernization affects [India] at many levels." He is only a mite resistant, however. For sure, in Europe he would be resisting Americanism; in India, he resists "western imposition."[5] Amaladoss is complex figure. In the Indian milieu, he can be identified as a Nehruvian socialist who feels much more at home in the West than, say, in Russia. In fact, he shows no cultural attraction to Russia, contrary to many Indians. His position, I argue, illustrates a dualism that continues to mark Indian Christianity, a rift between West and East, the rationalist and the romantic, one may say. Understanding this tension, I think, helps to explain why he is so eager to cut ties with the West and why he finds it difficult to do so.[6]

Amaladoss belongs to an extraordinary generation of theologians and spiritual seekers—George Soares-Prabhu, Kuncheria Pathil, George Nedungatt, and Duraiswami Simon Amalorpavadass, among others—who were born in India before the end of British colonialism and reached maturity during the Nehru era. At the very moment that Indians experienced greater freedom, an impulse emerged to identify more deeply with, and even take pride in, the nation's character of independence. This embrace of autonomy as a way forward also opened this generation to choosing national freedom—and therefore national identity—over individual freedom and consequently individual identity. The focus on national identity rather than individual identity set the goal on the relationship between nations, continents, and hemispheres rather than individuals. The concept that nations are the primary social entities and not congregations of individual human beings has forged Amaladoss's mental habitus and given

---

5   In Europe there is a minority, although an influential one, that identifies with anti-American sentiment. In brief, anti-Americanism is a systematic or essentialist form of prejudice targeting all Americans. Anti-Americanism is a field of study, with its dedicated experts, bibliographies, and schools of thought. For anti-Americanization as a field of study, see, for example, Ivan Krastev and Alan McPherson, eds., *The Anti-American Century?* (Budapest: Central European University Press, 2007).

6   Amaladoss falls into the same category of socialist or social-democratic theologians in Europe. In the British intellectual milieu, he could probably be aligned with personalities like the philosopher John Gray or the theologian John Milbank, who want change but in the shape of reform, not structural change. Amaladoss is a clerical socialist, that is, a Christian socialist.

CONCLUSION 161

him a sharp sense of the relationship between West and East. For him, the West-East connection is not a matter of peaceful conversation between individuals; it is a realm of power struggle between poles so that if the Eastern pole does not protect its autonomy, it will lose it. The ramifications of the above are crucial.

Let me return to Amaladoss's conviction that "no serious Indian (Asian) theology will emerge as long as we are tied to the apron strings of a Euro-American system." This is the Western-Indian divide that he not only pursues but also hopes for. It is a crucial issue for him. When one applies this specific vision to Catholicism, one understands why Amaladoss's work is marked by a certain degree of idealization of India and a high degree of antiwesternism that in his case is synonymous with anti-Europeanism. A Catholic Other emerges in his work as the presumed oppressor, not just of Indians but of all Asian Christianities: the shameless Western Christianity. Catholicism descended into symbolic warfare between two ecclesial, continental identities, one committed to dissociating itself from historical shame, the other dedicated to persisting in its mistakes. Amaladoss's peculiarity lies in this specific idea that the Eastern pole of Christianity and the Western pole are both, so to speak, the center of the world: both look at the world from a self-declared centrality. This complicated dispositive only makes sense as a result of an obvious desire of Westerners to avoid being considered colonialists and a natural desire of Easterners to avoid being considered inferior. Because the essence of such a dispositive is inherently incoherent—it condemns the West for being colonialist while insisting that the East does not need the acceptance of a colonialist West—the risk is inertia.

During my conversations with Amaladoss, I mentioned that some Western thinkers believe that non-Western Christianity (or, better, Christianities) are walking a historical path already walked by Western Christianities. What I had in mind was the work of an evangelical historian, Mark Noll, who sketched a picture of a non-Western Christian world that bears remarkable similarities to Christianity in the West. Beginning in the late sixties, historians and theologians suggested that centuries of cultural and religious imperialism by European and North American missionaries and colonial powers provide the explanation for the enduring resemblances of non-Western Christianity to Western Christianity. This is exactly the point of departure for thinkers like liberation theologist Gustavo Gutiérrez, who called for the liberation of theology from the Western grip. For Amaladoss and many others, these earlier explanations continue to resonate up to the present day, despite the fact the colonies achieved independence almost a century ago and now enjoy political sovereignty. For them, the influence of the West continues to prevail through paternalistic relationships and social, religious, and economic structures, thus propagating forms of Christianity that look very much like those of the West.

Noll challenges this opinion, suggesting instead that these similarities are primarily because of emerging social, economic, and political similarities. In brief, he believes that the non-Western Christianity is becoming more similar to Western Christianity because the non-Western world is economically, socially, and politically becoming more similar to the West.[7] For Gutiérrez and Amaladoss, the influence of the West is direct, but for Noll, it is indirect: this amounts to the fact that the great non-Western countries of the world increasingly resemble the Western countries. Here is hidden the main reason why non-Western Christianities are similar to Western Christianities: these days, the former are being shaped by the same kind of social, political, and economic circumstances that shaped the latter during the nineteenth and twentieth centuries. Noll argues that the primary reason for similarities between Western and non-Western Christianity stems from a shared historical occurrence, an occurrence of economic, social, and political forces once experienced in the West that now shape non-Western Christianity. The disadvantage of Noll's argument is that it downplays the fact the Western Christianity has maintained some degree of control over the shape of non-Western Christianity; it has the enormous advantage, however, to consider the members of the indigenous Church as the primary agency of their own destiny. In South Asia, colonization has been the major element of theological formation; it is no surprise that theologians tend to be critical of the West. Even today, young liberation theologians still somehow live in that era, although some recognize that local governments may be responsible for discrimination; injustices are not always the result of the legacy of Western forces.

---

7   Mark Noll, *The New Shape of World Christianity: How American Experience Reflects Global Faith* (Downers Grove, IL: InterVarsity, 2010).

CONCLUSION   163

Several years ago, Gerd-Rainer Horn wrote a book with a remarkable title: *Western European Liberation Theology: The First Wave (1924–1959)*.[8] His thesis was that the progressive and radical theology of the aftermath of the Council outside the West had its antecedent in the progressive Catholicism of preconciliar Europe. Horn is neither a theologian nor a Church historian; his specialization is the history of social movement in twentieth-century Europe. Anyone who knows the history of progressive and radical Catholicism in France and Italy, however, must recognize that the argument holds. Horn argued the existence of a continuity between two waves of progressive Catholicism, one before and the other after the Council, although he did not minimize the role of the Council: "But Vatican II did more than 'merely' bestow the official imprimatur on the ideologies and practices of left Catholicism of the preceding thirty-five years. Vatican II became the launching pad for an even more powerful 'second wave' of experiments in left Catholic politics and culture in the ensuing two decades."[9] The preconciliar progressive and radical European Catholicism struggled to de-inculturate Catholicism from the ecclesiastic rigorism of Neo-scholasticism and the residual traces of Christendom's grandeur and inculturate it into the living reality of the poor and marginalized: the sick, the rejected, the disadvantaged. They saw Europe as a *pays de mission*, as a continent to evangelize.[10] They opened political and ecumenical dialogues with the Soviet Union and China. They fought for justice and peace (during the Cold War). Most paid high prices for their perceived arrogance: the suffered forms of ecclesiastical repression or relegation, isolation, or even laicization on the part of the hierarchy. Some received rehabilitation, but others faded from the collective memory of Catholicism. Their names—Charles Boland, Primo Mazzolari, Lorenzo Milani, Zeno Saltini, and Jean Verdier—represent only a select few and may be unknown in India, but they can be considered the Italian and French versions of Kappen and Amaladoss. They were secular and religious priests, monks, friars, members of the hierarchy, or simple parish priests who worked to renovate

---

8   Gerd-Rainer Horn, *Western European Liberation Theology: The First Wave (1924–1959)* (Oxford: Oxford University Press, 2008).

9   Horn, *Western European Liberation Theology*, 291.

10   Henri Godin and Yvan Daniel, *France, pays de mission?* (Paris: Cerf, 1943).

monastic life, break down the division between clergy and laity, promote the Church of the poor, and open a dialogue with the different social and political components of society: in sum, they managed the secularization of the Church, which they considered a necessary target well before the opening of the Second Vatican Council.

Both Noll's and Horn's arguments can be expanded. According to John Gray, the non-West, and particularly Asia, cannot be conceived as intellectually severed from the West. Several facts contribute to corroborate this thesis. One is that it seems that both the West and the East are moving toward an illiberal horizon. Western liberalism has become illiberal, but ideologies originating in the illiberal West—Marxism, nationalism, the suppression or discrimination of minorities, the experiment in coercive nation-building, the emergence of nation-states asserting a right to self-determination whose closest historical parallels are in interwar Europe—dominate the scene in Asia. One may add the Marxist–Leninist philosophy of the Chinese party and its historical materialism; in India, the law is written in English. The Indian penal code is in English. It has never been translated into local languages because everybody knows that if one translates the law, one changes the law. This is Gray's thesis, and he claims it may be possible that Western liberalism, not Western civilization as many in Asia seem to believe, is largely defunct.[11] But in the case that Western civilization is decomposing, the ideas originated in the West still dominate the global debate so that the Asian counterpart is not alien civilization. Whether the Western power is vanishing remains a matter of contention, but Western ideas are alive in the Asian powers that now confront the West.

AMALADOSS AND THE CHURCH

In India, Christian theologians need to assume a kind of theological double vision. They must acknowledge the legacy of a millenarian religious tradition that is mostly unfamiliar without accepting its inevitability. In their projection of the future, what is possible must coexist with what

---

11   John Gray, "The West Isn't Dying: Its Ideas Live on in China," *The New Stateman*, July 28, 2021. https://tinyurl.com/45zcthae.

CONCLUSION   165

should be. This requires a careful synthesis of realist and utopian theological sensibilities. If there is an Indian thinker active in recent decades who clearly sought a third way between optimism and melancholia, hope and defeatism, while embodying this ambivalence, it is Amaladoss. His writing has oscillated from dark reflections on the cultural prison in which Indian Christianity survives to positive images of its liberation. His writings aim to create ideal conditions for a flourishing, truly Indian Christianity while revealing the audacity, and ultimately the improbability, of such an attempt. His work is both a framework for imagining the future of a fully integrated Christianity in the religious and cultural patchwork of South Asia and a lament—a sign of impotent frustration.

For radicals, theology consists of a concern for correcting obvious and addressable problems and an insistence that the Church's social doctrine can be extended to the limits. In this way, Kappen once declared, the "radical upsurge within Christianity" will "show that religions are . . . untapped reservoirs of energy which can be harnessed to humanized society."[12] For progressives, theology instead involves establishing a new innocence in relation to Western Christianity's past sins in India. By dissociating themselves from the past, progressives seek to supply moral authority to Indian Christianity. The two streams share the opinion that the future cannot be determined by the past; on the contrary, the future liberates a society from the past. In Christian thought and life, the faithful do not travel forward; they travel backward from the future to the present (and the past). The world is expecting the eschatological Christ who will come at the eschaton as the union of the created and the uncreated. One may be concerned with the social engagement and the political relevance of such an eschatological view. If the Church is, as some Indian theologians maintain, chiefly the remembrance of the future, an icon of the eschatological Kingdom, then does this future have any impact on the present social life of both the ecclesial community and wider society? Can the future be a cause of the present in the social realm, and, therefore, does it define the present, even partially?

---

12   Sebastian Kappen, "The Struggle of Fishermen in Kerala," in *Collected Works of Sebastian Kappen*, vol. 5, *Hindutva and Indian Religious Traditions*, ed. Sebastian Vattamattam (Delhi: ISPCK, 2021), 184.

Amaladoss acknowledges that radical political activity for the defense of the poor and the marginalized, alongside the victims of history, is an element missing or at least not explicitly developed in his work. He has not articulated a comprehensive political theology or political eschatology. His interest is more precisely centered in the destiny of the Church in India, and therefore, he works toward a comprehensive, so to speak, ecclesial eschatology. And yet, a large part of his writings reveals an underlying struggle with ecclesiastical authority. Once again, Amaladoss is not a radical; he does not contest the legitimacy of the authority of the Magisterium. He prefers to isolate, at least theoretically, Indian or Asian Catholicism from Rome so that a certain degree of autonomy is reached through a distance or a difference that is repeatedly emphasized. Here is one example: "The Federation of Asian Bishops' Conferences spelt out the mission of the Church in Asia as the building up of a local Church through a dialogue of the Gospel with its many poor, the rich cultures and the living religions—and it is not understood by the centre (of the Church in Rome)!"[13] By framing a cognitive gap between the center and the periphery, Amaladoss builds a gulf between legitimacy and legality. He does not contest the legitimacy, but rather the legality of such authority: he recognizes the authority of the Magisterium but resists the exercise of such authority.

Amaladoss has not articulated a comprehensive political theology, yet he has his own political theological view, a summary of which would probably go something like this: Europe and the West may be correct that a long history connects the present Christianity with the early Church, but thousands of miles away, in the world's second-largest country, that history looks quite controversial. That history carries out good and honorable episodes but also violent and unjust episodes. The Indians have had personal experience with the troubled and ambiguous character of that history. They have watched the rich and powerful Christianity in the Global North disregard Indians' views and preferences in pursuit of its own interests. Thus, Indian Christians have limited patience for Western—theological and doctrinal—narratives and affirm the right to build their own tradition. This right is not based on, say, the authority of an ancient episcopal see,

---

13   Amaladoss, *Peoples' Theology*, 21.

CONCLUSION 167

but, I suppose, self-determination. Indian Christianity's priority is to hear the voices of the poor and give voice to the marginalized; so, it is positioning itself in the heartland of the Global South to be a bridging presence that stands for harmony and justice. This perspective is not unique to Indian Christians. Many of the Asian Christianities are wary of being dragged into doctrinal discussions that originated in Europe. They are understandably more concerned about their level of poverty and discrimination, a pluralistic religious and cultural coexistence, climate vulnerability, and their need for better health care and education systems. For Asian Christianities, navigating this complex situation between their historical loyalty to Rome and their biological and cultural proximity to the people of Asia is difficult. The benefits, if successful, will be enormous—both for Asian Christianities and Christianity as a whole.

Given this context, it is no surprise that the priority of Indian Christianity is India. The ambition of Christians in India is to become a pole within global Christianity and a contributing community within the Indian nation. These efforts for emancipation have not been received as warmly in the West, but Indian Christianity sees these critiques as partisan. The West routinely put Indian theology under intense scrutiny while claiming that its critiques are guided by speculative concerns. This claim should be questioned, as the West has often acted in accordance with its interests. The East has every right to take the same approach, no matter what the West says. Moreover, the West should be aware that Christians in India are extremely sensitive to any badgering by Western subjects about Indian Christianity's own decisions. Indians do not have much tolerance for being hectored about their worship, doctrine, theology, and practice, especially from a part of the Christian world where problems abound.

So far, Indian Christianity has done an impressive job of maintaining its balancing act. The key point is that Indian Christianity does not accept to be envisioned as a peripheral entity of the Rome-centric Christian society. Of course, the Indian community is organically part of the Christian society, but Rome and the West should not mistake Indian Christianity's participation in Christian society for an unconditional adherence. Instead, Indian Christianity deserves attention on both sides of its complex identity: the Christian side and the Indian side. Indian Christianity is part of Christianity but also of India. Indian Christianity is learning to be assertive and displaying a newfound confidence. Whether it can continue to do so in the years ahead is an open question.

Amaladoss is correct to reject the concept of transferring knowledge and custom from the center to the periphery, as there are more advanced and less advanced, theologically speaking, realities. India cannot be a passive recipient of Western wisdom; Indian Christianity, instead, can engage with the received knowledge, altering and tailoring it to their own circumstances, a procedure that Amaladoss has mastered in his work. The complex process of alteration, adaption, and interaction between theological poles presents a more balanced image of theological dialogue than does the top-down concept of knowledge transfer. Amaladoss is correct in saying that Indian theology cannot be original as long as it is subaltern to Tradition, but it is wrong to believe that Indian theology can be truly original as long as it defines itself in opposition to Tradition. The mastermind of the nineteenth-century Catholic reactionary intellectuals is not necessarily the most obvious reference when it comes to Amaladoss. Yet, Joseph Marie, Comte de Maistre, had a point in saying that "a counter-revolution is not a revolution of the opposite sign but the opposite of a revolution."[14] What he meant is that in a relationship between two poles, one pole is always dependent on the pole it wants to oppose. Freedom is not doing something different from but rather doing something transcendent upon. To put it differently, Tradition is not an option for Indian theology to avoid but a problem for Indian theology to solve. If Amaladoss is serious about his intent to free himself from Western influence, he should free Tradition from Western influence, not try to separate himself from that Tradition. He should make Tradition no longer a property of the West by engaging Tradition and making it plural (if he thinks it is not already so). He should trust Tradition as a vehicle of liberation. Tradition is a sort of imaginative storehouse of Christianity. What happens to theologies that endure is that they address the storehouse in which is compressed an enormous amount of meaning, and then they try to unpack it once again. In fact, Vatican II clearly argued that Tradition is a living

---

14   Joseph Marie de Maistre, *Considerazioni sulla Francia* (Napoli: Il Giglio, 2010), 248 . The translation is my own.

process: always interrogated with new questions in the movement of history, Tradition always shows its virtualities, that is, the characteristic of Tradition to be inexhaustible and capable of reproposing the eternal truth in historically new forms.

Oedipus is a fundamental figure in Western literature and philosophy. Homer mentioned him in both *Odyssey* and *Iliad*. Aeschylus and Euripides wrote plays about the hero. In modern times, Hegel established Oedipus as an inaugural philosopher in his *Lectures on the History of Philosophy*. For Heidegger, Oedipus was the embodiment of his own definition of philosophy as the self-generating process of destruction and recreation. Oedipus is a man at the crossroads between being a puppet in the hands of the gods and being an individual responsible for his own fate, between being controlled and using his free will. I dare adopt Oedipus as an entry into what I believe is the mythical core of Amaladoss's thought. Here *mythos* stands for belief. For Amaladoss—my interpretation goes— the problem that affects Indian Christianity is a sort of Oedipus complex, a complex that is used to suppress authenticity in the service of normalization and control. On one side, in fact, a westernized Church is a kind of anti-oedipal institution that must colonize its members, repress their desires, and give them complexes as a way to function as an organizing principle of Christianity. On the other side, Indianness is the original, virginal state of Christianity in India. Like Oedipus, Indian Christianity finds itself at the intersection of being a puppet and being authentic. Oedipus means, through a subtraction operation, to kill the alien concepts, whatever is alien and alienating, and get back to the original, the native, the mother-birth, so to speak. Oedipus is naturally oriented to kill all those things in himself which are installed in him and are not of himself, because they are alien concepts that are not his. They must die. Amaladoss's effort is to liberate Indian Christianity from the Oedipus complex and move in the direction of authenticity rather than ancient customs and foreign religious traditions.[15]

---

15 As far as I know, there is no equivalent to the Oedipus in the Hindu mythology. The story of Devayani's husband, Yayati, works as a reverse-Oedipal complex, because in this case the father kills the son.

WHAT HAS BEEN LEFT OUT

It is difficult to summarize the extensive and diverse theological work of Amaladoss. In his career, he has published around eight million words. His output is monumental. By comparison, this study of 80,000 words amounts to merely one percent of his body of work. Omissions and simplifications are inevitable. I have limited myself to outlining three main axes that define his theological reflection and am content to offer a few sporadic references to the rest of his work. Some of his most beautiful books, in fact, have nothing to do with inculturation, religious dialogue, Christology, or the erection of a true Indian theology.

In 1994, Amaladoss wrote *A Call to Community*, a book against the caste system.[16] It is a plea for the liberation of the Dalits and the abolition of the caste system. The book was written in response to the emergence of Dalit theology and the Dalit Christian Liberation Movement.[17] Although the work offers a general overview of the problem, it focuses on the reality of Christian Dalits. Amaladoss invited Christianity to avoid any form of accommodation: "Many Dalit groups thought they would escape the burden of untouchability if they left Hinduism and joined other religions."[18] But, Amaladoss explained indignantly, they discover that the caste system has been assimilated within the Church of India. As a citizen, he called for political and economic interventions against inequality. As a Christian, he referred to the image of the reign of God as a path to conversion toward a wholly inclusive community. In the end, he sees the dimension of the religious to be called to be "a casteless community of fellowship and love."[19]

Amaladoss's book on integral spirituality originated from a series of lectures delivered in memory of his friend Amalorpavadass.[20] The title, *Towards Fullness*, may create confusion. Fullness, Amaladoss explained, is

---

16   Michael Amaladoss, *A Call to Community: The Caste System and Christian Responsibility* (Anand: Gujarat Sahitya Prakash, 1994).

17   Amaladoss, *Call to Community*, xii.

18   Amaladoss, *Call to Community*, 8.

19   Amaladoss, *Call to Community*, 137.

20   Michael Amaladoss, *Towards Fullness: Searching for an Integral Spirituality* (Bangalore: National Biblical, Catechetical and Liturgical Centre, 1994).

CONCLUSION   171

not a process but a state of liberation.[21] The study indeed covers an impressive range of themes—the world, the self, the vision and the way to reach fullness—but the book is relevant mainly because in it the author clarified his approach to both Hinduism and Christianity. I am a Hindu-Christian, Amaladoss declared, and this book was not an exposition of Christian or Hindu spirituality; in it, he took the liberty to use the Hindu and Christian terms "with my own nuances." Therefore, he concluded, "I can only request you to understand me in the context of my own reflections."[22] In other words, Amaladoss invited his readers to enter into his theological universe.

A precious study on the Jubilee was published in 2000.[23] In it, Amaladoss connected the biblical appreciation of the human caducity with the divine imperative of justice. The theological reflection covers both the biblical landscape of ancient Israel and the contemporary reality of economic, political, and even ecological dysfunction. The book hosts several themes that are recurrent in Amaladoss's writings: the caste system, economic inequality, the distinction between the Church and the Kingdom, the pluralistic reality of India, and the local Church. The 2000 Jubilee was an occasion for refocusing the Church on the interreligious dialogue and for contextualizing the role of the Eucharist. For Amaladoss, the Eucharist is "the symbol of [the] communion in life" as manifested in the Gospel of John (John 17:21–23).[24]

In a short essay, *The Challenges of Fundamentalism*, published in 2009, Amaladoss addressed the rising tide of Hindu fundamentalism.[25] The book is divided into two parts: an analysis of the phenomenon and a call to action. Amaladoss believes that a collective mobilization against communalism can work on several levels including education, communication and propaganda, and religious festivals. More importantly, fundamentalists should be isolated, their claims challenged, and a spirit of pluralism reenacted.

---

21   Amaladoss, *Towards Fullness*, 4.
22   Amaladoss, *Towards Fullness*, preface.
23   Michael Amaladoss, *A Call to Jubilee* (Dindigul: Vaigari Publications, 2000).
24   Amaladoss, *Call to Jubilee*, 125.
25   Amaladoss, *Challenges of Fundamentalism*.

The Dancing Cosmos was an ambitious project.[26] In it, Amaladoss offered his humble reflection on basic questions like, Why am I here? and, What is the meaning and purpose of life?[27] The book is not academic, and it does not come with the traditional apparatus of footnotes and a bibliography. It reads as a long monologue, the expression of a set of thoughts that had been fermenting for a long time. The theologian must excuse Amaladoss when the latter drafts poetic expressions that look vague or, on the contrary, disputable: in this book, the intention was not to convince scholars but to bring spirituality to all.

Finally, I provide a few examples of Amaladoss's versatility and range of interests. In *Vision and Value for a New Society*, he offered his theological contribution for a planetary society oriented to peace and harmony.[28] In *Making All Things New*, he invited readers to rediscover the relevance of mission as prophecy.[29] In *The Joy of Living*, Amaladoss enjoyed a lovely conversation with his friend and fellow Jesuit M. A. Joe Antony.[30] Two books, *Love or Justice?* and *Creative Conflict*, are more precisely a collection of eighty-one monthly columns that he published under the rubric "Theology and Life" in the bimonthly magazine *The New Leader*.[31] These collections show the other side of Amaladoss—not the specialist but the theologian who can speak to a popular audience. In his words, "If for some people at least God and religion do not become a burden but an experience worth living . . . my effort at carrying on these reflections on theology and life will be amply rewarded."[32]

---

26 Michael Amaladoss, *The Dancing Cosmos: A Way to Harmony* (Anand: Gujarat Sahitya Prakash, 2003).

27 Amaladoss, *Dancing Cosmos*, 4.

28 Michael Amaladoss, *Vision and Values for a New Society. Responding to India's Social Challenges* (Bangalore: NBCLC, 2004).

29 Amaladoss, *Making All Things New*.

30 Michael Amaladoss and M. A. Joe Antony, *The Joy of Living: Wisdom from the East and West* (Mumbai: St. Paul's, 2004).

31 Michael Amaladoss, *Creative Conflict: Theological Musings* (Bombay: St. Paul's, 1995) and *Love or Justice?* (Dindigul: Vaigarai, 1999).

32 Amaladoss, *Love or Justice?* 8.

UNANSWERED QUESTIONS

This study on Amaladoss has no ambition to be exhaustive; it covers only a few islands of the large archipelago of themes that in my mind represents his entire production. I left some stones unturned. One has to do with Amaladoss's writing style. Salman Rushdie once said:

> India is not cool. India is hot. It's hot and noisy and odorous and crowded and excessive. How could I represent that on the page? I asked myself. What would a hot, noisy, odorous, crowded, excessive English sound like? How would it read? The novel I wrote was my best effort to answer that question. The question of crowdedness needed a formal answer as well as a linguistic one. Multitude is the most obvious fact about the subcontinent. Everywhere you go, there's a throng of humanity. How could a novel embrace the idea of such multitude? My answer was to tell a crowd of stories, deliberately to overcrowd the narrative, so that "my" story, the main thrust of the novel, would need to push its way, so to speak, through a crowd of other stories. There are small, secondary characters and peripheral incidents in the book that could be expanded into longer narratives of their own. This kind of deliberate "wasting" of material was intentional. This was my hubbub, my maelstrom, my crowd.[33]

These are not words that can be applied to Amaladoss. In his writings, India is cool in the sense that it is organizable, intelligible, and cogent. Take this sentence for example:

> We should speak of Hindu communalism rather than of Hindu fundamentalism. This is not to say that there are no Hindu fundamentalists at all. But they may be a small core group of what is basically a communalist movement. The communalists can

---

33   Salman Rushdie, *Midnight's Children* (New York: Random House, 1981), xvi–xvii.

eventually marginalize the hard-core fundamentalists *if and when necessary* [emphasis added].[34]

Amaladoss's India is reasonable, not excessive; it is crowded but organized. It does what it is supposed to do. On the subject of Hindu fundamentalism, books are banned, individuals are silenced, pieces of history are taken away from syllabi, but no names of victims are remembered, no harassment is mentioned, and no sign of discomfort is shown. The theologian is a participant observer. Emotions, passions, and irrationality have no place in Amaladoss's theology or in the complex, aporetic, nuanced character of human life. This is not to say that Amaladoss is a man without pathos. On the contrary: he is a man of obvious and manifested pathos. As a writer, however, his pathos is less evident, replaced by a rational view of problems, events, and people that leaves no room for contingency, fatality, or paradox.

In the introduction of his book *Experiencing God in India*, Amaladoss made a clear point: "If I do want to write about God . . . I can engage in apologetics. . . . I can do systematic theology . . . [or] . . . I can look around at the different religions and see how people have experienced God, briefly present their experiences and reflect on them from my point of view."[35] How does Amaladoss look and see? His writing style reflects a certain way of seeing reality. I already mentioned that Amaladoss is a modern theologian with a distinct inclination for progressive history. What I did not investigate is how rationality and progressive history find their intersection on paper. This remains something that someone else needs to study. The question arises in the sense that, in Amaladoss's theology, a classificatory rationality offers guidance on social and religious matters; it provides order where there was chaos and meaning where there was incomprehensibility. "Hindu fundamentalism is, at least partially, a response to perceived Muslim fundamentalism. . . . They have to put an end to terrorist bombings. . . . At the same time . . . we should not resist the fundamentalists on their religious plane. They should be ignored."[36] The logic of discourse and the

---

34 Michael Amaladoss, "Fundamentalism in Religions," in *Fundamentalism in Religions*, eds. Pidota Rayappa John, John B. Mundu, and Joseph Lobo (Delhi: ISPCK, 2018), 10.

35 Amaladoss, *Experiencing*, 5.

36 Amaladoss, *Challenges of Fundamentalism*, 51.

CONCLUSION 175

consequentiality of the argument bring light where there was darkness. Thus, in Amaladoss, the theology of the lived experience, the object of his theological research, cannot be untied from a strict logic that frames and gives sense to such experiences. The explanation dominates the description; the normative surpasses the shame. This raises the question whether Amaladoss really develops his theological frameworks internally from experience, as he claims, or whether he applies some predefined frameworks to the living experience. In other words, the question is whether his rationality is descriptive or prescriptive. Are the aporias of the living experiences resolved logically or does logic leave such aporias outside the framework? Is logic constructed upon life or applied to life?

Another theme that deserves more research is Amaladoss's discussion on globalization, which he sees in terms of neocolonialism.[37] Here is an example:

> Many of the countries in Asia have masses of poor people. This is partly the result of past political and continuing economic colonialism, often supported by the local elite for their own benefit. Even in the developing countries the gap between the rich and the poor is increasing. The globalization based on the liberal market capitalism is only making the situation in the poor countries worse.[38]

More study is necessary to unveil the roots of such an interpretation of globalization. Is his view of the subject based on a historical or sociological investigation? Of course, globalization is primarily a paradigm, a set of ordering principles and internal and external political and economic relations. As a paradigm, it fosters expectation of economic and social modernization. But can it be seen as an empire, a planetary power, a form of neocolonialism? China proved that globalization is neither economic nor political colonialism. Globalization is an extension on a planetary scale of a certain mode of organizing society. It is a social framework that works as a model of reference. The primary role played by the United States in globalization is historically (although not necessarily morally) justified: at the

---

37 See Michael Amaladoss, ed., *Globalization and Its Victims as Seen by the Victims* (Delhi: Vidyajyoti Education and Welfare Society & ISPCK, 1999).

38 Amaladoss, "Together Toward the Kingdom," 3.

end of World War II, the United States was the single remaining sea power. Most of the world trade is carried by sea routes because moving things on water is about one-tenth the cost of moving things on land, but sea routes can be dangerous places. During the age of the colonial empires, European as well as Asian military fleets were used to patrol oceans and seas and protect their own trade. But with the dawn of the European and Japanese empires, the US Navy was the only force available to protect the global shipment of goods. Unlike the colonial empires, however, the United States offered to protect with their fleet not only their own ships but also those of any nation that agreed to use the US dollar as the denomination of trade and English as the lingua franca of global logistics. In exchange, the Navy would guarantee the security of the world's trade routes to all the nations of the world, including its competitors like Russia and China. Many countries signed the agreement, and others executed it in practice.

With naval protection, the oceans became home to an increasingly large number of valuable ships of immense size and slow speed, which in turn unlocked economies of scale that propelled efficiency and reduced product cost. Access to international trade generated the internationally free trade world, or globalization, as we know it. The key principles of globalization, at least in the beginning, were free trade and the opening of national markets to world trade. Globalization also implied the idea that a market society would develop within each state and lead to economic growth and the peaceful resolution of conflicts. Then came the financialization of trade, and one must admit that significant parts of the population of the countries involved in globalization were left in poverty. Economic growth driven by globalization has been supplanted by an austerity regime that has generated an array of populist reactions from the lower classes. But globalization has propelled countries like China to the top of the world, and this is the point I want to make. Kevin Rudd, former Australian prime minister and seasoned China watcher, observed that China's rapid ascent has been like "the English industrial revolution and the global information revolution combusting simultaneously and compressed not into 300 years, but 30."[39]

---

39 See Graham Allison, *Destined for War: Can America and China Escape Thucydides's Trap?* (New York: HarperCollins, 2017), 12.

CONCLUSION   177

India has never completely embraced globalization; this decision has protected a great deal of its political and economic autonomy from the West. The same decision, however, has placed India in a subordinate position to China.[40] Recent events have reversed the results of decades of globalization and suggested a return to a fragmented world. In short, the growing trend over the past thirty to forty years is running out of steam: this is an age of deglobalization. Collaboration has once again shifted to competition and growing conflict. The admittedly vague idea of a cultural assimilation to Western values has been replaced by a much more concrete military and political threat along the northern borders with China and in the midst of the Indian Ocean.[41] It becomes increasingly clear that the obstacles to a complete emancipation of India from foreign powers come more from the East than from the West. The position of Amaladoss on globalization requires additional study, but I wonder if at this point the entire debate on globalization should become a matter for historians, not theologians.

LEGACY

How do such appraisals hold up when evaluating Amaladoss's work today? There are several reasons he preserves an imposing presence in the Indian theological landscape. First, he created an imposing body of work that covers much ground and spans decades. Second, his quality writings are always lucid and penetrating. Third, the audacity of his theses, which may resonate as too risky for some, has fostered an ethos among younger theologians, a confidence that Indian theology has a unique contribution to make to the intellectual and cultural reality of Catholicism. This possibility can be realized only if Indian theology repents for its false humility. The pathos of modern theology is its false humility. If Indian theology no longer seeks to position, qualify, or criticize Western discourses, then it is

---

40   In his most recent book, former foreign secretary to the government of India Shyam Saran recognizes that China envisions India as a subordinated power in a China-dominated Asia. See Shyam Saran, *How China Sees India and the World* (New Delhi: Juggernaut, 2022).

41   For a historical study of the Sino-Indian conflict on the northern border, see Avtar Singh Bhasin, *Nehru, Tibet and China* (New York: Penguin, 2021).

inevitable that these discourses will position Indian theology. For Indian theology, this must be a fatal mistake, because once it surrenders its ambition to be a metadiscourse, it can no longer serve the Indian Church. This is the message of Amaladoss to the young generations of theologians: an Indian theology positioned by Western theology suffers characteristic forms of confinement.

In the seventies and eighties, society became the theologians' predominant concern. Although the spiritual struggles of individuals received some coverage, the social problem clearly dominated the theological conversation. Thus, one has in the theology of the last decades of the century a kind of shift from an escapade into the boundless and unseen world of the spirit to the concrete society marked by contrary interests of economic growth and unequal wealth redistribution, extension of democracy and legacy of the caste system, rich and poor, socialism and liberalism, colonialism and postcolonialism, and West and East. The task has become an attempt to forge a compromise or reconciliation of the contraries into a dynamic of changes without the extremes of radicalism. This is the world in which Amaladoss's theology flourished. Indeed, from the mid-eighties onward, the inculturation-religious dialogue stream of theology that Amaladoss embodies so well seemed embarrassingly dated. Far from producing equality and justice, the socialist Indian state had abandoned significant parts of its population to the margins. This marginalization became the primary concern of theology. The theological shift gave the impression that Amaladoss can be pictured as an aging scholar from old India in the new India. However, when considering Amaladoss's twenty-first-century legacy, his work looks more relevant than ever. His theology is characterized by the presence of a revolutionary core. Despite his adamant support for the ideals of peace and harmony, he maintains that an ecclesial revolution is needed. This is partly what gives his prose its distinctive, bittersweet cadence: he can denounce the wrongs within the present without overstating his ability to correct them. But Amaladoss's vision of a truly Indian Christianity has nonetheless exposed a chasm between the real and the possible. His contemporary legatees must keep it open.

It should be clear at this point that colonialism is not, in Amaladoss's frame of reference, one phase of the history of the country and, as such, it lays, like any other moments in the millennial history of the country, in the

CONCLUSION   179

Indian collective consciousness. In the end, Amaladoss's legacy depends on the survival of the category of colonialism. In Amaladoss, Indianness does not stand on its own right but is related to colonialism. Amaladoss has decided to make colonialism not an element to be placed in history, but the evaluation criterion of history, arriving at a peculiar historical and theological understanding of Christianity in this postcolonial era. Postcolonialism is the time of the emancipation of Indian Christianity and of the efforts of Western Christianity to resist such emancipation. India is a subject in the process of emancipation in the double sense that Indian Christianity is emancipating itself (historical phenomenon) and emancipation is the characteristic trait of Indian Christianity (ontology, the thing in itself). The same can be said of the colonial West: Western Christianity resists the emancipation of India, and being colonial defines Western Christianity.

A shifting memory in India is underway. The current Indian leadership has spoken frequently of freeing Indians from the colonial mindset left by the British Empire and of removing the relics of that rule. In mobilizing the memory of a glorious past that precedes the eras of foreign invasions and domination, the Indian nationalist government offers a new reading of the recent and ancient histories of India. For example, Hindu nationalists perceive Nehru as a member of the Indian bourgeoisie that had inherited a British mindset and sought to turn India into a successor of Britain in South Asia, so that India could fill the vacuum left by a British exit from the region. One can disagree with this political use of the past but still cannot underestimate its impact on the wounded memory of India.[42] The nationalist leadership encourages optimism and faith that the golden age of India is yet to come—that the twenty-first century will be India's.[43] Time will tell whether this leadership can really insert the country into the realm of Asian major powers. The narrative, however, marks a shift away from recalling the past trauma of colonization to anticipating

---

42   According to V. D. Savarkar, "Hindutva is not a word but an history." See Vinayak Chaturvedi, *Hindutva and Violence: V. D. Savarkar and the Politics of History* (New York: State University of New York Press, 2022), 31.

43   See, for example, Aditya Mukherjee, *Imperialism, Nationalism and the Making of the Indian Capitalist Class 1920–1947* (New Delhi: Sage, 2002) and Ravinder Kaur, *Brand New Nation: Capitalist Dreams and Nationalist Designs in Twenty-First-Century India* (Redwood City, CA: Stanford University Press, 2020).

the imminent attempts to restore national greatness.[44] I do not claim that Indian Christianity will take its lead from nationalism; I am rather saying that time goes on. When India achieved independence, the history textbooks were rewritten, and the villains became the heroes, and the heroes became the villains. Now the history textbooks are rewritten again.[45] Every generation rethinks the past to align it to its interests; every age rewrites the past to make it suitable to the present. Historical truth is the output of intellectual and even political battle. These adjustments in remembrance demonstrate for Indian theologians that the past is not a mere encumbrance but a productive resource for change. Efforts for the decolonization of the Christian past are already in progress.[46]

Two conflicting processes are at work within Indian society these days. On one side, Hindu nationalism, with its emphasis on religious traits and differences, seems to preserve and confirm the crucial role that religion plays in Indian society. Against those who believe that Hindu nationalism is a deviation from Indian mainstream, it will soon become clear that Hindu nationalism belongs to the Indian mainstream. It is not a political force against the mainstream; it is a cultural diaspora within the mainstream. The first option creates the familiar image of an Indian culture that, in its main part, is overpowered by a political minority; it is a comforting image. The second option offers a more troubling image of a modernist movement that is both religious and secular: religious in its emphasis on religion as a discriminating principle within Indian society and secular in its materialistic

---

44   Mohamed Zeeshan, *Flying Blind: India's Quest for Global Leadership* (New York: Vintage, 2021).

45   I refer to the changes for syllabus rationalizing of the social science textbooks for grades six through twelve in India, occurred in India. Among the changes, one attracted my attention: a book asserts that the Mughal Emperor Akbar, who was the monarch when the Mughal Empire was at its zenith, "didn't win the Haldighati battle against Maharana Pratap" in 1576. The book maintains the "victory of the Mughal forces was not certified." See Seema Chisthi, "Rewriting India's History through School Textbooks," *New Lines Magazine*, March 9, 2023, https://tinyurl.com/5cm3xmdj.

46   Here I refer to the work of Clara Joseph that aims to connect Indian Christianity to its precolonial heritage. See Clara A. B. Joseph, *Christianity in India: The Anti-Colonial Turn* (New York: Routledge, 2020).

goals. On the other side, however, the construction of an affluent society makes religion irrelevant. In the present age of Hindu nationalism, religious pluralism seems no longer necessary to build an affluent society. The point can be extended: Hindu nationalism is neither a secular nor a religious movement; it is a secular religion. As such, it is uninterested in the marginalization of religion(s) but rather in the desacralization of it. Hindu nationalism is uninterested in denying the historical manifestations of religion(s), rather its supernatural foundations. In reframing the history and nature of Indian religions, Hindu nationalism works to replace the transcendental vision of religions with an immanent vision of reality. Indian theologians will be forced to reflect on this new context and particularly on the main question that emerges from it: the dissolution of the distinction between the temporal and the supernatural, that is, the secularization of the sacred. The relevant, theological questions are no longer those of injustice or integration but those involving the negative effects of materialism. As India and its leaders revisit the past, theologians correct and refocus their memory to align with present needs and concerns.

IN PLACE OF A CONCLUSION

Over a history spanning two millennia, Christianity has shown a remarkable ability to reform itself. Born as a near Middle East religious movement, it found its home in a Mediterranean empire. When the empire collapsed, the people from the North seemed to threaten the very survival of Christianity. What happened instead was that these people opened northern Europe to the gospel. Thus, in the fourteenth century, Christianity extended from Lisbon to Moskva, from the old lands of the Vikings to the borders of Islam. Then, globalization—with its alliance of state and Church—brought Christianity all over the globe. Sad as it may be, colonialism was instrumental in producing global Christianity.[47] Today, Christianity is experiencing one of these pivotal periods in its history. To an increasingly less Christian Europe corresponds an increasingly more Christian world. It is possible that we are witnessing the eclipse of the great synthesis

---

47   David Emil Mungello, *The Catholic Invasion of China: Remaking Chinese Christianity* (Lanham, MD: Rowman and Littlefield, 2015).

182 MICHAEL AMALADOSS AND THE QUEST FOR INDIAN THEOLOGY

of the Scripture and Hellenism, Jerusalem and Athens, so that the gospel is exculturated from Hellenism and inculturated in the great world cultures. It is also possible that the late Samuel P. Huntington was correct in suggesting that globalization will not be driven by the West, and, therefore, it will not produce a more accentuated westernization of the non-Western societies. The opposite, he argued, is true: "As their power and self-confidence increase, non-Western societies increasingly assert their own cultural values and reject those 'imposed' on them by the West."[48] One must think of the new reality of Asian nationalism and Chinese triumphalism rising and Western power in Asia declining. Although maintaining the traditional nonaligned stance, India is pursuing strategic autonomy through an increasing assertiveness in its international appearances, especially in its role as an emerging superpower.

Huntington was even more specific here: "Further modernization then alters the civilizational balance of power between the West and the nonwestern society and strengthens commitment to the indigenous culture."[49] Finally, it is also possible that Huntington was correct to distinguish the line between modernization and westernization so that non-Western societies can be modern in their own terms.[50] This book is not the place to confirm or reject these theses. I mention these theses not only for the obvious reason that they resurface in Amaladoss's theology but also because the legacy of his theology depends on these theses and on the emergence of a less westernized Christianity. What remains certain is that at the conclusion of this transformational age, hundreds of years in the future, Christianity will be there. From a theological point of view, in fact, Christians know that the witnesses of revelation will not disappear (Matt 16:18, *portae inferi non prevalebunt*). However, they also know that they will be defeated, because the victory belongs not to them but to Christ on His glorious return (Mark 13:26).

---

48   Samuel P. Huntington, *The Clash of Civilizations and the Remaking of World Order* (New York: Simon & Schuster, 1996), 21, 28.

49   Huntington, *Clash of Civilizations*, 76.

50   "Modernization is distinct from Westernization and is producing neither a universal civilization in any meaningful sense nor the Westernization of nonwestern societies." See Huntington, *Clash of Civilizations*, 3.

POST SCRIPTUM

EXCUSATIO

The scope of this post scriptum is to say what has been left unsaid in the main body of the book, that is, the underlying metatheological background of this study. *Metatheology* is the self-reflective inquiry into the nature and rules governing theology, its methods and styles, and the relationship among different streams of theology. More specifically, I address the Western-Indian divide in Catholic theology. This post scriptum is a short and necessary essay in normative metatheology, that is, reflection on theology that is not limited to the description of how theology is or has been, but that aims to suggest how it ought to be. Descriptive (i.e., what actually is) metatheory is important, no doubt, but in addressing the Western-Indian divide that is the underlying metatheological background of this study, normative (i.e., what it should be) metatheory helps explain why I see the theological divide as a problem. Here I dedicate more space to the Indian pole because this book is concerned with Indian theology. Furthermore, readers should forgive the excessive generalization of the sociological categories Western theologians and Indian theologians as well as the intellectual categories Western theology and Indian theology. I use these categories as proxies, not entities.

EXEGETICAL PROBLEM

I am the most improbable exegete of Michael Amaladoss. For starters, he is a priest; I am a layman. His reminiscences go back to an almost totally Hindu village in Tamil Nadu where his family was the only Christian presence. I carry memories of the last generation of Italian Tridentine priests who enthusiastically embraced the spirit of the Second Vatican Council in the sixties. He is part of the clerical world's closeness he tried to escape; I am a born-again Californian who enjoys a constant sense of freedom and easiness. He identifies himself first as a Tamil, then as an Indian: he has a strong sense of his roots. In fact, his work can be seen as a form of resistance against an outside attempt to strip him of his identity. As he told me, he needs to defend his identity from the "rest," or whatever is not Indian. I did not allow my birthplace to define my destiny. I ran away from my roots a long time ago, and now I borrow the label *cosmopolitan* as a cheap term for self-identification. He is an Indian who went temporarily abroad. I am an immigrant who permanently left his country of birth. He is monocultural; I am multicultural. Amal does not side with globalization; I am a self-conscious product of it. How can I get Father Amal right?

I am not an Indian theologian. This is, so to speak, a personal exegetical problem. I am not Indian. I do not theologize in India, that is, I do not write theology through the living encounter with the multidimensional, pluralistic reality of India, as Father Amal has done for most of his life. More importantly, I do not theologize like an Indian theologian; in fact, in my work I do not apply the hermeneutics of the experience, in which theology emerges from below. How can I successfully decode the thought of an author who celebrates Indianness if I am not Indian? How can I penetrate the thought of an Indian theologian who has spent his life objecting to the distorting effect that foreign modes of thinking have on Indian theology without making this work vulnerable to the same objection? Can a Western theologian like me get to the bottom of the thought of an Indian theologian such as Father Amal?

Western theologians might find the exegetical problem defined in the above terms difficult to take seriously. Theologians read de Lubac without being French, and they study von Balthasar without any concern for his Swiss passport. Italian theologians write and publish in the United States, and North American theologians discover the riches of the German theological tradition. Theologians happen to be French, Spanish, or Canadian and write and teach in French, Spanish, or English, but they consider themselves part of the same theological conversation. But this is exactly the objection that Indian theologians advance: "the same theological conversation," they protest, is another expression for "Western conversation." If Indian theology belongs to the conversation of Western theologians, it belongs in effect to a Western conversation, which is exactly the condition Indian theologians are trying to avoid. In India, or at least in the limited domain of the local Catholicism there, the problem for theologians is not to become part of a larger conversation already established by Western theologians but to find their autonomous voice. If I take Indian theologians at face value, Western theologians show a universalistic mentality, namely, Western modes of theologizing are the universal way to do theology. Therefore, my responsibility is to protect this book from being vulnerable to the same criticism.

It must be clear at this point that the exegetical problem I raise also has a more general extent. European traditions of theologies are not linked to a principle of national identity. Since the end of the Second World War, the three main European theologies—German, French, and Italian—have been characterized by a process of deterritorialization. Many young people are trained in foreign universities and institutions, and scholars entertain more and more frequently intense and continuous relationships with research centers in the world. The internationalization of scholarship, with the consequent inclination to study authors of languages and theological traditions different from their own, has fused these distinct traditions. There is no national and identity connotation in European theologies. The opposite is true in India. In fact, in the last three decades or so, a belief emerged in India that Indian theology is unconcerned with empathetic or sympathetic hermeneutics, but pathetic hermeneutics, namely, with a specific epistemological approach to, and a genuine firsthand experience of, Indian reality. Such a direct, unfiltered experience is both necessary and propaedeutic in order to perform Indian theology. Some theologians interpret this statement literally: Indian theology is theology of the Indians by the Indians for the Indians. For those who know their James Cone well, the statement resonates: only Black people can do Black theology; only Indian people can do Indian theology.[1] In other words, Indians and only Indians have the right to be the subject of their theology. Others are more open to consider the possibility that even if Indian theology remains primarily a field for Indian thinkers, others can contribute. The status of non-Indian theologians doing Indian theology is controversial, to say the least.

---

[1]   James Cone, *A Black Theology of Liberation* (Maryknoll, NY: Orbis, 1964).

Pathetic knowledge belongs to theologians who learned from their own social and living experience as Indian-born, their pastoral experience in the Church of India, and their educational path within Indian seminaries and institutions. Pathos is the primary hermeneutical key to Indian theology. This is theology from within that is produced by Indians. Empathetic knowledge is for those theologians who, although they are not Indian, can empathize with the Indian reality. This is the theological contribution to Indian theology of the expats. They leverage their subjective knowledge of India. They are Indian theologians in the sense that they are committed to the emergence of a truly Indian theology, a theology embedded in Indian context. India has produced an outstanding series of European theologians, scholars of religion, and spiritual authors who moved to South Asia and became so captivated with the local religiosity to embrace it without reservation; consider Monchanin, Abhishiktananda, Griffiths, Dupuis, Panikkar, Francis Acharya, Pierre Charles, SJ, Klaus K. Klostermaier, and George Gispert-Sauch, SJ. They are Western priests and monks who went to India and attempted to harmonize their Western minds with the experience in India. Some broke from their Western frames of thought to conform to the Indian way of life. Others remained firm in their Western mindset and missed the chance to align with Indian culture. Most were more interested in making Christianity more genuinely Indian than making India more authentically Christian. Some genuinely believed in the possibility of a true Indian theology. They composed brilliant, fascinating pieces of work, both theological and spiritual.

One name comes to mind because I had the fortune of knowing him personally: theologian and Indologist Father George Gispert-Sauch, SJ (1930–2020) was born in Catalonia and landed in India by age 19. Father Gispert's understanding of India was quite different from that of other European scholars who considered Hinduism a field of study. First, he became an authentic interpreter in postindependence India of Hinduism's ancient wisdom; then he confronted the marginalized soul of India. In his scholarly work, he moved beyond Hinduism's philosophical categories to reach the poor and their struggles. He came to see Hinduism not as a religion but as a pervasive culture in which Christians can live as a community in communion. In the same terms of Amaladoss and others, Father Gispert approached Hinduism as a civilizational matrix in which several religions have taken shape. Hinduism is a religion, a culture, a tradition of philosophy and theology, and it is a way of life. As a religion, it is an umbrella term that denotes the religions of the majority of people of India who refer to themselves as Hindus. Thus, Hinduism encompasses a range of religious beliefs and practices: for example, the householder and the renouncer are two distinct realms. As a culture, the term *Hindu* is used to denote the culture of the high-caste Brahmins in contrast to other cultures. Christianity was not generated in India, but a hinduized Indian culture nurtured Indian Christianity for centuries so that Christianity assumed a Hindu character. To borrow a phrase from Panikkar, "Most cultures have a certain trans-religious validity because they are not necessarily bound up with one particular religion."[2]

Finally, sympathetic knowledge is for theologians who, although they are not Indian, want to intellectually advance Indian Christianity.[3] These theologians have objective knowledge of Indian society and write about it. In this case, ethos is the hermeneutical key to Indian theology. Although empathetic and sympathetic knowledge may provide the right to participate in the Indian theological project, I am sure Indian theologians still advocate the primacy of pathetic knowledge, a firsthand, knowledge from experience of Indian pathos, or they at least maintain a three-layered hierarchy in their minds.

WESTERN-INDIAN THEOLOGICAL DIVIDE

The exegetical problem, that is, whether a Western theologian can proficiently interpret the work of an Indian theologian, arises from a growing distance between Indian and Western theologies. No literature exists about the Western-Indian theological divide. As far as I know, there is no canonical appraisal of the problem, so I feel compelled to specify what

---

2   Raimon Panikkar, *The Unknown Christ of Hinduism: Towards an Ecumenical Christophany* (Maryknoll, NY: Orbis, 1981), 41.

3   I borrowed the three modes of knowledge from Nirmal, although I made a few changes to adapt to the situation. See Nirmal, "Doing Theology from a Dalit Perspective," in *A Reader in Dalit Theology*, ed. Arvind P. Nirmal (Madras: Gurukul Lutheran Theological College & Research Institute, 1990), 142.

exactly the Western-Indian divide is meant to be. The distinction between Western and Indian theologies is a historiographical and metatheological distinction in the sense that it involves both history and culture. I have addressed the topic at length elsewhere.[4] Here I present a brief overview. The increasingly evident Western-Indian theological divide is twofold. On one hand, few Western theologians pay attention to the work of Indian theologians, or worse, they equal them en bloc to liberation theologians. It is rare to find in Western scholarly articles on Indian Christianity a list of references that shows a serious engagement with the nuances and variety of Indian theological positions. A few scholars, including this author, have engaged Panikkar and other Western expats in India, but they mostly interpret him according to Western categories of thought. On the other hand, Indian theologians pay little attention to the work of their Western colleagues. For example, Western scholars are responsible for much of the literature on Hindu-Christian dialogue and religious pluralism. They produce remarkable pieces of scholarship that are highly influential among their colleagues in the Western circuit, but their work does not necessarily fly in the same orbit with reference to Indian theologians. Of course, Indian theologians maintain that there is a place for textual analysis within the study of Indian religion and philosophy, but gone are the days when Western scholars can study Śaṅkara's commentary on the Brahma Sūtras and claim it is the royal way to penetrate the Hindu mindset.

Although Western theologians may take their tradition for granted as normative for theologians around the world, Indian theologians have reconceptualized and radically expanded the boundaries of their own theological tradition. Such theological tradition does not derive its inspiration from Western models but from abundant Indian religious and cultural resources. Theologians like Amaladoss pronounce valid only the theology that is placed in the context of the threefold dialogue with the cultures, the religions, and the poor of India and then measured against the social and theological concepts of justice. To paraphrase a statement from the FABC, a voluntary association of episcopal conferences in South, East, Southeast, and Central Asia, theology must become truly Indian in all

---

4   Enrico Beltramini, *Indian Theologians between Hinduism and Western Theologies* (forthcoming).

POST SCRIPTUM   189

aspects.[5] To become Indian, theology must inevitably become local, that is, deal with the domestic reality of the Indian people: the places they visit, the houses in which they live, the injustices they suffer, the culture they share, and their ways of life. Theology, however, becomes Indian not only because local religious, cultural, and social resources are accepted as material for theology, but more importantly because the theological logic and language are shaped by indigenous philosophy and culture. Thus, Indian theology means, by and large, a truly inculturated and embodied theology. Indian theology in India must be Indian.[6] Indian theology is Indian both in the sense that the social reality at the center of its investigation and the epistemological categories that infuse such an investigation are unique and intrinsically Indian. Indian theologians are developing a theological tradition to be able to express themselves in their own voices amid the ebb and flow of Indian contexts and in dialogue with other religions.

The word *tradition* (instead of trend or school) needs to be taken with caution. A tradition implies a series of canonical authors, a distinct mode of theologizing, a particular style of writing and studying authors, and a distinguished way of relating theology to culture and politics (*lato sensu*). Other considerations include a specific form of theological training and a conception of what theology is and ought to be. The Indian tradition is still a work in progress. Amaladoss believes that "although it is true that we do not have an Indian theology as a well-articulated system, I think that a framework is emerging. There are questions and reflections that are new. There are elements of method that are different."[7] Clearly, modern Indian theologians as a sociological group share certain methodological and epistemological assumptions regarding the manner of theologizing and preferential topics to address. For Indian theologians, to be Indian and to theologize in an Indian fashion in an Indian context is important, and one aim of this book is to explain why. Indian teachers, preachers, pastoral ministers, and theologians take to heart a mandate that Pope Paul

---

5   The original quote reads, "Asian Churches then must become truly Asian in all things." See *FAPA*, vol. 1, 72.

6   Once again, I paraphrase from the documents of the FABC. The original quote reads, "[His] Church in Asia must be Asian." See *FAPA*, vol. 1, 22.

7   Michael Amaladoss, "An Emerging Indian Theology," *VJTR* 58, no. 8 (1994): 473.

VI delivered to the FABC in April 1974. Pope Paul VI called the Church to make herself in her fullest expression native to the Asian countries, cultures, and races, and to "draw nourishment from the genuine values of the venerable religions and cultures."[8] The search for ways to make the Catholic Church more Asian and to theologize in an Asian way has since been the driving force behind the FABC's efforts to foster solidarity.

The instinct in the West is to make the world more Christian; in India, instead, it is to make Christianity more Asian. For both Western and Indian theologians, the context is a resource and a starting point for theological reflection. But for the former, Christian sources—i.e., Scripture and Tradition—are used to shed light on the signs of the times, but for the latter, the signs of the times shape the interpretation of Scripture and Tradition.[9] As long as it embodies and manifests the presence and action of God and His spirit, the context opens to Indian theologians additional hermeneutical opportunities regarding the interpretation of Scripture and tradition.[10] To better position the notion of hearing the Spirit at work in the realities of Asia through cultural and religious resources and a call to read the Scriptures in solidarity with all who lack peace, I borrow a line from an official document issued after a consultation among bishops, Bible scholars, and pastoral workers drawn from different parts of Asia-Oceania: "This calls for a contextual reading of the Christian scriptures done with sensitivity to the Spirit who whispers in mysterious and unbounded way, through the rich cultural and religious resources of Asia."[11] The Church

---

8   Pope Paul VI, "Address to the First General Assembly of the Federation of Asian Bishops' Conference" (Rome, April 20, 1974).

9   To place these features of Indian theologizing in the much wider Asian context, see *FAPA*, vol. 3, 355–64; Peter C. Phan, "Current Trends and Future Tasks of Christian Theology of Asia: In Celebration of the 50th Anniversary of the Foundation of the FABC," *Jnanadeepa: Pune Journal of Religious Studies* 21, no. 4 (2021): 11.

10   See *FAPA*, vol. 3, 356: "Context, or contextual realities, are considered resources of theology (*loci theologici*) together with the Christian sources of Scripture and Tradition. Contextual realities become resources of theology insofar as they embody and manifest the presence and action of God and his Spirit. This is recognized through discernment and interpretation. It calls for theological criteria to recognize and assess the loci."

11   *FAPA: Federation of Asian Bishops' Conferences Documents from 2002–2006*, vol. 4, ed. Franz-Josef Eilers (Quezon City: Claretian, 2007), 269.

pays attention to the signs of the times and discerns the truths of the Scripture through the inspirations and whispers of the Holy Spirit.

A theological divide implies two distinct traditions. I can provide a few examples: authors such as Augustine, Thomas Aquinas, and Karl Rahner belong to the Western canon but can be ignored by Indian theologians; recall when Amaladoss stated, "We are convinced that no serious Indian (Asian) theology will emerge as long as we are tied to the apron strings of a Euro-American system." Rayan, Kappen, and Felix Wilfred belong to the Indian canon and can be ignored by Western theologians. References to science, technology, or secularism are standard in Western works but are irrelevant for Indian works, and references to the social transformation or to the pluralistic cultural and religious context gives typical premises to Indian arguments but are hardly mentioned in Western texts. Western theologians generally address their academic colleagues, as all scholars do, but Indian theologians have the Church and ecclesiastic matters as their primary audience, with scholarly readers on occasion. Western theologians generally prefer to dialogue with either Western theology or patristics, generally ignoring or underrating the notion of theology coming out of the encounter with the social reality, which is typical of Indian theologians. Western theologians receive their theological education mostly from Catholic or secular universities, but seminaries are the primary source of theological education in India. A conception of theology as speculation in the West is marked by the ideals of clarity, rigor, and argumentation, but in India, theologians embrace a conception of theology as a social enterprise committed to social improvement.

Telluric movements of epochal magnitude together with a certain tendency of the Church toward decentralization show a clear and unquestionable tendency to make the divide more prominent. A sort of duplication of the theological domain is emerging, as if Catholic theology is divided into two traditions, one in the West and one in India (or Asia). If someone wants to know something about a theological problem, and if one wants to gain exhaustive information about it, one must refer to two bibliographical repertories. The distance between Indian and Western theologies is a sign of an advancing effort to emancipate Indian theologians from Western modes of theologizing. The push belongs to a larger theological attempt of Asian Catholicism to incarnate and inculturate the gospel in the very reality of Asia. This attempt, fully legitimized by the documents of the Church's Magisterium—for example, the important guidelines in Pope John Paul II's postsynodal exhortation *Ecclesia in Asia*—and the contribution of the Asian bishops. It includes the work of theologians, social workers, priests and nuns, members of religious orders, and the laity and is instrumental in building a shared and accepted Catholicism with an Asian face, that is, an Asian Church with specific Asian values and an Asian worldview. Their efforts resemble the efforts of European theologians before and after the Council to adapt the Christian message to a secular, modern society.

EPISTEMIC FRAMEWORKS

Besides being an interesting phenomenon of historical and sociocultural relevance, the mentioned theological divide implies an epistemological problem: the growing distance between Indian and Western theologies raises the problem of incommensurability. Clearly, one can object that there are no such things as Western and Indian theologies; there are only theologies done by Indians in India in Indian modes and theologies done by Westerners in the West in Western modes. But in framing Western and Indian modes of Catholic theology on a trajectory to become reciprocally estranged rather than mutually enriching, one detects the epistemic problem. In the words of Helle, the distance "would perhaps render Asian or Western theology non-available for students or scholars outside of these geographical borders."[12] This brings me back to my original question: can a Western theologian proficiently study an Indian theologian? Or, is a theologian whose intellectual and cultural categories have been shaped in a non-Indian context a competent and reliable judge of an Indian theologian? If the West and India are conceived in terms of two distinct theological poles, one must be aware of the epistemic obstacles a Western theologian faces in penetrating and unveiling the movements of an Indian theological mind.

Clearly, nobody disputes the legitimacy of both Indian and Western theologians to reflect on all things Indian. The work of Western religious

---

12   Helle, *Towards a Truly Catholic*, 84, 54.

scholars, theologians, historians of Christianity, sociologists, and experts of interreligious dialogue can make useful contributions to compensate for the deficiencies of an approach that is focused merely on native issues. One might envision not one but two epistemological stances: one favors a form of methodological nationalism and the other adopts a transnational approach to Indian theology.[13] Indian theologians undoubtedly produce Indian theology. The claims made by Indian theologians are part of the social and psychological fabric of Christian communities that have given them life and that have had, and still have, profound personal significance for people within them. But Indian theology is not only the result of the work of Indian theologians. Indian theology is not purely the self-understanding of Indian theologians within the narrowed terms of theology of India for India by Indians, but it is also the construction of non-Indian theologians attempting to make sense of the reality of India, including the plurality of Indian religious phenomena. One can detect in Indian theology not one but two distinct intellectual streams: on one hand, an autonomist orientation that identifies Indian theology as rooted in the experience of India, and on the other, an effort that is not in terms of opposition but of complement and enhancement toward the construction of a Western theological reflection of India.

Two streams of Indian theology—one constructed with Indian resources and the other with Western materials—ultimately constitute Indian theology. An enormous potentiality exists within the realm of Indian theology if it reckons with the entirety of the scholars, geographies, and histories that it comprises. The advantage in formulating the theological reflection in broadly national (or local) and transnational (or global) terms is that each approach complements and corrects the epistemological limits of the other. An epistemic framework predetermines certain master narratives for theologically engaging India and defines the boundaries of what is theologically relevant. If this epistemic framework is designed

---

13   Andreas Wimmer and Nina Glick Schiller, "Methodological Nationalism and Beyond: Nation-State Building, Migration and the Social Sciences," *Global Networks* 2, no. 4 (2002): 301–34; Andreas Wimmer and Nina Glick Schiller, "Methodological Nationalism, the Social Sciences, and the Study of Migration: An Essay in Historical Epistemology," *The International Migration Review* 37, no. 2 (2003): 576–610.

according to national concerns and resources, it becomes the axiomatic knowledge that protects a certain idea of India; to this end, it tacitly directs and informs the work of theologians in a way that secures the reproduction of determined tropes and approaches in theology to ultimately solidify a national canon.[14] The framing of Indian theology as rooted in a particular, historic, and above all, social demarcation, construed in terms of a biologically existing people occupying a certain space and, over time, developing norms of engagement, implies the risk that this theology assumes the form of a national theology, a risk that Amaladoss himself explicitly refuses. This is the potential benefit of a transactional Indian theology in the sense that it is directed precisely toward opening this entrenched epistemic frame of Indian theology to Western academic contributions.

To put this in more general terms, India and Indian theology can be considered not just as objects of study but also epistemic frameworks, namely epistemic knowledge regimes that may be consciously held and explicitly elaborated into historical-theological and social-cultural projects, projects of social change and critiques to power. Indian theologians have constructed an epistemic framework that governs ways of knowing India and doing Indian theology, deciding what is worth knowing and what is acceptable practice in their given communities. As a framework that in a specific way governs how India is to be approached and theologically engaged, it carries the social representations and the symbolic codes that position Indian theology in, and connect it to, a specific social-historical *time-space*—a defined society marked by assumed characters and values. As knowledge-producing professionals, Indian theologians are responsible for constructing India and Indian theology as frameworks both for their own community and for those outside it. At the same time, they must prepare for continuous confrontations with the construction of these frameworks through engagement with Indian academics in their own or other fields, social activists and politicians

---

14 I recognize my debt to Andy Byford for the concept of "epistemic framework." Professor Byford has used the concept in numerous articles, most recently in "Russia as an Epistemic Frame," *Ad Imperio* 23, no. 1 (2022): 73–84. I use the concept in a slightly different way: he used the terms in the sense of tacit framework, and I use them in reference to an explicit framework.

who might be claiming India as "theirs," Asian intellectuals and specialists, and Western clerical and lay individuals. To paraphrase a line from Andy Byford, if India and more specifically Indian theology are to be understood as epistemic constructs, then transnationalizing Indian theology is itself an epistemic project—an interrogation and deconstruction of epistemic boundary work involved in constructions of India and Indian theology.[15]

The option that two streams of Indian theology constitute Indian theology—one constructed with Indian materials and the other with Western resources—is particularly useful if one looks more deeply into the Indian context in which theologians work and their relationship with both Western theology and universal doctrine. Of course, every generalization fails to recognize the ample variety of situations, orientations, and degrees at work in the phenomenon under investigation. This is true in this analysis of the current Indian theological landscape. On one side, there are the Western-trained scholars who recognize themselves in the traditional ecclesiastical and theological frameworks and teach theology in theological seminaries in Western fashion. On the other side are the scholars who believe that academic life is lethargic and meaningless if it is not combined with a committed ministry for a radical change that happens in the concrete flux of human history. The former reads the Indian context through the biblical and theological lens; the latter reads the Scripture through the prism of the Indian context. In the middle, between the two sides of the conservative and radical theologians, are the theologians who express some degree of criticism against Western institutions and frameworks but are animated by a spirit of compromise and complement. The few theologians who teach permanently or temporally in Western institutions fall disproportionally into the three camps.

Although divided along political lines, all theologians share the same life of service and sacrifice. Almost all are part of the clergy. Most theologians serve as instructors in seminaries, but others are asked to take administrative roles in those seminaries and other educational institutions. When

---

15 Andy Byford, Connor Doak, and Stephen Hutchings, "Introduction: Transnationalizing Russian Studies," in *Transnational Russian Studies* (Liverpool: Liverpool University Press, 2019), 10.

free from these appointments, their main concern is to provide parishes and communities with some theological sustenance and training. Most of the Christian parishes deal with the poor, marginalized, and underdeveloped, and the theological concerns are focused on basic questions of social justice. In the words of P. R. John, theologians "face a lot of questions when confronted with the negatives of life. . . . If faith exists only in the life of celebration, then the question [what does faith seek to understand] is pointless."[16] Thus, Indian theologians are called to understand the depths of pain and the torments of injustice. They serve by offering healing and promoting change; they raise their voices to protest, contest, and syntonize the message of the gospel to the reality of desperation and frustration of many. The time and urgency for metaphysical reflection, so to speak, are uncommon.

It is important to distinguish the correspondence between Indian theologians and the universal Church and her Magisterium on one hand, and on the other, the correspondence between Indian theologians and Western theologians. Only the second association is the subject of this post scriptum. The first association belongs to the much broader discourse about the supposed priority of the universal over the local dimension of the Church for contemporary Catholic theology. The dependence of the local Indian Church on the universal Church has implications for both its institutional structure—worship, theology, Western-trained leadership—and its economic survival.[17] Although dioceses from the United States, Italy, and Germany, among others, contribute with donations to the financial needs of the universal Church, India is among the Asian dioceses that have received financial support from the universal Church. Lazar captured the situation with frank and synthetic words: "The Catholic Church in India is still dependent on Rome or on the generosity of the rich dioceses in Europe or from the USA, not only for spiritual and administrative guidance but also for economic subsidies. Since there is no proper economic security for the local church the entire business of generating income and

---

16   Pudota Rayappa John, "Towards Indian Christology," in *Seeking New Horizons: Festschrift in Honour of Dr. M. Amaladoss, S. J.*, ed. Leonard Fernando (Delhi: Vidyajyoti Education and Welfare Society & ISPCK, 2002), 55.

17   *FAPA*, vol. I, 337.

maintaining rests on the local bishop."[18] It is no surprise that in such a situation, power is very much centralized with the bishops at the top of the pyramid of the ecclesiastical structure, and the most radical voices are restrained. To borrow a phrase from another theologian who shall remain anonymous, "Rome treats us as a Third World Church. She uses the money she sends to finance the local churches as a means to exercise control." This relationship between the local and the universal, or between Indian theologians and the teaching of the Church as articulated by the Magisterium, also refers to the divergences around worship and theology. Regardless of the call for inculturation, Indian Christianity is still an importer of cultural and intellectual frameworks and conserves the liturgical forms and the ecclesiastical structures of the Latin Church. Despite the commitment to take Asian religions and cultures seriously and develop "an indigenous theology . . . so that the life and message of the Gospel may be ever more incarnate in the rich historic cultures of Asia," Indian theologians are still forced to rely on what they see as European ways of theologizing to access the gospel.[19]

The second association refers to Western and Indian Catholicism seen in terms of relationship among local theologies in the universal Church. I have studied the gap between European and Indian modes of theologizing in India at length in another book, and I can be brief here. The conversation between Western and South Asian modes of Catholic theology has been historically monodirectional. In the first half of the twentieth century, Indian theological reflection was a pure and simple application of European forms and theories of theology to the local context. In the decades immediately before and after the Second Vatican Council, however, an attempt was made to reciprocally influence both European and Indian modes of theologizing. The attempt was based on the parallel roles of Christian and Hindu sources of revelation. A double hermeneutical circle between the sources of Christianity and those of Hinduism would stimulate the Christianization of India and the Indianization of European Christianity. This bidirectional approach flourished in India for some time; on one hand, it allowed the contemporary birth of an Indian theology

---

18   Lazar, "Five Years of Pope Francis," 5.

19   *FAPA*, vol. 1, 9.

linked with patristic roots, and on the other, the renewal of the European theology fruitfully contaminated with Asian contributions. Probably the best example of this approach is Panikkar's work. Starting in the eighties, however, a different approach gained traction among Indian theologians, no longer based on engagement with the classical tradition of texts (patristics, Vedas) but with the living tradition of the people of India and their pacific coexistence with the different religions, cultures, languages, and customs that populate South Asia. The adoption of life (or context) as the primary access to Tradition has empowered Indian theologians but it has also diminished the link between Indian and Western theologies. In turn, Western theologians show limited interest in Indian theology. The result is mutual estrangement.

This mutual estrangement takes different forms. I already mentioned two of them in passing; now it is time to elaborate. The first form can be framed as follows: although the relationship between Western and Indian modes of theology is, in effect, a relationship between local dimensions, Western theologians often behave as if their mode encompasses the whole universal Church. The Church has her own universal doctrine and culture, and it is helpful to not equate the universal with the local.[20] The problem is that Western theologians have a general tendency to privilege the universal over the local. They frequently identify the universal with the Western, that is, they believe that the Western practices of abstraction support their effort to universalize their theological tradition. To put it differently, sometimes Western theologians identify their theology, rooted in patristics and developed in dialogue with continental philosophy, with theology tout court. This way of thinking may lead to an understanding in which Western theology is identified as mainstream and Indian theology as peripheral. This understanding implies that Western theologians master a universal language that can marginalize the place of the local in theology and sever the association between thought and concrete modes of life. Indian theologian Felix Wilfred has discussed at length the "tendency and claim" of Western theologians "to present a single universal picture of Jesus."[21] A case

---

20   Pope Benedict XVI, "Regensburg Address."

21   Felix Wilfred, "Jesus-Interpretations in Asia: Fragmentary Reflections on Fragments," *East Asian Pastoral Review* 43, no. 4 (2006).

in point might be this book: the adoption of Western modes of theologizing allows the author to penetrate the movements of thought of an Indian theologian because, in the end, Western modes are universal.

The second form refers to the object of the Indian theologians' criticisms. The Western audience can easily misunderstand those criticisms against Western theology as referring to Catholic lay-academic theology, but often, they refer to clerical-institutional theology instead. A different valuation of both lay-academic theology and clerical-institutional theology is at stake. In the West, academic theologians believe they are influential. This has always been true in the Protestant world. When it comes to Catholicism, however, it is quite another matter. For a long time, academic theology has not been exactly the place to be if one wants to leave a mark on Catholic theology. This realm, dominated by lay theologians, has played a secondary role in the articulation of Catholic theology. It was an established tradition in Catholicism that theology is a realm of priests and members of the religious orders. It is, in other words, a clerical business pursued in seminaries and houses of study. Without looking back at Augustine and Thomas Aquinas, it is sufficient to say that the pantheon of twentieth-century theologians is filled with priests. Catholic theology was dominated by clerical theologians who taught at the pontifical universities and seminaries and spoke with authority to the hierarchy, even when they displeased the hierarchy. They were perceived as legitimate players because they are priests and were ultimately subject to clerical command and control. This likely had something to do with the evangelical imperative that no one can serve two masters (Luke 16:13; Matt 6:24): devotion to the Church hierarchy and faithfulness to scholarly craft.

Things, however, have changed in the West: as mentioned, the faculties of the departments of theology and religious studies have replaced those of the seminary as the decisive producer of theological content. Men and women, and eventually married people who are not ordained but nevertheless have been trained as theologians, are taking elevated roles within the hierarchy. Lay theologians who are practicing members of the Church and conserving an ecclesial commitment offer a lay reflection on theological subjects that matter to the Church and society at large. They play an unofficial role in the Church and are recognized as such. All things considered, Catholic theology as a product of lay people is growing and is more relevant to the world of the celibate clergy. This is different in India, where most theologians belong to the clergy, and religious education is delegated to private religious organizations. Consequently, most of the theological work is done in seminaries.

POLITICS OF IDENTITY

Theoretically, nobody contests the idea that both Indians and non-Indians contribute to the discipline of Indian theology. However, I suspect this generic declaration of intent is of no help in getting to the bottom of the problem. More precisely, the problem is that at a practical level, the two streams seem to resist intersection. Western theologians tend to privilege theology framed in universal, abstract, and ultimately Western categories of thought; Indian theologians maintain that language is contextually and historically contingent. Western scholars carry on ways of thinking and doing theology that Indian theologians believe are foreign approaches to theology and, as such, incompatible with an articulation of the Indian face of Christ. The expression stands for a theological style rooted in the cultural, religious, and social context of India.[22] Once that context is elevated to be the proper *loci theologici*, the work of Western scholars is perceived as alienated from the salient contextual realities of India and fails to enter into dialogue with that of their Indian counterparts.[23]

To put it another way: nobody refuses the idea of a complementarity between Indian and Western theologians when it comes to reflecting theologically on India. Together, Western theologians—who maintain not only a scholarly interest but a sincere, deep affection for the South Asian people and history—and Indian theologians can play different roles: the former like outside observers, and the latter like inside participants. Moreover, the theological work of Indian scholars and that of Western scholars reflects different aims, modes, and audiences. In practice, however, Western

---

22   In 2004, the Office of Theological Concerns arranged a colloquium on "the Asian Faces of Christ." In the FABC's theology, the Asian faces of Jesus are rooted in the Asian cultural, religious, and social context. See *FAPA,* vol. 4, 287.

23   The comment on the *loci theologici* is borrowed from Helle, *Towards a Truly Catholic,* 91.

theologians are perceived by their Indian counterparts as vehicles for a style of theology that is inadequate for, and incompatible with, Indian contexts. It is a style of theology that is considered to persist with a sense of foreignness to the Christian faith in India and to confirm the feeling generally held in India that Christianity is a religion of Westerners. In fact, those familiar with the current Indian theological landscape know that the theologians more praised by Western theologians for their work in Hindu-Christian dialogue are practically ignored by their Indian colleagues. Monchanin, Abhishiktananda, and Panikkar, who are the object of a cottage industry of spiritual and theological studies in the West, are almost forgotten in India because they failed in their writings to comply with the fundamental criteria of the current Indian theologizing: the removal of the Western mediation. Panikkar's colleagues in India do not necessarily consider him an Indian theologian, as he never permanently settled in South Asia and instead became famous for his prestigious appointments at North American universities. Panikkar has been considered, so to speak, not Indian enough. Most of the theological work of Indian theologians in last decades is built on assumptions of the dominance of Western constructions of theology, the marginality of Indian constructions, and the imperative of a rebalancing between the two. Indian theologians are involved in the effort to reformulate theologies free from their dependency on theological categories designed by the West.

At the core of the formulation of Indian theology as theology in India, of India, and for India, is a distinct politics of identity. With the word *identity*, I mean a specific articulation of the relationship between being Indian and being Catholic. The articulation refers to the struggle Indian Christians face when remaining true to Indian culture and way of life while conforming to a frame of thought that they perceive as foreign and alienating. The problem can be seen as an organic by-product of the historical formation and diffusion of theological development in Catholicism, in which knowledge moves from Europe to India and not the other way around. The problem in the constitution of Christian India is a social-cultural construct, but it is also a fixed and persistent form of consciousness. The double-consciousness figure manifests a certain tension between an innate orientation for the Indian world and a theoretical mindset grounded in a Western system of thought. Although a sociocultural construct, it is consciousness that fails to merge its double self into a better and truer self. It is a peculiar sensation, this double consciousness, this sense of always looking at oneself through the eyes of others. It is no surprise that Indian theologians respond to this sensation by doing the very thing that placed them at risk of isolating themselves from Western theology: striving for full recognition of Indian freedom, humanity, and equality.

With the word *politics*, I signify the adoption of a method of theological thinking that uses political concepts to identify the place of Indian theologians within Catholicism. In brief, politics stands for the framing of the difference between Indian and Western theologies in political terms. In India, Western influences are not only dismissed; they are also criticized. In other words, Indian theologians hold a theological bias against the influences of the theological West. Indian theology must be different from its Western counterparts in order to escape, as described by the FABC, "the trappings of Western culture and signs of the colonial era."[24] Frequently found in the comments of Indian theologians is a certain degree of reticence toward Christian history as it has unfolded in India. Here the question is no longer about the foreignness of Christianity, but rather its historical alliance with European colonialism in India. The colonial origins of the Catholic Church of India lay a heavy burden not only on the Christian faith but also on Christian theology. Father Samuel Rayan, a dominant figure in the postindependence Indian theological landscape, wrote insightful lines about the imperative of a decolonization of Indian theology.[25] Although Western theologians may think of themselves as universalists, in Father Rayan's opinion, their intellectual production can more correctly be framed as "ethnocentric and culture-bound, and not universalist as it has been claiming to be." Western theology "has been a handmaid of Western expansionism, and an ally, however unwilling, of the exploitation of other continents by

---

24   OTC, "On Being Human in the Changing Realities in Asia," *FABC Papers* 133 (2011): 44.

25   Samuel Rayan, "Decolonization of Theology," *Jnanadeepa: Pune Journal of Religious Studies* 1, no. 2 (1988): 140–55. For a comprehensive understanding of Rayan's theological thought, see Nicholas Tharsiuse, *Christian Faith: A Liberation Praxis: Theology of Samuel Rayan* (Delhi: ISPCK, 2015).

POST SCRIPTUM   203

Europe and America."[26] Western theologians are inherently colonialist, although they may not recognize it.

Father Rayan was a priest, a Jesuit, and a liberation theologian. His writings do not represent the entire constellation of positions, sensibilities, and styles present in Indian theology. For example, in the documents of the FABC, the heritage of colonialism is mentioned as responsible for the foreignness of Christianity in Asia; the responsibility, however, is not extended to theologians. Amaladoss was unafraid to call the influence of Western hermeneutical strategies in Indian theology a "Western imposition." However, he concluded that Indian theologians need to resist the "imposition," not reject it. But Father Rayan was a highly respected theologian, and his statements carried weight.[27] "Decolonization needs decolonizing," he claimed, then added, "We have little or no knowledge of colonists withdrawing except when thrown out."[28] What Father Rayan meant by the first statement is that decolonization will be matched with wrangle; therefore, embarking on a decolonization project is, for an Indian theologian, like enlisting in the military. The opposition to Western theologies is instrumental in the attempt to create a truly Indian theology: the defeat of the colonial influence on Indian theology makes room to search for ways to create indigenous modes of theologizing. In Father Rayan's writings, words are bullets. When fired on Western theologians, those words can obviously do harm. He was unafraid to depict the current generation of Western theologians, whether consciously or not, as imperialists at heart.

Politics of identity is a distinct formulation of Indian theology that marks its difference from Western theology in political terms for sense of identity. Indian theology is not simply a scholarly field: it is also a matter of authority and of positioning. It refers to how the theological meaning of images and depictions in the specific context of India is established and controlled. Consequently, Indian theology is theological reflection, struggle for authority, and right of positioning, that is, to see India in a certain way. It would certainly be incorrect to interpret the attempts to create a truly

---

26   Rayan, "Decolonization of Theology," 145.

27   Felix Wilfred, "Obituary—Samuel Rayan, SJ (1920–2019)," *Mission Studies* 36, no. 2 (2019): 187–89.

28   Rayan, "Decolonization of Theology," 140.

Indian theology merely as opposition to the hegemonic theologies of the West, but certainly the India-West relationship plays a crucial role in such attempts. Amaladoss frames the problem in simple terms: "I have to defend my identity against the rest." It seems that part of the identity of Indian theologians depends on the relationship with the rest, mainly the West, and is thus the result of a category of difference. If so, the heart of the matter is the Indian theologians' perception of an identity, which is the result of a category of difference designed by the West.[29] The crux of the matter is who controls, between Western and Indian theologians, the category of difference. The gap between the aspiration of a truly Indian theology and the reality of intellectual dependency has been framed in the problematic terms of being genuinely Indian and authentically Catholic.[30] Only a category of difference between Western and Indian theology designed by Indians would liberate them from their dependence on a view of India built by Westerners. It is through the control of the category of difference that the narrative can be turned around, namely, Indians become the subject and Westerners become the object of the narrative. It is through this operation that Indian theologians would be free to build their own theological realm and remove it from Western vestiges.

In conclusion, who is an Indian theologian? Who is a Western theologian? What is the link between culture and location, and how do the considerations of culture and location impact the construction of the self and its other(s)? The category of Western theology has played a crucial role in the Indian theological imagination. It has operated as a specific marker of difference from what is considered to be the essence of Indian theology; not surprisingly, it has become a constitutive aspect of the modern Indian theological self. It should be clear at this point that Indianness is not a peripheral attribute when it comes to study or a fortiori to engage Indian theologically. Indianness is the prior criterion for recognizing and assessing the authenticity and credibility of a piece of theological work in and about India. *Indianness* is a term that stands for true Indianness as well as

---

29   Ruben Mendoza, "A Church in Dialogue with Peoples of Other Faiths: A Journey to the Kingdom in the Spirit: The Federation of Asian Bishops' Conferences, 1970–2007" (PhD diss: Catholic University of Louvain, 2008), 10.

30   Helle, *Towards a Truly Catholic*, 3.

the rejection of colonialism in its multiplicity of forms: historical, ecclesial, ecclesiastical, dogmatic, and, of course, epistemological. Indianness is the marker of a difference that embraces politically engaged theology to critique the West and its colonialist orientation.[31]

INTRA-CATHOLIC THEOLOGICAL DIALOGUE

The question addressed in this post scriptum is an exegetical problem that has a personal, but most importantly, an epistemological and ultimately a political dimension. The problem is rooted in the present status of estrangement (for Western theologians) and at times conflicting (for Indian theologians) relationship between Western and Indian modes of theology in Catholicism. I previously mentioned that for Father Amal, no serious Indian theology will emerge as long as Indian theologians are in dialogue with the Euro-American system. It is a bold statement and deserves attention: Father Amal longs for the construction of an alternative (to the Western) theological, cultural, and ecclesial pole of reference. In this study, I took certain pains to justify the existential and intellectual motives of this statement. It raises the question whether the construction of Indian theology indeed requires opposition rather than dialogue with Western theology. It is time to say that I disagree with Father Amal: instead of pursuing a mutual estrangement, or worse, a bipolar, confrontational relationship between West and East, Western and Indian theologians should mutually fertilize each other. Of course, the statement must be extended to each and every local theology: all local theologies benefit from mutual enrichment.

The present status of estrangement and even conflict between Western and Indian modes of theology in Catholicism has created the need for some metatheological reflection on the future of the relationship among local theologies in world Catholicism of the twenty-first century. Surely it means neither the coexistence of a variety of national theologies nor a unique standard universal theology; it can only mean having local theologies in dialogue to mutually complement and enhance one another. The Church is a communion. In the specific case of India, a distinct

---

31   On Indianness, see Paul M. Collins, *Context, Culture and Worship: The Quest for "Indian-ness"* (Delhi: ISPCK, 2006).

intra-Catholic dialogue between Western and Indian theologies would amend the reciprocal estrangement and fuel mutual enrichment. A proper dialogue would bridge the distance between the two theological traditions and make one intelligible to the other. It would also dismiss both universalist temptations on one hand, and on the other, the option of a self-contained, autonomous local theology. Each and every local theology is complementary. I label this option "intra-Catholic dialogue" with Panikkar in mind.[32] An intra-Catholic dialogue in theology is a two-faceted process in which there are both encroachment and opening to the globe as well as collocation and localization. When Indian theology lands in European and North American departments, the thought of Indian authors is reworked and reframed within a Western horizon. However, this reframing produces feedback and challenges Indian authors to rethink their assumptions. An original and autonomous reception of some important European authors could only benefit Indian theologians.

A critic of the West, Amaladoss looks at a bipolar Christian order against the illusions of the universalist Christianity. He reminds his readers that the Christian world is a pluriverse, not a universe. If so, some reflections on the relationship between the different universes of Christianity is necessary. The dialogue between East and West has been going on for three thousand years and has influenced both regions. In the words of Goethe, "East and West cannot be separated."[33] The same orientalism that has been so significantly criticized is not only the expression of Western imperial power but also of admiration for civilizations from which the West has learned and still learns.[34] Indian scholars have investigated the ambivalence of the European-Indian relationship in several disciplines. The historian Gyan Prakash has explored such an ambivalence in his book on science. Science, he has argued, was

---

32   Panikkar suggested the term "dia-topical hermeneutics" to deal with the challenge of interpreting across traditions (*dia-topoi* meaning literally "across places") that do not share a common cultural or religious worldview. In this case I refer to the cultural worldview. See Raimon Panikkar, *Myth, Faith and Hermeneutics* (New York: Paulist, 1979), 9.

33   See John James Clarke, *Oriental Enlightenment: The Encounter Between Asian and Western Thought* (New York: Routledge, 1997), 3.

34   Clarke, *Oriental Enlightenment.*

POST SCRIPTUM   207

instrumental for the construction of a colonized India and, simultaneously, of an indigenous nationalist elite that fought for independence.[35] Here I offer an example of such ambivalence: Indian theologians' use of social theory.

Although all theologies are contextual, not all contextual theologies are the same. Contextual theologies could be those of the Western Churches dealing with the hypersecularization of affluent societies or those of the minority Churches of Asia that exist in religious and cultural pluralistic societies. Indian theologies are contextual not only in the sense that they focus on the concrete, circumstantial experience of the people of India but also that that experience is neither merely spiritual nor purely materialistic, but rather simultaneously spiritual and materialistic. Here the idea is to move beyond a narrow view of the discipline of hermeneutics, which is limited to written (biblical and nonbiblical) texts, to include the interpretation of social phenomena such as economy and politics. A true Indian theology emerges when indigenous theologians dismiss the hermeneutics that homologates them and find new meanings for their intellectual search. In other words, an authentic Indian theology emerges when Indian theologians are free to define themselves in their context. In fact, in India, social realities are considered more important than doctrinal reasoning and religious belonging; therefore, it is not philosophy but social theory that informs theology. The interdependence arises because social theory is a Western—more specifically, French—theory. Directly or indirectly imported to India, social theory is a European discipline that brings all the conjectures and limits of the European way of thinking. It is ironic that Indian authors use the academic tools of the Western scholarly tradition for the very purpose of developing an Indian theological style that is inherently distinct from the Western one. The truth is that a pure Indian context does not exist, and, therefore, a pure Indian theology cannot exist, nor can a pure French theology or a pure German theology. All theologies arise at the expense of sacrificing purity. Against any separation between the West and the East, as if they were different worlds with no mutual interdependence, Father

---

35   Gyan Prakash, *Another Reason: Science and the Imagination of Modern India* (Princeton: Princeton University Press, 1999).

Saju Chackalackal, CMI, pointed out a few years ago that no Christianity is an island.[36]

It is imperative that both sides endeavor to de-essentialize, that is, to historicize the West-East theological relationship. I offer an example on the Indian side: the persistent reference to colonialism. Theologians in Europe are working from the heritage of the theologies that created the reality of Christendom they want to leave behind. Somehow, a similar statement can be made for the theologians in Latin America, who did not directly experience Christendom but instead the colonial brutality of Catholic empires. In Latin America, the altar and the throne worked together against natives. Indian theologians who emulate Latin American theologians forget that India has neither been part of Christendom, the Christian civilization of medieval Europe, nor of a Catholic empire. The British Empire was not Catholic. Indian theologians can obviously protest the authoritarian organization of the Catholic Church; they can contest as Indians the heritage of the colonial era. But they cannot put the words *colonial* and *Church* in the same statement. They cannot speak of Christendom in India because, with the temporary and limited exception of the Portuguese and the French colonies, no alliance between altar and throne has been seen in India. The British Raj responded to the queen and the Catholics to the pontiff, and the two were not friends. Indian Christianity may be built on an authoritarian, medieval, theocratic Latin Church but not on a colonialist Church.

Moreover, Indian theologians can contest the Latin roots of Christianity but not the Latin roots of India. A line can be drawn between European and Latin American theologians on one side, and Indian theologians on the other, in the sense that the former live in a context that is (or at least was) Christian, but the latter live in a context that is not. This is a well-known point of Indian theologians, who use it as a differentiator with the secular, post-Christian condition of the West. But the difference is relevant in another way, too: the Tradition cannot be seen as the primary source for what is wrong in India. European and Latin American theologians return

---

36   Saju Chackalackal, "Dharmaram Vidya Kshetram: Door of Faith to the Indian Church" (inaugural address of the president, Pontifical Athenaeum of Philosophy, Theology, and Canon Law, Bangalore, June 3, 2013).

to the Tradition to find new interpretations that allow them to overcome the old interpretations, because the old interpretations were the foundation of Christendom and Catholic empires. In other words, they reinterpret the source in order to blame and surpass the old interpretations. But Indian theologians do not have old interpretations to blame, because India has never been a Catholic empire. I borrow this critique from Paulson Pulikottil, a Pentecostal pastor and theologian who drew a sharp difference between theologians in the West and those in India; the former are justified in their reinterpretation of the Bible because they believe the Bible is responsible for what they want to dismiss and overcome. The latter cannot blame the Bible; they should blame other religious traditions that are responsible for what they want to overcome. Accordingly, Pulikottil invites Indian theologians to venture outside the Bible to scrutinize the Hindu scriptures that created and perpetuated the social and religious conditions in India.[37]

Pulikottil's critique can be broadened. The colonial past of India, as tragic as it may be, is only one element of a much more complex history. Political theorist Ananya Vajpeyi has offered a nuanced clarification of the point: "I am situated in an intellectual context—the Indian academy— that is torn between its precolonial inheritance, its colonial legacy, and its postcolonial aspirations, making any engagement with European ideas a fraught exercise, a ligature of self with another who is not quite other, but not quite self either."[38] A proper context of Indian theology must include the pre-Christian, pre-British eras, the Christian and British eras, and of course the post-British era. Accordingly, the responsibility of the shortcomings of India (regarding caste discrimination, for example) requires a much larger net that covers the precolonial, colonial, and postcolonial eras.[39] To read India exclusively through the lens of colonialism equals

---

37 Paulson Pulikottil, *Beyond Dalit Theology: Searching for New Frontiers* (Minneapolis: Fortress, 2022), 31–32. Pulikkottil directs his critique to Dalit theologians alone; I extended it to all Indian theologians who share the same mindset.

38 Ananya Vajpeyi, *Prolegomena to the Study of People and Places in Violent India* (New Delhi: WISCOMP, 2007), 36.

39 In his beautifully written article on the life of Catholic priest Swami Ishwar Prasad, San Chirico reveals the extent of the caste mentality that has been a regular feature of Indian society and the Church. See Kerry P.C. San Chirico,

reading the entire history of Italy through the prism of the foreign powers that dominated the country in the modern era, Germany through the lens of the subordination to the House of Austria, and Ireland through the prism of the British domination. Italy reached independence in 1861, Germany in 1866, and Ireland in 1917. And Italians, Germans, and Irish rapidly forgot their colonized status after independence and moved on.[40]

Most Indian theologians are committed to acquiring the right to their own narrative, but it is matter of discussion whether the present introversion of Indian theology is the prerequisite for growth or a sign of provincialism. Is it too much to hope that a serious Indian theology will progress in dialogue with Western theology and any other local theology in the synodal Church? After the Gregorian model, the Tridentine model, the juridical-corporate model, and the people of God model, it is time for the synodal model of the Church. I do not address this theme because it is subjected to constant changes, almost from month to month. However, it seems that Pope Francis intends to establish a preferential, permanent axis between synodality and the synod of bishops—to extend synodality as the "supreme regulatory criterion of the permanent government of the Church," superior to both episcopal collegiality and the primatial authority of the pope.[41] The return to the conciliarist orientation of Constance and Basel, the councils celebrated in the first half of the fifteenth century, assumes a horizontal and cooperative organization, no longer vertical and

---

"The Grace of God and Challenges of Indian Catholic Identity," *Journal of Global Catholicism* 1, no. 1 (2016): 60–61.

40 Here I am basically paraphrasing former Foreign Minister of India (2006–2009) Shivshankar Menon, who recently argued: "We've been independent 75 years now. We're grown up. I think we take responsibility for what we do. It's convenient to say this is all left over from history and blame the British for whatever there is and we're not responsible. And maybe it opens up space to compromise. But it's time, I think, that leaders . . . took responsibility for what they do and say." See: Brookings Institution, "A Big-Picture Look at the India-China Relationship," inaugural episode of the podcast *Global India*, hosted by Tanvi Madan. Washington, D.C., September 20, 2023. https://www.brookings.edu/articles/a-big-picture-look-at-the-india-china-relationship.

41 The literature on the synodal Church is growing. I took these notes from Carlo Fantappiè, professor of canon law at the Gregorian University. See Carlo Fantappiè, *Metamorfosi della sinodalità* (Venezia: Marcianum, 2023).

clerical. In turn, this type of organization favors dialogue among the realities of the particular churches to avoid isolation and fragmentation.

At a ceremony commemorating the fiftieth anniversary of the institution of the Synod of Bishops in 2015, Pope Francis spoke of a synodal Church as a Church in which everyone has something to learn. The faithful people, the college of bishops, and the bishop of Rome listen to each other, and all are listening to the Holy Spirit, the "Spirit of truth" (John 14:17), in order to know what He "says to the Churches" (Rev 2:7). This is Pope Francis's vision. How does anybody dare say that Asian Christianity and Western Christianity have nothing to learn from each other?[42] One thing that the recent tragic past has taught Western theologians is that there is no such thing as ideological neutrality. One is part of the solution or part of the problem, and to be part of the solution in the present divide between Western and Indian theologies, one must be an instrument of "harmony," to borrow a term from the FABC, for to be anything less is to be part of the problem.[43]

Hearts can be changed, minds can be purified by the vestiges of the past, and efforts can be made to successfully bridge the divide between Western and Indian theologians. An effort to decenter Indian theology from its customary self-absorption and isolationism and propel the discipline into a broadened engagement with Western theology is as desirable as a serious engagement of Western scholars to Indian theology. A commitment of Western theologians with Indian and other modes of theologizing can only produce an inclusive discipline and a complexity of cartographies and temporalities from which Catholic theology emerges as dynamic and interpenetrated. Western theologians should pursue a patient provincialization of their frameworks based on a willingness to listen to non-Western modes of theologizing. This is particularly true if the future of Catholicism is in Asia, as Pope Francis reportedly said to Cardinal

---

42   Pope Francis, "Address of His Holiness Pope Francis" (ceremony commemorating the 50th anniversary of the Institution of the Synod of Bishops, Rome, October 17, 2015), https://tinyurl.com/bdz8bcek.

43   Herman Punda Panda, *Towards Living Together in Harmony: A Study of Interreligious Dialogue as an Effort to Promote Harmony among Believers of Various Religions Based on the Federation of Asian Bishops' Conferences (FABC) Documents from 1970 to 1996* (Rome: Pontifical Urbaniana University, 2001).

Luis Antonio Tagle during his pastoral visit to the Philippines in 2015.[44] If the future of Catholicism is in Asia, Indian theology is no longer an exclusive realm of knowledge of the Indian theologians. If the center is the new periphery and the periphery is the new center, India is a matter of interest for all theologians, Indian and Western alike. The entire world's geopolitical center of gravity, not only Catholicism's, is in fact moving East. India is located at the center of the crucial region of the Indo-Pacific, which in turn is the epicenter of global economic activities and of most trading routes. The Indo-Pacific is also significant in terms of climate change and biodiversity because of its economic and demographic weight and its wealth of natural resources, including energy. And with the center of the geopolitical order moving from the West to the East, remarkable shifts that outline the newly emerging reality of the Asian century are going to modify the landscape of South Asia.

---

44   "Card. Tagle: Pope Francis Told Me That the Future of the Church is in Asia," *Asia News*, July 23, 2015, https://tinyurl.com/yc28xdwy.

BIBLIOGRAPHY

BOOKS BY MICHAEL AMALADOSS

The Asian Jesus. Chennai: Maryknoll, NY: Orbis, 2006.

Becoming Indian: The Process of Inculturation. Bangalore: Dharmaram Publications, 1992.

Beyond Dialogue: Pilgrims to the Absolute. Bangalore: Asian Trading Corporation, 2008.

Beyond Inculturation: Can the Many Be One? Delhi: Vidyajyoti Education and Welfare Society and ISPCK, 1998.

Blessed Are the Peacemakers—Theological Reflections. Chennai: New Leader Publications, 2012.

A Call to Community: The Caste System and Christian Responsibility. Anand: Gujarat Sahitya Prakash, 1994.

A Call to Jubilee. Dindigul: Vaigari Publications, 2000.

The Challenges of Fundamentalism. Chennai: IDCR, 2009.

Creative Conflict: Theological Musings. Bombay: St. Paul's Publications, 1995.

The Dancing Cosmos: A Way to Harmony. Anand: Gujarat Sahitya Prakash, 2003.

Dire la fede ai piedi dell'Himalaya. Villa Verucchio: Pazzini, 2020.

Do Sacraments Change? Variable and Invariable Elements in Sacramental Rites. Bangalore: Theological Publications in India, 1979.

Experiencing God in India. Anand: Gujarat Sahitya Prakash, 2016.

Faith, Culture and Inter-Religious Dialogue. Ideas for Action Series 2. New Delhi: Indian Social Institute, 1985.

Inigo in Indi: Reflections on the Ignatian Exercises by an Indian Disciple. Anand: Gujarat Sahitya Prakash, 1992.

Interreligious Encounters: Opportunities and Challenges. Maryknoll, NY: Orbis, 2017.

(with M. A. Joe Antony), *The Joy of Living: Wisdom from the East and West*. Mumbai: St. Paul's, 2004.

Lead Me On. Chennai: Blink, 2016.

Life in Freedom: Liberation Theologies from Asia. Maryknoll, NY: Orbis, 1997.

Living in a Secular Society. Chennai: IDCR, 2010.

Love or Justice? Dindigul: Vaigarai, 1999.

BIBLIOGRAPHY

Making All Things New: Dialogue, Pluralism and Evangelization in Asia. Maryknoll, NY: Orbis, 1990.

Making Harmony: Living in a Pluralist World. Delhi: ISPCK, 2003.

Missão e inculturação. São Paulo: Edições Loyola, 2000.

Mission Today: Reflections from an Ignatian Perspective. Anand: Gujarat Sahitya Prakash, 1989.

Our Faith, Our Religion. Dindigul: Vaigarai, 2008.

Palsamaya Otthuzhaipu. (Tamil). Dindigul: Vaigarai, 2008.

Peace on Earth. Mumbai: St. Paul's, 2003.

Peoples' Theology in Asia: Collection of the Lectures, East Asia Theological Encounter Program (2006–2018). Phnom Penh: Jesuit Conference of Asia Pacific, 2021. https://tinyurl.com/2p8na6vc.

Quest for God: Doing Theology in India. Anand: Gujarat Sahitya Prakash, 2013.

Towards Fullness: Searching for an Integral Spirituality. Bangalore: National Biblical, Catechetical and Liturgical Centre, 1994.

Uyirum Uravum. (Tamil). Palayamkottai: Tamil Nadu Jubilee Committee, 2000.

Vision and Values for a New Society: Responding to India's Social Challenges. Bangalore: NBCLC, 2004.

Walking Together: The Practice of Inter-Religious Dialogue. Anand: Gujarat Sahitya Prakash, 1992.

We Believe: Understanding the Roots of Our Faith. Mumbai: St. Paul's, 2005.

Yesuve En Vazhvu (Tamil). Dindigul: Vaigarai, 2008.

BOOKS EDITED BY MICHAEL AMALADOSS

For Others, with Others: Arrupe Challenges Indian Jesuits. Anand: Gujarat Sahitya Prakash, 2007.

Globalization and Its Victims as Seen by the Victims. Delhi: Vidyajyoti Education and Welfare Society & ISPCK, 1999.

Religions in Society in Asia: Conflict and Convergence. Chennai: IDCR, 2017.

Taming the Violent: Narratives of Conflict Resolutions. Chennai: IDCR, 2010.

(with P. Arockiadoss). *Equal and Free: Dalit Quest for Liberation: Theological Reflections.* Dindigul: Vaiharai, 2010.

(with M. Joseph Britto). *Festivals and Social Change.* Dindigul: Vaiharai, 2002.

(with Rossino Gibellini). *Teologia in Asia.* Brescia: Queriniana, 2006.

(with T. K. John and G. Gispert-Sauch, eds). *Theologizing in India: Selection of Papers Presented at the Seminar Held in Poona on October 26–30, 1978.* Bangalore: Theological Publications in India, 1981.

Arokiasamy, S. *Life for All: Ethics in Context.* Anand: Gujarat Sahitya Prakash, 2012.

ARTICLES AND OTHER MATERIAL BY MICHAEL AMALADOSS (QUOTED IN THIS BOOK)

"Address to the Forum for Liberation Theologies." November 30, 2011.

"Asian Theology: Bilan and Perspectives." Paper presentation, Louvain-la-neuve, May 1, 2001.

"Attaining Harmony as a Hindu-Christian." In *In Search of the Whole*, edited by John Haughey, 99–110. Washington, DC: Georgetown University Press, 2011.

"Being a Hindu-Christian." In *Toward A Planetary Theology: Along the Many Paths of God*, edited by Jose Maria Vigil, 3–37. Montreal: Dunamis, 2010.

"Can One Be a Hindu-Christian?" *Ishvani Documentation and Mission Digest* 15, no. 1 (1997): 88–93.

"The Church Open to the World from Vatican Council II to Pope Francis with Special Reference to Asia." In *Towards Renewing Church and World: Revisiting Vatican Council II Through the Eyes of Pope Francis*, edited by Francis Gonsalves, Arjen Tete, and Dinesh Braganza, 59–69. Delhi: ISPCK, 2020.

"Contextual Theology and Integration." *East Asian Pastoral Review* 40, no. 3 (2003): 266–71.

"Culture and Dialogue." *International Review of Mission* 74, no. 294 (1985): 169–77.

"Dialogue and Mission, Conflict or Convergence." *VJTR* 48, no. 2 (1986): 62–86.

"Dialogue between Religions in Asia Today: 40 Years of Vatican II and the Churches of Asia and the Pacific—Looking Back and Moving Forward." *East Asian Pastoral Review* 42, no. 1–2 (2005): 45–60.

"Dialogue with Cultures and Religions." In *Born Again: Jesuits back in Tamil Nadu*, edited by Leonard Fernando and Bernard D'Sami, 259–66. Dindigul: Jesuit Madurai Province, 2002.

"Double Religious Identity and Pilgrim Centres." *Word and Worship* 43, no. 1 (2010): 5–22.

"Double Religious Identity: Is It Possible? Is It Necessary?" *VJTR* 73, no. 7 (2009): 519–32.

"Editorial—Imaginary and Inter-Faith Dialogue." *Horizonte* 15, no. 45 (2017): 11–17.

"An Emerging Indian Theology: Some Exploratory Reflections." *VJTR* 58, no. 8 (1994): 473–84; 559–72.

"Freedom in the Spirit and Interreligious Dialogue." *Studies in Interreligious Dialogue* 8, no. 1 (1998): 5–18.

"Fundamentalism in Religions." In *Fundamentalism in Religions*, edited by Pudota Rayappa John, John B. Mundu, and Joseph Lobo, 1–19. Delhi: ISPCK, 2018.

"The Future of Mission in the Third Millennium." *Mission Studies* 5, no. 1 (1988) 90–97.

"Inculturation and Dialogue." *Vatican II 20 Years Later*, 151–76. Rome: Centre of Ignatian Spirituality, 1986.

216 BIBLIOGRAPHY

"Inculturation and Ignatian Spirituality." *The Way Supplement* 79, no. 1 (1994): 39–47.

"Indian Christian Theological Issues in the Context of Interreligious Dialogue." In *Windows on Dialogue*, edited by Ambrogio Bongiovanni, Leonard Fernando, Gaetano Sabetta, and Victor Edwin, 33–42. Delhi: ISPCK, 2012.

"Interreligious Dialogue 50 Years after Vatican II: Challenges and Opportunities." *VJTR* 79, no. 2 (2015): 85–99.

"Is Christ the Unique Saviour? A Clarification of the Question." In *What Does Jesus Christ Mean?* Edited by Errol D'Lima and Max Gonsalves, 6–17. Bangalore: Indian Theological Association, 1999.

"Jesus Christ as the Only Saviour and Mission." *The Japan Mission Journal* 55, no. 1 (2001): 219–26.

"Jésus Christ, le seul sauveur, et la mission." *Spiritus* 41, no. 2 (2000): 148–57.

"L'église en Inde: Vingt ans après Vatican II." In *Le retour des certitudes*, edited by Paul Ladrière and René Luneau, 13–33. Paris: Centurion, 1987.

"The Limitation of Theology." *VJTR* 51, no. 11 (1987): 521–29.

"The Liturgy: Twenty Years after Vatican II." *VJTR* 47, no. 5 (1983): 231–39.

"Mission from Vatican II into the Coming Decade." *VJTR* 54, no. 6 (1990): 269–80.

"Mission in a Post-Modern World." *Mission Studies* 13, no. 1 (1996): 68–79.

"My Pilgrimage in Mission." *International Bulletin of Missionary Research* 31, no. 1 (2007): 21–24.

"The Mystery of Christ and Other Religions: An Indian Perspective." *VJTR* 63, no. 5 (1999): 327–38.

Review of *Do Not Stifle the Spirit: Conversations with Jacques Dupuis*, by Gerard O'Connell. *Horizons* 46, no. 2 (2019): 413–15.

"Secularization and India: Modernization and Religion in an Eastern Country." *Exchange* 21, no. 1 (1992): 34–48.

"A Spirituality of Creation According to Pope Francis." *VJTR* 79, no. 8 (2015): 565–78.

"Together Toward the Kingdom: An Emerging Asian Theology." 2005–2008 INSeCT Project. Accessed May 2, 2023. https://tinyurl.com/4jvt55xy.

"Toward an Indian Theology." In *Theological Explorations: Centennial Festschrift in Honour of Josef Neuner, SJ*, edited by Jakob Kavunkal, 18–34. Delhi: ISPCK, 2008.

"The Trinity on Mission." In *"Mission Is a Must": Intercultural Theology and the Mission of the Church*, edited by Frans Wijsen and Peter Nissen, 99–106. Amsterdam: Rodopi, 2002.

"Which Is the True Religion? Searching for Criteria." In *Co-Worker for Your Joy: Festschrift in Honour of George Gispert-Sauch, SJ*, edited by Sebastian Painadath and Leonard Fernando, 45–60. Delhi: Vidyajyoti Education and Welfare Society & ISPCK, 2006.

"Who Do You Say That I Am?" *VJTR* 60, no. 12 (1996): 782–94.

BOOKS, ARTICLES, AND OTHER MATERIAL ON MICHAEL AMALADOSS (QUOTED IN THIS BOOK)

Amaladoss, Michael. "Michael Amaladoss and Lucette Verboven." Interview by Lucette Verboven. March 29, 2000. Video, 30:38. https://tinyurl.com/4kw6vj7z.

Antony, M. A. Joe. "Amal the Person." In *Seeking New Horizons: Festschrift in Honour of Dr. M. Amaladoss, S. J.*, edited by Leonard Fernando, 1–8. Delhi: Vidyajyoti Education and Welfare Society & ISPCK, 2002.

Beltramini, Enrico. "The 'Wisdom Writer': Michael Amaladoss and His Thought," *Religions* 12, no. 6, 396 (2021). https://doi.org/10.3390/rel12060396.

John, Pudota Rayappa. "Towards Indian Christology." In *Seeking New Horizons: Festschrift in Honour of Dr. M. Amaladoss, S. J.*, edited by Leonard Fernando, 53–76. Delhi: Vidyajyoti Education and Welfare Society & ISPCK, 2002.

"Michael Amaladoss." Accessed May 22, 2022. https://tinyurl.com/mryhe54j.

Segatti, Emis. "The Christological Thought of Michael Amaladoss," *Archivio Teologico Torinese* 7, no. 2 (2001): 345–62.

Skudlarek, William. Review of *Interreligious Encounters: Opportunities and Challenges*, by Michael Amaladoss, edited by Jonathan Tan, *Dilatato Corde* 7, no. 2 (December 2017). https://tinyurl.com/4kcubjd6.

Vagdevi: Journal of Religious Reflection 11, no. 1 (January 2017).

BOOKS (QUOTED IN THIS BOOK)

Abhishiktananda. *Ascent to the Depth of the Heart: The Spiritual Diary (1948–1973) of Swami Abhishiktananda*. Delhi: ISPCK, 1998.

Allison, Graham Tillet. *Destined for War: Can America and China Escape Thucydides's Trap?* New York: HarperCollins, 2017.

Aquinas, Thomas. *Summa Theologiae*. Steubenville, OH: Emmaus Academic, 2018.

Asif, Manan Ahmed. *The Loss of Hindustan: The Invention of India*. Cambridge, MA: Harvard University Press, 2020.

Barnes, Julian. *Flaubert's Parrot*. London: Picador, 1984.

Bassett, Ross. *The Technological Indian*. Cambridge, MA: Harvard University Press, 2016.

Beltramini, Enrico. *Indian Theologians between Hinduism and Western Theologies*. Forthcoming.

Benigni, Mario, and Goffredo Zanchi. *Giovanni XXIII: Biografia ufficiale*. Milan: San Paolo, 2000.

Bhasin, Avtar Singh. *Nehru, Tibet and China*. New York: Penguin, 2021.

Blanchard, Shaun, and Stephen Bullivant. *Vatican II: A Very Short Introduction*. Oxford: Oxford University Press, 2023.

BIBLIOGRAPHY

Borghesi, Massimo. *The Mind of Pope Francis: Jorge Mario Bergoglio's Intellectual Journey*. Collegeville, MN: Liturgical, 2018.

Bosch, David J. *Transforming Mission: Paradigm Shifts in Theology of Mission*. Maryknoll, NY: Orbis, 1991.

Bowersock, Glen. *Hellenism in Late Antiquity*. Ann Arbor: Michigan University Press, 1990.

Bultmann, Rudolf Karl. *Neues Testament und Mythologie: Das Problem der Entmythologiesierung der neutestamentlichen Verkündigung*. München: Kaiser, 1985.

Burrow, Bill. *Jacques Dupuis Faces the Inquisition*. Eugene, OR: Wipf & Stock, 2012.

Chakrabarty, Dipesh. *Provincializing Europe: Postcolonial Thought and Historical Difference*. Princeton: Princeton University Press, 2000.

Chatterjee, Partha. *Lineages of Political Society: Studies in Postcolonial Democracy*. New York: Columbia University Press, 2011.

Chaturvedi, Vinayak. *Hindutva and Violence: V.D. Savarkar and the Politics of History*. New York: State University of New York Press, 2022.

Clarke, John James. *Oriental Enlightenment: The Encounter between Asian and Western Thought*. New York: Routledge, 1997.

Clarke, Sathianathan. *Dalits and Christianity: Subaltern Religion and Liberation Theology in India*. Delhi: Oxford University Press, 1998.

Collins, Paul M. *Context, Culture and Worship: The Quest for "Indian-ness."* Delhi: ISPCK, 2006.

Cone, James. *A Black Theology of Liberation*. Maryknoll, NY: Orbis, 1964.

De Maistre, Joseph Marie. *Considerazioni sulla Francia*. Napoli: Il Giglio, 2010.

Dewart, Leslie. *The Future of Belief: Theism in a World Come of Age*. New York: Herder and Herder, 1966.

Dirlik, Arif. *Global Modernity: Modernity in the Age of Global Capitalism*. Boulder, CO: Paradigm, 2006.

Du Bois, W. E. B. *The Souls of Black Folk*. New York: Gramercy, 1994.

Dupuis, Jacques. *Christianity and the Religions: From Confrontation to Dialogue*. Translated by Robert Barr. Maryknoll, NY: Orbis, 2002.

———. *Toward a Christian Theology of Religious Pluralism*. Maryknoll, NY: Orbis, 1997.

Fantappiè, Carlo. *Metamorfosi della sinodalità*. Venezia: Marcianum, 2023.

Gaonkar, Dilip P., ed. *Alternative Modernities*. Durham, NC: Duke University Press, 2001.

Godin, Henri, and Yvan Daniel. *France, pays de mission?* Paris: Cerf, 1943.

Gonzales, Justo L. *Christian Thought Revisited: Three Types of Theology*. Nashville: Abington, 1989.

Gramsci, Antonio. *Quaderni dal Carcere*. Torino: Einaudi, 1975.

Helle, Jukka. *Towards a Truly Catholic and a Truly Asian Church*. Boston: Brill, 2022.

BIBLIOGRAPHY 219

Horn, Gerd-Rainer. *Western European Liberation Theology: The First Wave (1924–1959)*. Oxford: Oxford University Press, 2008.

Huntington, Samuel P. *The Clash of Civilizations and the Remaking of World Order*. New York: Simon & Schuster, 1996.

John, Mary. *Indian Catholic Christians and Nationalism*. Delhi: ISPCK, 2017.

Joseph, Clara A. B. *Christianity in India: The Anti-Colonial Turn*. New York: Routledge, 2020.

Kappen, Sebastian. *Jesus and Cultural Revolution: An Asian Perspective*. Mumbai: Build, 1983.

Kappen, Sebastian, ed. *Jesus Today*. Madras: All India Catholic University Federation, 1985.

Kaur, Ravinder. *Brand New Nation: Capitalist Dreams and Nationalist Designs in Twenty-First-Century India*. Redwood City, CA: Stanford University Press, 2020.

King, Richard. *Orientalism and Religion: Postcolonial Theory, India and "the Mystic East."* New York: Routledge, 1999.

Krastev, Ivan, and Alan McPherson, eds. *The Anti-American Century?* Budapest: Central European University Press, 2007.

Kuhn, Thomas S. *The Structure of Scientific Revolutions*. 3rd ed. Chicago: The University of Chicago Press, 1996.

Kuttianimattathil, Jose. *Practice and Theology of Interreligious Dialogue: A Critical Study of the Indian Christian Attempts Since Vatican II*. Bangalore: Kristu Jyoti Publications, 1995.

Lapide, Pinchas E., und Raimon Panikkar. *Meinen Wir denselben Gott?* München: Kösel Verlag, 1994.

Léon-Dufour, Xavier. *Lecture de l'Evangile selon Saint Jean*. Vol. 1. Paris: Seuil, 1988.

Monchanin, Jules. *Théologie et spiritualité missionnaires*. Edited by Edouard Duperray and Jacques Gadille. Paris: Beauchesne, 1985.

Mong, Ambrose. *A Tale of Two Theologians: Treatment of Third World Theologies*. Cambridge: James Clarke, 2017.

Mukherjee, Aditya. *Imperialism, Nationalism and the Making of the Indian Capitalist Class, 1920–1947*. New Delhi: Sage, 2002.

Mungello, David Emil. *The Catholic Invasion of China: Remaking Chinese Christianity*. Lanham, MD: Rowman and Littlefield, 2015.

Nietzsche, Friedrich. *Richard Wagner in Bayreuth*. Translated by Anthony M. Ludovici. Glasgow: Good Press, 2021.

Noll, Mark. *The New Shape of World Christianity: How American Experience Reflects Global Faith*. Downers Grove, IL: InterVarsity, 2010.

O'Collins, Gerald. *On the Left Bank of the Tiber*. Leominster: Gracewing, 2013.

O'Connell, Gerard. *Do Not Stifle the Spirit: Conversations with Jacques Dupuis*. Maryknoll, NY: Orbis, 2017.

BIBLIOGRAPHY

Panikkar, Raimon. *Christianity*. Opera Omnia, vol. 3, no. 2. Maryknoll, NY: Orbis, 2016.

———. *Entre Dieu et le Cosmos Entretiens avec Gwendoline Jarczyk*. Paris: Albin Michel, 1998.

———. *Myth, Faith and Hermeneutics*. New York: Paulist, 1979.

———. *The Unknown Christ of Hinduism: Towards an Ecumenical Christophany*. Maryknoll, NY: Orbis, 1981.

Phan, Peter C. *Christianity with an Asian Face: Asian American Theology in the Making*. Maryknoll, NY: Orbis, 2003.

Phan, Peter C., ed. *The Asian Synod: Texts and Commentaries*. Maryknoll, NY: Orbis, 2002.

Pieris, Aloysius. *The Christhood of Jesus and the Discipleship of Mary: An Asian Perspective*. Colombo, Sri Lanka: Logos, 2000.

———. *Fire and Water*. Maryknoll, NY: Orbis, 1996.

Prakash, Gyan. *Another Reason: Science and the Imagination of Modern India*. Princeton: Princeton University Press, 1999.

Pulikottil, Paulson. *Beyond Dalit Theology: Searching for New Frontiers*. Minneapolis: Fortress, 2022.

Punda Panda, Herman. *Towards Living Together in Harmony: A Study of Interreligious Dialogue as an Effort to Promote Harmony Among Believers of Various Religions Based on the Federation of Asian Bishops' Conferences (FABC) Documents from 1970 to 1996*. Rome: Pontifical Urbaniana University, 2001.

Rowland, Tracey. *Ratzinger's Faith: The Theology of Pope Benedict XVI*. Oxford: Oxford University Press, 2008.

Rushdie, Salman. *Midnight's Children*. New York: Random House, 1981.

———. *One Thousand Days in a Balloon, in Imaginary Homelands: Essays and Criticism, 1981–1991*. New York: Penguin, 1992.

Said, Edward W. *Orientalism: Western Conceptions of the Orient*. New York: Vintage, 1978.

Samuel, Vilakuvelil Cherian. *The Council of Chalcedon Re-Examined*. Delhi: ISPCK, 1971.

Saran, Shyam. *How China Sees India and the World*. New Delhi: Juggernaut, 2022.

Sullivan, Francis A. *Salvation Outside the Church?* New York: Paulist, 1992.

Tharsiuse, Nicholas. *Christian Faith: A Liberation Praxis: Theology of Samuel Rayan*. Delhi: ISPCK, 2015.

Toulmin, Steven. *Return to Reason*. Cambridge, MA: Harvard University Press, 2001.

Vagaggini, Cyprian. *Doing Theology*. Bangalore: IJA, 2003.

Vagneux, Yann. *Co-esse: Le mystère trinitaire dans la pensée de Jules Monchanin (1895–1957)*. Paris: Desclée de Brouwer, 2015.

———. *Indian Portraits: Eight Christian Encounters with Hinduism*. New Delhi: Nirala Publications, 2021.

———. *A Priest in Banaras*. Translated by Roderick Campbell Guion. Varanasi: ATC, 2020.

Vajpeyi, Ananya. *Prolegomena to the Study of People and Places in Violent India*. New Delhi: WISCOMP, 2007.

Vattamattam, Sebastian, ed. *Hindutva and Indian Religious Traditions*. Vol. 5 of *Collected Works of Sebastian Kappen*. Delhi: ISPCK, 2021.

Von Balthasar, Hans Urs. *Romano Guardini: Reform from the Source*. San Francisco: Ignatius, 2010.

———. *The Theology of Henri de Lubac: An Overview*. San Francisco: Ignatius, 1991.

Von Harnack, Adolf. *Das Wesen des Christentums*. Edited by Trutz Rendtorff. Gütersloh: Kaiser/Gütersloher Verlagshaus, 1999.

Zeeshan, Mohamed. *Flying Blind: India's Quest for Global Leadership*. New York: Vintage, 2021.

ARTICLES, BOOK CHAPTERS, AND BOOK REVIEWS (QUOTED IN THIS BOOK)

Abraham, Kochurani. "The Emergence of Local Churches." In *Seeking New Horizons: Festschrift in Honour of Dr. M. Amaladoss, S. J.*, edited by Leonard Fernando, 31–52. Delhi: Vidyajyoti Education and Welfare Society & ISPCK, 2002.

Al-Azm, Sadiq Jala. "Orientalism and Orientalism in Reverse." *Khamsin, Journal of the Revolutionary Socialists of the Middle East* 8, no. 1 (1981): 6–25.

Armus, Seth D. "The Eternal Enemy: Emmanuel Mounier's Esprit and French Anti-Americanism." *French Historical Studies* 24, no. 2 (Spring, 2001): 271–304.

Bauman, Chad, Arun W. Jones, Brian Pennington, Joseph Prabhakar Dayam, and Michelle Voss Roberts. "Hinduism and Christianity." *Oxford Bibliographies* (2012). http://doi.org/10.1093/obo/9780195399318-0042.

Bertone, Tarcisio. "A proposito della ricezione dei Documenti del Magistero e del dissenso pubblico." *L'Osservatore Romano* (Vatican City), December 20, 1996.

Bilimoria, Purushottama, and Devasia Muruppath Antony. "Raimon Panikkar: A Peripatetic Hindu Hermes." *European Journal of Humanities and Social Sciences* 3, no. 2 (2019): 9–29.

Brookings Institution, "A Big-Picture Look at the India-China Relationship," inaugural episode of the podcast *Global India*, hosted by Tanvi Madan. Washington, D.C., September 20, 2023. https://www.brookings.edu/articles/a-big-picture-look-at-the-india-china-relationship.

Byford, Andy. "Russia as an Epistemic Frame." *Ad Imperio* 23, no. 1 (2022): 73–84.

222   BIBLIOGRAPHY

Byford, Andy, Connor Doak, and Stephen Hutchings. "Introduction: Transnationalizing Russian Studies." In *Transnational Russian Studies*, 1–34. Liverpool: Liverpool University Press, 2019.

"Card. Tagle: Pope Francis Told Me That the Future of the Church Is in Asia." *Asia News*, July 23, 2015. https://tinyurl.com/yc28xdwy.

Carola, Joseph. "La metodologia patristica nella teologia preconciliare dell'Ottocento." *Gregorianum* 97, no. 3 (2016): 605–17.

Center for the Study of the Second Vatican Council. *Archives conciliaires de Gérard Philips*, 123, CT 5/61:41.

Chackalackal, Saju. "Dharmaram Vidya Kshetram: Door of Faith to the Indian Church." Inaugural address of the president, Pontifical Athenaeum of Philosophy, Theology, and Canon Law. Bangalore, June 3, 2013.

Chandran, J. Russel. "Methods and Ways of Doing Theology." In *Readings in Indian Christian Theology*, vol. 1, edited by R. S. Sugirtharajah and Cecil Hargreaves, 4–13 (Delhi: SPCK, 1993).

Chisthi, Seema. "Rewriting India's History Through School Textbooks." *New Lines Magazine*, March 9, 2023. https://tinyurl.com/9xcfh98c.

Chui, Nick. "Is Roman Theology Neo-Scholastic? A Genealogical Reply to Michael Amaladoss." *Trinity Theological Journal* 21, no. 1 (2013): 43–60.

Congar, Yves. *De Ecclesia, Quomodo exponi exprimique possit nexus inter homines extra Ecclesiam visibilem extantes et Corpus Mysticum*, May 18, 1961.

———. "Pour une histoire sémantique du terme 'magisterium.'" *Revue des sciences philosophiques et théologiques* 60 (1976): 85–97.

Darmaatmadja, Julius. "A New Way of Being Church in Asia." *VJTR* 63, no. 12 (1999): 887–91.

Dirlik, Arif. "Revisioning Modernity: Modernity in Eurasian Perspectives." *Inter-Asia Cultural Studies* 12, no. 3 (June 2011): 284–305.

Du Bois, W. E. B. "Strivings of the Negro People." *The Atlantic*. August 1897.

Essen, Georg. "Hellenisierung des Christentums? Zur Problematik und Überwindung einer polarisierenden Deutungsfigur." *Theologie und Philosophie* 87, no. 1 (2012): 1–17.

Faggioli, Massimo. "Vatican II: Bibliographical Survey 2016–2019." *Cristianesimo nella Storia* 40, no. 3 (2019): 713–38.

Franzoni, Giovanni. "Concilio Tradito. Concilio Perduto?" Address to the 31st Congress of the Asociación de Teólogos y Teólogas Juan XXIII. Madrid, September 18, 2011.

Frost, Robert. "A Group of Poems." *The Atlantic Monthly*, August 1915. https://tinyurl.com/yrsnssex.

Gravend-Tirole, Xavier. "An Examination of the Indigenisation/Inculturation Trend within the Indian Catholic Church." In *Constructing Indian Christianities:*

Culture, Conversion and Caste, edited by Chad M. Bauman and Richard Ford Young, 110–37. New Delhi: Routledge India, 2014.

Gray, John. "The West Isn't Dying—Its Ideas Live on in China." *The New Stateman*, July 28, 2021. https://tinyurl.com/45zcthae.

Griffiths, Bede. "The Mystical Dimension in Theology." *Report of the First Annual Meeting of Indian Theological Association* 14 (1977): 229–46.

Hankey, Wayne J. "One Hundred Years of Neoplatonism in France: A Brief Philosophical History." In *Levinas and the Greek Heritage Followed by One Hundred Years of Neoplatonism in France: Brief Philosophical History*, edited by Jean-Marc Narbonne and Wayne J. Hankey, 97–248. Leuven: Peeters, 2006.

Kappen, Sebastian. "The Struggle of Fishermen in Kerala." In *Collected Works of Sebastian Kappen*. Vol. 5, *Hindutva and Indian Religious Traditions*, edited by Sebastian Vattamattam. Delhi: ISPCK, 2021.

Kaviraj, Sudipta. "An Outline of a Revisionist Theory of Modernity." *Archives of European Sociology* 46, no. 3 (2005): 497–526.

Kunnumpurum, Kurien. "Theology in India at the Crossroad." In *Theologizing in India Today*, edited by Michael Amaladoss, T. K. John, and G. Gispert-Sauch, 208–16. Bangalore: Theological Publications in India, 1981.

Lazar, Roy. "Five Years of Pope Francis—Insights for Indian Christians." Unpublished paper, 2018.

Markschies, Christoph. "Does It Make Sense to Speak about a 'Hellenization of Christianity' in Antiquity?" *Church History and Religious Culture* 92, no. 1 (2012): 5–34. http://doi.org/10.1163/187124112X621581.

Matties, Gordon. "Biblical Interpretation in India." Unpublished manuscript. Accessed March 2, 2021. Microsoft Word file. https://tinyurl.com/bdewp2w7.

Mendoza, Ruben. "A Church in Dialogue with Peoples of Other Faiths: A Journey to the Kingdom in the Spirit: The Federation of Asian Bishops Conferences, 1970–2007." PhD diss., Catholic University of Louvain, 2008.

Ning, Wang. "Orientalism versus Occidentalism?" *New Literary History* 28, no. 1 (1997): 57–67.

Nirmal, P. Arvind. "Doing Theology from a Dalit Perspective." In *A Reader in Dalit Theology*, edited by Arvind P. Nirmal, 139–44. Madras: Gurukul Lutheran Theological College & Research Institute, 1990.

———. "Towards a Christian Dalit Theology." In *Readings in Indian Christian Theology*, vol. 1, edited by R. S. Sugirtharajah and Cecil Hargreaves, 53–70. Delhi: SPCK, 1993.

Panikkar, K. N. "Alternative Historiographies: Changing Paradigms of Power." In *The Struggle for the Past: Historiography Today*, edited by Felix Wilfred and Jose D. Maliekal, 11–20. Chennai: Department of Christian Studies, University of Madras, 2002.

BIBLIOGRAPHY

Panikkar, Raimon. "The Dream of an Indian Ecclesiology." In *Searching for an Indian Ecclesiology*, edited by Gerwin van Leeuwen, 24–54. Bangalore: Asian Trading Corporation 1984.

Parappally, Jacob. "Theologizing in Context." In *Theologizing in Context: Statements of the Indian Theological Association*, edited by Jacob Parappally, 23–53. Bangalore: Dharmaram, 2002.

Phan, Peter C. "Current Trends and Future Tasks of Christian Theology of Asia: In Celebration of the 50th Anniversary of the Foundation of the FABC." *Jnanadeepa: Pune Journal of Religious Studies* 21, no. 4 (2021): 8–30.

Raj, Selva J. "Being Catholic the Tamil Way." In *Vernacular Catholicism, Vernacular Saints: Selva J. Raj on "Being Catholic the Tamil Way,"* edited by Reid B. Locklin, 1–16. Albany: State University of New York Press, 2017.

———. "Dialogue 'On the Ground': The Complicated Identities and the Complex Negotiations of Catholics and Hindus in South India." In *Vernacular Catholicism, Vernacular Saints: Selva J. Raj on "Being Catholic the Tamil Way,"* edited by Reid B. Locklin, 177–94. Albany: State University of New York Press, 2017.

———. "An Ethnographic Encounter with the Wondrous in a South Indian Catholic Shrine." In *Vernacular Catholicism, Vernacular Saints: Selva J. Raj on "Being Catholic the Tamil Way,"* edited by Reid B. Locklin, 115–40. Albany: State University of New York Press, 2017.

Rayan, Samuel. "Decolonization of Theology." *Jnanadeepa: Pune Journal of Religious Studies* 1, no. 2 (1988): 140–55.

———. "Doing Theology in India." In *Theologizing in Context: Statements of the Indian Theological Association*, edited by Jacob Parappally, 11–22. Bangalore: Dharmaram Publications, 2002.

San Chirico, Kerry P. C. "The Grace of God and the Travails of Contemporary Indian Catholicism." *Journal of Global Catholicism* 1, no. 1:3 (2016): 56–84.

Sullivan. Francis A. "Introduction and Ecclesiological Issues." In *Sic et Non: Encountering Dominus Iesus*, edited by Stephen J. Pope and Charles Hefling, 47–56. Maryknoll, NY: Orbis, 2002.

Sunderland, Jabez T. "The New Nationalist Movement in India." *The Atlantic*, October 1908. https://tinyurl.com/bdh9u8wh.

Tracy, David W. Review of *Jesus-God and Man*, by Wolfhart Pannenberg, Lewis L. Winkins, and Duane A. Priebe, and review of *Revelation as History*, by Wolfhart Pannenberg and David Granskou. *Catholic Biblical Quarterly* 31, no. 2 (1969): 285–88.

Vagneux, Yann. "Abhishiktananda: A Priesthood in the Spirit." *VJTR* 83, no. 8 (2019): 625–38.

———. "A Marriage with Hinduism." Translated by Roderick Campbell Guion. *Dilatato Corde* 10, no. 1 (January–June 2020). https://tinyurl.com/tbu6zk67.

———. "'The One in Greece and the Indies': An Unpublished Work by Jules Monchanin." *Revue des sciences philosophiques et théologiques* 96, no. 3 (2012): 514–56.

Wilfred, Felix. "Jesus-Interpretations in Asia: Fragmentary Reflections on Fragments." *East Asian Pastoral Review* 43, no. 4 (2006).

———. "Obituary—Samuel Rayan, SJ (1920–2019)." *Mission Studies* 36, no. 2 (2019): 187–89.

Wimmer, Andreas, and Nina Glick Schiller. "Methodological Nationalism and Beyond: Nation-State Building, Migration and the Social Sciences." *Global Networks* 2, no. 4 (2002): 301–34.

———. "Methodological Nationalism, the Social Sciences, and the Study of Migration: An Essay in Historical Epistemology." *The International Migration Review* 37, no. 2 (2003): 576–610.

CHURCH DOCUMENTS (QUOTED IN THIS BOOK)

Congregation for the Doctrine of the Faith. "Declaration *Dominus Iesus* on the Unicity and Salvific Universality of Jesus Christ and the Church." Rome, August 6, 2000.

Congregation for the Doctrine of the Faith. "Doctrinal Note on Some Aspects of Evangelization." Rome, December 14, 2007.

Congregation for the Doctrine of the Faith. "Instruction *Donum Veritatis* on the Ecclesial Vocation of the Theologian." Rome, May 24, 1990.

Congregation for the Doctrine of the Faith. "Notification on the Book *Toward a Christian Theology of Religious Pluralism* (Maryknoll, NY: Orbis, 1997) by Father Jacques Dupuis, SJ." Rome, January 24, 2001.

"First Plenary Assembly: Statement and Recommendations." Federation of Asian Bishops' Conferences. Taipei, Taiwan, April 22–27, 1974.

For All the Peoples of Asia: Federation of Asian Bishops' Conferences Documents from 1970 to 1991. Vol. 1. Edited by Gaudencio Rosales and C. G. Arevalo. Quezon City: Claretian, 1997.

For All the Peoples of Asia: Federation of Asian Bishops' Conferences Documents from 1997 to 2001. Vol. 3. Edited by Franz-Josef Eilers. Quezon City: Claretian, 2002.

For All the Peoples of Asia: Federation of Asian Bishops' Conferences Documents from 2002–2006. Vol. 4. Edited by Franz-Josef Eilers. Quezon City: Claretian, 2007.

1985 Extraordinary Synod. *The Final Report of the 1985 Extraordinary Synod*. Rome, 1985. https://tinyurl.com/26p2zeb2.

Office of Theological Concerns, "On Being Human in the Changing Realities in Asia," *FABC Papers* 133 (2011).

Pope Benedict XVI. "The Regensburg Address." Regensburg, Germany, September 12, 2006.

———. *Verbum Domini*. Post-Synodal Apostolic Exhortation. Rome, September 30, 2010.

226 BIBLIOGRAPHY

Pope Francis. "Address to the Students of Gregorian University." Rome, April 10, 2014.

———. "Address of His Holiness Pope Francis." Ceremony Commemorating the 50th Anniversary of the Institution of the Synod of Bishops. Rome, October 17, 2015. https://tinyurl.com/bdz8bcek.

———. *Gaudete Et Exsultate*. Apostolic Exhortation. Rome, March 19, 2018.

———. *Praedicate evangelium*. Apostolic Constitution. Rome, March 19, 2022.

———. "Ma il Cammino è ancora lungo." *La Repubblica*, October 2, 2022.

———. "Pope Francis' Letter to New Doctrine Chief Archbishop Manuel Fernández." Catholic News Agency. Rome, July 1, 2023. https://tinyurl.com/yck4e45e.

Pope John Paul II. "Address on the Occasion of the Meeting with the Exponents of Non-Christian Religions." Madras, February 5, 1986.

———. "Christmas Address to the Roman Curia." *Bulletin of the Secretariats for Non-Christians* 64 (1987): 54–62.

———. *Redemptoris Missio*. Letter Encyclical. Rome, December 7, 1990.

———. *The Pope Speaks to India* (Bombay: St. Paul, 1986).

Pope Paul VI. *Lumen Gentium*. Dogmatic Constitution on the Church. Rome, November 21, 1964.

———. *Nostra Aetate*. Declaration on the Relation of the Church to Non-Christian Religions. Rome, October 28, 1965.

———. *Dei Verbum*. Dogmatic Constitution on Divine Revelation. Rome, November 18, 1965.

———. *Gaudium et Spes*. Pastoral Constitution on the Church in the Modern World. Rome, December 7, 1965.

———. "Udienza Generale." Rome, September 24, 1969.

———. "Address to the First General Assembly of the Federation of Asian Bishops' Conference." Rome, April 20, 1974.

Pope Pius IX. *Dei Filium*. Dogmatic Constitution of the First Vatican Council. Rome, April 24, 1870.

Pope Pius XII. *Humani Generis*. Letter Encyclical. Rome, August 12, 1950.

Ratzinger, Cardinal Joseph. "Christ, Faith and the Challenge of Cultures." Address to the presidents of the Asian Bishops' Conference. March 3, 1993. https://tinyurl.com/mrxvm2d7.

Theological Advisory Commission of the Federation of Asian Bishops' Conferences. "Theses on Interreligious Dialogue: An Essay in Pastoral Theological Reflection." *FABC Papers* 48 (1987).

"Towards a Theology of Religions: An Indian Christian Perspective." Statement of the Twelfth Meeting of the Indian Theological Association. In *Religious Pluralism: An Indian Perspective*, edited by Kunchria Pathil, 324–37. Delhi: South Asia Books, 1991.

INDEX OF NAMES

Abhishiktananda (also Henri le Saux), 43n, 46, 55–56, 66, 69, 96, 100, 186, 201
Acharya, Francis, 186
Aeschylus, 169
Al-Azm, Sadiq Jalal, 29
Alexander the Great, 138
Amalorpavadass, Duraiswami Simon, 77, 160, 170
Antony, M. A. Joe, 6n, 172
Aquinas, Thomas, 35, 93, 133, 146, 191, 199
Arockiasamy, Soosai, 44,
Asif, Manan Ahmed Asif, 3n
Augustine, 90, 93, 133, 191, 199

Barnes, Michael, 58n
Benedict XVI, Pope (also Joseph Ratzinger), 39, 44n, 68, 77, 134, 138, 147, 150, 152–53
Bertone, Tarcisio, 150
Bilimoria, Purushottama, 9
Blanchard, Shaun, 62n
Blondel, Maurice, 45
Boff, Leonardo, 9
Boland, Charles, 163
Borghesi, Massimo, 62n
Bowersock, Glen, 137
Bullivant, Stephen, 62n
Bultmann, Rudolf Karl, 22, 126–29
Byford, Andy, 194n, 195

Chackalackal, Saju, 208
Chakrabarty, Dipesh, 28
Charles, Pierre, 186
Chui, Nick, 43–44n
Clarke, Sathianathan, 57
Clooney, Francis X., 58n
Cone, James, 185
Congar, Yves, 45, 90
Cornille, Catherine, 58n

Darmaatmadja, Julius, 108
De Lubac, Henri, 4, 28, 45, 156, 184
Del Noce, Augusto, 24
De Maistre, Joseph Marie, 168
Dewart, Leslie, 135
Du Bois, W. E. B., 14, 14n
Dupuis, Jacques, 1, 9, 36–38, 45, 52, 62, 116, 186
Dussel, Enrique, 99

Emmanuel, Pierre, 66
Essen, Georg, 137
Euripides, 169

Faggioli, Massimo, 65n
Fantappie, Carlo, 210n
Flaubert, Gustave, 20
Francis, Pope (also Jorge Mario Bergoglio), XIX, 36n, 50, 68, 152, 186, 210–11
Franzelin, Johann Baptist, 38n
Franzoni, Giovanni, 151, 152n
Frost, Robert, 39

228 INDEX OF NAMES

Gadamer, Hans-Georg, 41, 41n
Gandhi, Mohandas Karamchand, 63, 141
Gispert-Sauch, George, 186
Griffiths, Bede, 55, 85, 186
Gramsci, Antonio, 70
Grant, Sara, 55
Gray, John, 160n, 164
Guardini, Romano, 4n
Gutierrez, Gustavo, 44n, 162

Hegel, Georg Wilhelm Friedrich, 169
Heidegger, Martin, 41, 169
Helle, Jukka, 60–61, 192
Hicks, John, 98n
Hirudayam, Ignatius, X, 31–36, 52, 71,
    101, 157
Hobbes, Thomas, 83
Homer, 169
Horace, 82
Horn, Gerd-Rainer, 163–64
Huntington, Samuel P., 182

John, P.R. (Pudota Rayappa), 101, 196
John, T.K, 77
John XXIII, Pope, 153
John Paul II, Pope (also Karol Wojtyla),
    25, 39, 79n, 91, 107, 117, 118n, 122, 124,
    125–26, 152–53, 192

Kappen, Sebastian, 72–75, 163, 165, 191
King, Richard, 29
Klostermaier, Klaus K., 186
Knitter, Paul, 58n
Kochappilly, Paulachan, 58n
Kolvenbach, Peter-Hans, IX, 8, 47–48
Kuhn, Thomas, 145
Kung, Hans, 9
Kunnumpuram, Kurien, 58n, 84
Kuttianimattathil, Jose, 60

Lazar, Roy, 67, 196
Leo XIII, Pope, 38
Leon-Dufour, Xavier, 116–17

Levinas, Emmanuel, 41n
Locke, John, 83

Maharshi, Ramana, 100
Marx, Karl, 50, 50n, 72
Matties, Gordon, 59n
Mazzolari, Primo, 163
Menon, Shivshankar, 210n
Milani, Lorenzo, 163
Milbank, John, 160n
Monchanin, Jacques, 43n, 66, 133–34,
    186, 201
Mounier, Emmanuel, 25
Muruppath, Devasia, 9

Nandy, Ashis, 139
Nedungatt, George, 160
Neuner, Josef, 17, 132
Newman, John Henry, 133
Nicolas, Adolfo, 44
Nietzsche, Friedrich, 137
Ning, Wang, 29
Nirmal, Arvind, 57, 76, 184n, 187n
Noll, Mark, 161–62, 164

O'Connell, Gerard, 36n
Origen, 133

Painadath, Sebastian, 58n
Parappally, Jacob, 79
Panikkar, Raimon, 1, 5, 9, 55–56, 67–68,
    67n, 68n, 70–72, 75, 100, 102, 115,
    186–88, 198, 201, 206, 206n
Passaglia, Carlo, 38n
Pathil, Kuncheria, 160
Paul, St., 148
Paul VI, Pope, 60, 144n, 152, 190
Perrone, Giovanni, 38n
Peter, St., 148
Pieris, Marian Aloysius Reginald, 32
Pius XII, Pope, 146n
Prakash, Gyan, 206
Pulikottil, Paulson, 209, 209n

INDEX OF NAMES 229

Raj, Selva, 11–12
Rayan, Samuel, 80, 156, 191, 202–203
Rahner, Karl, 43, 191
Ricoeur, Paul, 41, 41n
Rousseau, Jean-Jacques, 83
Rudd, Kevin, 176
Rushdie, Salman, 51, 173

Said, Edward, 28
Saltini, Zeno, 163
San Chirico, Kerry P.C., 209n
Saran, Shyam, 177n
Schauf, Heribert, 38n
Schrader, Clemens, 38n
Scotus, Duns, 133
Sobrino, Jon, 9
Soares-Prabhu, George M., 59n, 160

Skudlarek, William, 45n
Sullivan, Francis A., 120, 121n, 123
Sunderland, Jabez T., 63n

Tagle, Luis Antonio, 212
Tagore, Rabindranath, 63
Toulim, Steven, 145
Tracy, David, 138

Vagneux, Yann, 66
Verboven, Lucette, 33
Verdier, Jean, 163
Von Balthasar, Hans Urs, 4n, 28, 43, 184
Von Harnack, Adolf, 137

Wilfred, Felix, 58n, 191, 198

INDEX OF SCRIPTURES

Matthew
4:26–32, 86
5:3–12, 103
6:24, 199
7:15, 96n
21:12, 80
25, 110

Mark
13:26, 182

Luke
2:19, 151
2:51, 151
7:21, 103
16:13, 199
23:43, 103
24:13, 107

John
1:2–5, 116
1:17, 117

1 Corinthians
2:16, 148
12, 80
13:13, 103
15:28, 100, 122

Philippians
2:6–13, 81

Revelation
2:7, 211
2–3, 106